THE
CONTRACT and FEE-SETTING GUIDE for CONSULTANTS and PROFESSIONALS

HOWARD L. SHENSON, CMC

WILEY

JOHN WILEY & SONS
New York • Chichester • Brisbane • Toronto • Singapore

in association with

University Associates Inc.

UNIVERSITY ASSOCIATES INC.

Copyright © 1990 by Howard L. Shenson
Published by John Wiley & Sons, Inc. in association with
University Associates Inc.

This publication is designed to provide accurate and authoritative
information in regard to the subject matter covered. It is sold
with the understanding that the publisher is not engaged in
rendering legal, accounting, or other professional service. If
legal advice or other expert assistance is required, the services of
a competent professional person should be sought. *From a
Declaration of Principles jointly adopted by a Committee of the
American Bar Association and a Committee of Publishers.*

Library of Congress Cataloging-in-Publication Data:

Shenson, Howard L.
    The contract and fee-setting guide for consultants and
professionals / Howard L. Shenson.
        p.   cm.
    Includes bibliographical references.
    ISBN 0–471–50660–5. — ISBN 0–471–51538–8 (pbk.)
    1. Consultants—Fees.   2. Professional employees—Fees.
I. Title.
HD69.C6S517   1989
658.8' 16—dc20   89–36305
                                                     CIP

Printed in the United States of America

20 19 18 17 16 15 14 13 12 11

Introduction

This book provides you with detailed strategies for conducting your consulting practice. These are proven strategies that have a track record of producing successful results. We will cover the business of consulting — from fee-setting, through proposal writing, to drawing up the contract and issuing reports. A successful consultant produces satisfied clients, and the surest way to keep your clients satisfied is through good business practices.

Too many consultants place nearly all of their emphasis on their special talents. Certainly possessing those talents is one of the main features that set consultants apart from ordinary workers. But you must keep in mind that your clients are people in business and they know the difference between good business practices and sloppy work.

A brilliant, creative project can be ruined by poor record keeping and substandard reports. A merely competent consultation can produce very satisfied clients if it is executed with precision and attention to detail.

We will begin with fee-setting. People in business know about money and they will respect you if you are aware of your worth and aren't ashamed to ask for fair payment. The section on fees will lay out all that you need to know for determining your monetary value as a consultant who is running a business. Then you will learn how to establish a fee structure that will give you the greatest profit while producing truly satisfied clients. When you are done with the fees section, you will know what to charge and how to charge it.

The rest of the book follows a functional flow diagram that starts with a prospective interested client and takes you through writing a proposal, selecting the right contract, and determining the frequency and format of reports. This integrated approach shows you in diagrammatic form the entire business structure of a consulting practice. You take your talents and combine them with this business structure to ensure client satisfaction and a successful consulting practice.

For many consultants, developing written proposals is the least appealing aspect of a consultation. Yet it can be a very important element in securing contracts and producing satisfied clients. A well-written proposal can be your most effective marketing instrument. It also lays out the structure of the proposed consultation and can guide you through the entire project from the initial marketing to submission of the final report.

Because writing and submitting a quality proposal is so crucial to success, the process of constructing the proposal is covered in great detail. You will learn how to structure a proposal for maximum marketing effect, as well as how to use it as the first step in producing a satisfied client, one who will want to retain your services again in the future and who will recommend you to others.

The section on contracts shows how the flow diagram that produced a proposal also leads to selecting the right form for your contract. You will learn when and how to use letters of agreement, letters of engagement, and formal contracts in your practice. This is also where you combine your knowledge of fee-setting with the drafting of the contract to determine the right structure for payment for a given project.

The last section covers reports. You will learn when to issue reports and what kind of report to write. Reports are a written record of your consultation and can enable the client to apply the results of your work long into the future. Interim reports keep the client up to date on the progress of your work, which fosters improved communication and enhances client satisfaction.

The final report is one way — a very important way — for a consultant to deliver the project in a physical form. It summarizes your project, makes recommendations for the future, and reminds the client that you did quality work. When properly constructed and delivered, the final report and progress reports become effective devices for encouraging follow-on and referral business.

The appendices give examples of fees charged by consultants and samples of the kinds of written work you are expected to produce as a consultant. A careful review of each appendix will reward you by increasing your understanding of that aspect of consulting and by guiding you by direct example.

Consulting is one of the most exciting areas of business, and it is much more rewarding if you understand the business end of consulting. This book can make the difference between just getting by and really succeeding.

HOWARD L. SHENSON

Woodland Hills, California
September, 1989

Contents

PART I

Setting Your Fees

CHAPTER 1

The Fee-Setting Process

Determining your fee structure is probably one of the most important steps in building and maintaining a consulting practice. You will be selling your services to other people in business and, if you want to be seen as responsible, reliable, and desirable, you have to know and communicate the real value of your services. Setting your fees too low conveys the message that you don't value your services adequately. It may also communicate that you may not be able to provide quality service.

Fee setting is actually an element of marketing your services. A realistic fee announces that you are going to deliver quality service for dollars spent. It also communicates that you are confident in your abilities and the worth of your services. By explaining the basis of your charges, you let your prospective clients know how valuable your consultation is.

A low fee may get you some business initially, but it will cost you in the long run because it forces you to work at a rate of compensation that cannot support your practice. It also sets you up for future business at the same low, unrealistic rates. The problem is that low fees lead to poor service. It's easy to quote a low fee at the beginning of a project, but when the realities of overhead and the demands on your time become obvious, the usual response is to cut back on the quality of your work. This is especially true if you get several projects based on low estimates. It isn't possible to make a living and deliver quality work to several clients at once when your fees are set below market value.

The time to set fees is at the very outset of your business. Your fee is based on your skills, the need for your talents, and the assumption that you will give your clients state-of-the art services. Then you should regularly review and adjust your fees based on market realities and your increasing knowledge and skill.

THE STATE OF THE ART

People in business don't contract with consultants to get the same tired, old solutions and approaches. They want and deserve the benefit of the state of the art. If the client's work calls for computerized handling, you are not rendering a proper service by cranking out the data on a desk calculator over the weekend. Not only is cutting corners a disservice to the client, it can also reflect poorly on you in the long run. Asking clients to pay for cheap, short-cut methods is almost as unethical as overcharging them for top-notch processes.

For example, the compilation of field survey data is best done on a computer. The work may be done quickly on a table-top microcomputer or by a large-scale computer service. How much computerization you bring in depends on the amount of data and the processing requirements, as well as on the budget.

The same principle applies to human resources. Given an opportunity to use someone who is going to charge you a lower fee and enable you to make a greater profit, your concern must be whether you are short-changing the client. If the same talent and ability can be purchased at lower cost, so be it. No one suffers and you prosper. If your judgment tells you that the lower-priced talent does not meet the specifications of the contract or your own requirements, you are not giving your client the "state of the art" in human resources.

NAMING YOUR PRICE

Don't be afraid to lay your fee on the table. If you select one or more of the fee-setting methods outlined in this section, you should not allow the quoted fee to be negotiated. Given a change in requirements or specifications, which in turn lowers the amount of time or the level of expertise required, the cost of a particular contract is certainly negotiable. But your base rate and your underlying calculations are not.

As a consultant, you may find yourself about to lose a contract award to a competitor on the basis of cost. In general, bidding lower to keep the assignment is not good policy. It gives the impression that your original bid was inflated in the first place. The logical and probably unasked question in the client's mind is, ''Why didn't I get this price the first time?'' Making a second, lower bid may give the impression that you are hungry or needy. No one wants to entrust a vital responsibility to someone so needy that he or she can't get business at a fair market price.

From your point of view, if your fee contains a reasonable profit in the first place, then you should not settle for a less-than-reasonable profit.

Competitors who underbid dramatically tend to have short business lives. They *might* have a secret formula that enables them to survive, or perhaps even thrive, on lower fees. If so, then they deserve the contract. More likely they are underpricing themselves just to get the work, which often turns out to be less than satisfactory to the client. So even if these low-ball competitors stay in business, they can become your best advertising. In such cases, you will see the client again.

Don't be afraid to stick by your fee, as long as it is reasonable.

DETERMINING THE DOLLAR VALUE TO BE CHARGED

Going into business as a consultant means just that—going into business. The experienced consultant knows that expenses must be controlled and accounted for. Profits must be calculated and monitored. As the owner/operator of a product-oriented business, you would be concerned with inventories, raw material costs, depreciation, and other expenses related to manufacturing or shipping. In a service-oriented business, you must be just as concerned about expenses and profits, even though they take on a different form.

If you feel you should be earning, say, $300 a day (about $75,000 a year), you might have to bill $500 to $900 per day. The difference accounts for something that is a reality in every business—overhead. You cannot price yourself as a laborer because you have an office to support.

Setting a fee, or a "price," for your services involves several steps:

1. Establishing your *daily* labor rate, which is the value of your time and the time of others involved in the project.
2. Determining your *overhead,* which is the expense of being in business.
3. Determining what percentage of your budget should go toward marketing. (Marketing is included as part of overhead.)
4. Setting your *profit,* which is the value you place on the risk you take by being in business.

To the beginning consultant it may seem that the fees charged by established firms are high. But the senior partner of a major CPA firm who charges $1,500 or more a day is not getting rich quickly. Large firms have high overhead. Overhead may be lower in a start-up operation, but the financial realities are the same.

A typical management consulting firm breaks down its fees approximately into thirds. One-third covers the cost of the job, one-third covers the nonmarketing overhead, and one-third covers the marketing overhead. If we add in profit, the usual fee can be broken down as follows:

	%
Labor and direct expenses	30 to 40
Marketing	20 to 30
Overhead (nonmarketing)	20 to 30
Profit	10 to 20

These figures establish a range that varies according to the practices of the consulting firm and its needs. For some firms, labor is a major consideration. In other fields of consulting, marketing might take more time and money.

Another way to figure roughly the overhead of a large firm is simply to apply what is known as the *200% overhead rate.* If the firm incurs a direct labor dollar expense of $1,000, it multiplies that expense by 200% and adds the resulting $2,000 to its direct labor expense. The bill will come to $3,000.

If you are just starting in the consulting business, your overhead will probably be lower because certain expenses such as fringe benefits will be lower. But overhead has a way of creeping up after a consultant has been in business for a while. You need to monitor overhead expenses continually to keep them from becoming too large.

The fee-setting process begins by determining the value of your labor, the daily labor rate.

The Daily Labor Rate

Figuring the daily labor rate starts with deciding on the yearly amount that you are "worth." That annual figure is then converted to a daily amount, which is added to overhead and profit to determine your fee.

> Example: Jane Smith is resigning her position as a computer systems analyst with a major firm and becoming a consultant. Her position paid $48,000 a year and she would like to earn at least that much to start as a consultant. She has determined her annual "worth."
>
> She plans to be paid for 261 days a year. To arrive at her daily labor rate, all she does is divide her annual salary by the number of paid days.
>
> $$\$48,000 \div 261 = \$183.91$$
>
> Her daily labor rate can be rounded off to $185.

Overhead

Overhead includes the expenses that you have regardless of how much work you do. These expenses are fixed at pretty much one level whether you are working on one project or several. Of course, if your business expands greatly, the overhead will increase accordingly. Overhead usually includes the rent for the office, the lease payments on the photocopier, the office assistant's salary, the fee for your accountant, marketing expenses, and the like.

Expenses of another type, called direct expenses, vary with the work you do. They are related directly to the work on a particular project and are not included in your overhead. Direct expenses might include the daily labor rates of associates, travel expenses on an assignment, long-distance phone charges related to the client's project, supplies for mock-ups or presentations, and so on.

There are some expenses that you can choose to classify either as overhead or direct expenses. Travel expenses can constitute a direct expense if they were incurred on a particular, contracted assignment. You had to travel to do that work. On the other hand, let's say you traveled to meet with a prospect or two without the assurance that you would actually get a contract. In such a case, the travel expense would become part of your overhead. In general, the nature of the expenditure does not determine how it is classified, but its purpose does. The discriminating question is, "Can this expense be related directly to an assignment?"

Each type of expense, overhead or direct, is handled differently. Overhead is best converted to a fixed percentage and added to your daily labor rate. It is not recalculated for each job. As a general rule of thumb, it usually falls between 80% and 150% of the daily labor rate. Direct expenses are calculated for each job and are not included in determining the overhead rate.

Calculation of Overhead. The percentage of overhead charged by consultants depends on the costs or expenses that they incur. Although the amounts charged differ from one consultant to another, Figure 1.1 contains a realistic, not a contrived or theoretical, example.

Let's look at some of the overhead items in more detail.

Clerical Expenses. Clerical expenses can be billed partly as direct expenses and partly as overhead. In the example, 60% of the monthly salary for clerical work was charged as overhead. The remaining 40% will be billed as a direct expense, depending on how much clerical support is required for each project. Usually, up to two-thirds of the clerical work is charged directly to the client for such activities as typing reports, reducing survey data, and so on. The rest is spent on tasks such as answering the phone that have to be done routinely and are part of overhead.

Office Rent. Office rental is clearly part of overhead. Even if, as a consultant, you avoid paying rent, perhaps because you work from a spare room at home, you should include as part of the overhead budget the amount of rent that would normally be paid for an office. Otherwise you will seriously underprice your services. The same principle holds true for any other overhead expenses you obtain without direct charge or at a discount.

FIGURE 1.1
A typical overhead calculation

John Jones, full-time consultant
Daily labor rate = $450

Overhead

	Monthly
Clerical ($1,800)	$ 1,080
(60% of clerical salary charged to overhead)	
Office rent..	750
Telephone..	250
Postage and shipping..	120
Automotive	375
Employment taxes	650
Personnel benefits...	575
Insurance	140
Business licenses and taxes	110
Marketing	
Direct.............. $ 350	
Personnel........... <u>1,800</u>	2,150
Professional development....................................	200
Dues and subscriptions.....................................	70
Printing and photocopying	130
Stationery and supplies.....................................	110
Accounting and legal..	200
Practice management..	700
Other expenses...	<u>400</u>
Total overhead	$ 8,010

Telephone. As with office rent, telephone bills can be divided into overhead and direct expenses. Many consultants charge each client directly for telephone expenses incurred as part of that client's project. The balance is listed as overhead. The amount of expenses classified as overhead will be lower as more expenses are charged to clients directly. However, many consultants prefer to avoid charging clients directly for most expenses.

Automotive. The charge for automotive expenses covers the cost of leasing and maintaining an automobile for business purposes. When the automobile is used in behalf of clients, they are charged directly by the mile. Most consultants use the per-mile charge permitted by the IRS.

Benefits. You are still entitled to the normal and customary fringe benefits that you would receive from an employer, even though you are self-employed. Your overhead budget should therefore contain a charge for such expenses as:

- Paid vacation
- Health insurance
- Life insurance
- Paid sick leave
- Retirement plan

These expenses are normal and routine in American business. The cost of such items usually falls between 21% and 33% of direct salaries.

Marketing. In Figure 1.1, Jones charges $2,150 to overhead every month for marketing expenses. The $1,800 amount is categorized as "personnel," and the balance of $350 is called "direct." The total amount represents what this consultant feels he must spend to market his services and comes to 27% of all overhead.

The $1,800 for personnel represents four days' worth of income to Jones. He plans to spend these four days on marketing projects of his choosing. Somehow, those days have to be included in his overhead as a cost of doing business to account for the days on which he is not billing clients.

In contrast, a few consultants attempt to charge each client for the actual marketing costs they incurred to get the client by billing directly for some of the marketing money spent on prospects who did not become clients. This practice is neither wise nor recommended. Is is like the taxi driver who throws the meter before the passenger closes the door. This practice usually produces poor and rushed marketing.

You might regard allocating so much for marketing expense as a bit too much. It is not. You should give marketing the same time and care that you give your most important client. No matter how busy you become with client work, you must religiously set aside time each month for marketing. Failure to do so inevitably results in a kind of yoyo cycle, in which you go from feast to famine.

Figure 1.2 shows how this feast and famine cycle works. At the low points, you have no clients and no business. What do you do? You spend time marketing. You do so well that you become overloaded with

FIGURE 1.2
The feast and famine business cycle resulting from poor marketing

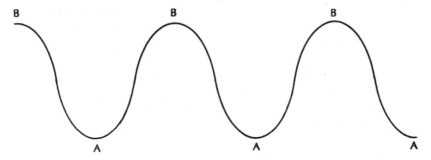

work. Your work load becomes so heavy that you have no time to market. As a result you come back to a low point of no work. And so the cycle repeats itself.

This cycle is not only a poor business practice, it is also psychologically unsettling. It is far better to discipline yourself to market in a consistent and regular fashion to create a business cycle that looks like the one in Figure 1.3. The flatter type of cycle gives you a smoother cash flow and greater peace of mind.

Professional Development. To maintain and improve your professional standing, you normally must spend money and time for courses, seminars, books, audio cassette training programs, and the like. These expenses arise either from legal requirements or from the need of the professional to keep abreast of the state of the art. These expenses are almost always treated as overhead. Clients must expect such costs to be included in your charges, as they are, for example, in the fees paid to the family doctor.

FIGURE 1.3
The more regular business cycle that results from good marketing

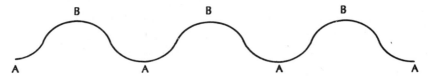

The Overhead Rate. In the professional services, overhead is always expressed either as a dollar amount per day or as a percentage. To determine the daily dollar value for overhead, divide the total overhead amount by the number of days that you expect to be billing clients. The resulting dollar amount must be added to the client's invoice for each day the client is billed.

> *Example:* Jones's overhead rate is calculated by taking the total dollar amount for his monthly overhead, $8,010, and dividing that by the number of days he expects to bill clients each month, 15 days. Dividing $8,010 by 15 days gives $534, which is his daily overhead charge. The daily overhead charge must be added to the charge for time and profit to cover the expense of doing business.

To find the overhead rate as a percentage, simply divide the daily dollar value for overhead by the consultant's daily labor rate.

> *Example:* Jones's daily labor rate is $450. The calculation is $534 divided by $450, which equals 1.186 or approximately 118%. An overhead percentage rate is then applied to the daily labor rate charge for each day. In this case you multiply the daily labor rate by the overhead percentage. Suppose you worked four and one-half days:
>
> $$\$450 \times 4.5 = \$2,025$$
> $$\$2,025 \times 1.186 = \$2,389.50$$
>
> This amount ($2,389.50) is added to the daily labor rate to give the subtotal for daily charges. The profit is then computed from this subtotal, as shown in the section on profit. The profit is then added to the subtotal to give the daily fee.

Adding Perks. Perks (perquisites) are the not-so-necessary items that are very appealing to you and that you feel can be paid for as part of your overhead. You may want a fancy office or additional vacation time. These are nice to have, but take care that you don't price yourself out of the market by living too well. Be reasonable before loading something onto your overhead rate.

Bureaucratic Growth. As your business gets on in years, it tends to grow. With growth comes higher overhead. Increased overhead is a reality of business life. As a practice becomes larger, it requires more labor to meet client demands.

On the surface this growth seems obvious and even more profitable. Lower-paid people may be used to handle less demanding tasks. Yet just the addition of personnel requires more management, more supervision, more communication—and more risk. The larger practice has more of a reputation to protect and the control of it is less direct than when its founder started it. Additional expenditures have to be over-viewed, supervised, and controlled. Many of these added expenses might well be judged as wasteful or as an indication of poor management to all but the most seasoned bureaucrat. As they grow, organizations tend to accumulate flab in their overhead rates.

Watching Overhead. To keep your overhead at a level that is appropriate to your size, you should compare your current actual expenses to those in the past. Where did the money go? Where did expenses go down? What new expenses appeared? Which ones dropped off the list? During the first year in business, six months is the longest you want to go without checking your actual expenses. For better control you should do so each quarter.

After the first year, reviewing your expenses once or twice annually should be frequent enough. If sudden or radical changes take place in your practice, more frequent comparisons are warranted. If you are expanding your practice and taking on new partners and employees, you should audit expenses more frequently to control overhead.

Profit

Over and above your daily labor rate and overhead, you should charge a profit. Many consultants overlook the need for profit. Their rationale is that, since they are charging for their labor, charging a profit would be immoral or improper.

One minor reason profit is overlooked is that it has recently acquired a negative connotation. Somehow it has become associated with the supposed evils of "Big Business." Most people resent the profits of the oil, utility, and phone companies, and this resentment carries over into small business.

The major reason for failing to charge a profit is that some people don't really understand how the free enterprise system works. Profit is the purpose for running any kind of business and contributes to the accumulation of societal profit and well-being by producing investment for future growth. Consultants who don't understand this point seem to think that all they have coming to them is their labor rate.

Profit is the reward for the risk of being in business. Even if consultants invest little or no capital in their businesses, they are still investing their time, which translates ultimately into money. They place their valuable time at risk, and they deserve to profit by that risk.

Consultants must distinguish between their labor rates and profits. They deserve their labor rates whether they work for someone else or for themselves. Their profits belong to them by reason of their being in business.

Typically, consultants charge between 10 and 20% of the combined sum of the daily labor rate and overhead charge. Some consultants charge more and some less. The rate depends on whatever the consultant judges to be fair and appropriate.

Example: So far we have established Jones's daily labor rate and overhead. If he wants to earn a profit of 15%, he can determine the daily profit by first adding the daily labor rate and the overhead.

Daily labor rate	$450.00
Overhead	507.00
Subtotal	$957.00

The profit is determined by multiplying the subtotal by 15%

$$\$957.00 \times .15 = \$143.55$$

The daily profit is $143.55.

DETERMINING THE DAILY FEE

The daily fee is established by adding the profit to overhead and the daily labor rate: The result is the daily fee for services.

Example: In Jones's case, the computation is as follows:

Daily labor rate	$ 450.00
Overhead	507.00
Profit	143.55
Daily fee	$1,100.55

The daily fee can be rounded off to $1,100.00. This is the amount he will charge for his services plus any direct expenses incurred for a particular client. You can get a good idea of the average (mean) fees charged by consultants in different fields in Appendix A. Go through the calculations in this chapter to determine your daily fee and then compare that amount with those listed in Appendix A.

THE GOVERNMENT CLIENT

The rules for calculating fees and overhead are often different when you are contracting with a government agency. To get a government consulting contract, you have to be sensitive to the special requirements, policies, and attitudes of different agencies.

Often you find yourself dealing on two levels: the official level and the realistic level. Officially, policy or law may entitle you to only this much profit or that labor rate. Realistically, the program managers for the government agency recognize that you simply cannot adequately or profitably perform the services within the confines of the policy. They are caught between the rock-like policy and the hard place of getting the programs going.

Some government consultants have worked out ways of handling this dilemma. Often it is a matter of understanding how agencies handle costs and define terms. We can list approaches used by some consultants and consulting organizations, but it is your responsibility to become fully acquainted with the procedures and legal requirements of any government agency you contract with.

When a government agency is a client, unique rules often govern the consultant's disclosure of the fee to the client. Given the legal and procedural considerations that govern procurement by government agencies, you sometimes have to make your responses strategic. Your chief considerations are:

1. The maximum on labor rates
2. The client's understanding of overhead
3. The acceptability of overhead charges
4. The acceptability of profit

Maximum Limitation on Labor Rates

Some government agencies have maximum acceptable labor rates. Whether established by executive decision or legislative mandate, these agencies can pay only so much per day. In such cases consultants should be sure that the labor rates they disclose to the client do not exceed the allowable maximum. If the agency is not permitted to pay any employee more than $200, consultants would not want even to hint that their daily labor rate is $250.

You might assume that the solution is to use a fixed-fee contract. However, working with a fixed-fee contract is sometimes not possible. And even when allowed, most government agencies require full disclosure of all estimated price breakouts, even if the contract has a fixed price. In the private sector those who hire a consultant on a fixed-price contract are usually not told anything other than the total dollar amount of the contract. But most government agencies work on line-item budgets. The entire pricing sheet must be shown to the governmental client.

Suppose that you cannot work on a fixed-price contract and that your labor rates exceed the limits of acceptability. Some consultants consider rearranging the work responsibilities so that the lower-compensated personnel can do more of the work. If the professionals and associates are obliged to work at a lower rate, you can keep this time to a minimum. The total billed amount can then come out the same, but the distribution of the workload changes to meet the agency's requirements.

What of the propriety of accepting lower labor rates and rearranging the workload? Officially, these practices are neither recognized nor advocated, particularly by the fiscal personnel in the government agency client. In reality, the program management people often accept such adjustments "to get the project through."

Client's Understanding of Overhead

Because consultants must reveal their pricing details to the governmental client, they must be sure that the client program personnel understand the nature of overhead and the process by which it is calculated. Because their divisional budgets don't include charges for accounting, rent, and the like, they may not be accustomed to thinking about overhead.

In government agencies many personnel are not experienced in buying consultant services. They may regard your charges as excessive and unreasonable. You may have to instruct them on the nature of overhead and its method of calculation.

Acceptability of Overhead Charges

Some government agencies don't accept certain expense items as overhead charges. Expenses such as marketing, entertainment, and interest are typical. If your contract is subject to certain audit provisions, these expenses will not be accepted. So inquire about the acceptability of such items before submitting a bid for services.

Acceptability of Profit

Some agencies have policies governing the acceptable rate of contractor profit. Others lack specific policies, but their employees have "personal" policies about such matters. You must ensure that the profit charged is acceptable to the client organization's policies or to the client's representatives.

To find out about policies or attitudes on profits, you might use precise questioning or fact finding. Or you might ask the client to provide you with a copy of one or more prior consulting contracts that it has awarded in a similar situation.

However you get your information, suppose that profit rates of 5% or 10% are required or expected. *Should* you work at such low rates of return? Many consultants would answer, "Technically yes, but in reality no."

Do consultants really work for government clients for such low returns? Rarely. Fortunately the personnel working for many government agencies have realistic attitudes toward contracting out for services. They recognize the economic need for legitimate profitability. Consequently, while the profit line may reflect a low percentage, some consultants often hide the extra profitability elsewhere in the budget. It may consist of a higher labor rate than actually paid, more labor days than actually expended, higher direct costs than are actually incurred, or the like.

Of course, if the contract is auditable, consultants take greater care to ensure that the expenses claimed are supported by evidence. If you anticipate substantial work on auditable government contracts, study the subject in detail.

Some consultants use another means to get the additional profit without showing it on the profit line. They create an additional category of expense, such as a general and administrative expense (G&A), that government agencies are often used to paying but that small consulting

practices rarely have. G&A is an expense that is handy for large
businesses to account for things like corporate-wide auditing and communications.

> *Example:* Jones charged 15% profit in computing the daily fee. If he is
> working for a government agency that allows only a 10% profit rate, he
> could change his billing by adding a 5% G&A charge.

Usual Procedure for Computing Daily Rate:

Daily labor rate	$ 450.00
Overhead	507.00
Profit	143.55
Daily fee	$1,100.55

Amended Computation of Daily Rate

Daily labor rate	$ 450.00
Overhead	507.00
Subtotal	957.00
G&A	47.85
Profit	95.70
Daily fee	$1,100.55

It is obvious that the computations give the same daily fee.

Although such practices certainly won't be found in the policies
and procedures manual of government procurement agencies, they are
relatively widespread. The facts of dealing with government agencies are
that sometimes the requirements are unrealistic to the point that no
consultants could afford to work for agencies, and that, as long as your
proposal is fairly estimated and the total cost to the agency reasonable,
some accommodation to these requirements must be expected. Whether
the fiscal personnel within government agencies recognize these practices
is not always known. Most program personnel who seek out the
consultant's services know about it, even if they do not generally admit
it. Sometimes the Administration makes half-hearted attempts to police
this situation, but it really doesn't know how without cutting off the
agencies from the benefits of hiring consultants.

PART II

Creating an Effective Proposal

CHAPTER 2

Finding the Right Payment Structure

When you are pricing a consulting project, there are two main considerations in setting up the structure for payment of your fee:

What is the appropriate payment structure for this project?

What is the most profitable payment structure?

With a short-term project such as a one-day presentation you may arrange for a simple lump-sum payment. A consultation that takes several months or a year calls for several payments. But the timing of payments is only one part of determining the structure of your fee payment.

The financial relationship between consultant and client can take a number of forms:

1. Fixed-price contract
2. Fixed fee plus expenses
3. Daily rate
4. Time and materials
5. Cost reimbursement
6. Retainer

Each type of payment structure deserves your attention because each is useful at one time or another, depending on the situation and the demands of a particular project.

FIXED-PRICE CONTRACTS

The fixed-price contract is very simple. After determining the client's precise needs, you tell him or her that you can perform the services required for a flat dollar amount of your choosing. Once the fixed price is accepted and a contract is drawn, you are then bound to deliver the services for that amount. If you handle the work efficiently and the services cost you less than you estimated, then you make more profit than expected. If your expenses are higher than estimated, you lose some profit.

Payment is linked to your performance. At the conclusion of the work, if the contract has not been fulfilled by the consultant, not only could the final payment be withheld, but also the progress payment amounts might have to be returned.

Clients run little or no risk with a fixed-price contract. The consultant assumes nearly all the risk. Why would consultants do that? The reason is that the fixed-price contract is usually more profitable than other types of contracts. In a survey of the consulting profession by *The Professional Consultant,* the practices of 76 consultants were analyzed in depth:

1. Those working exclusively on a fixed-price basis had 87% higher profits than those working on a daily or hourly basis.
2. When profits and salary were added together, the fixed-price group had profits and salary that were 95% greater than their daily-rate colleagues.
3. For those consultants using both daily rates and fixed-price contracts, profits were 32% higher, and profits and salary 36% higher.

The profit motive makes the fixed-price contract very attractive. But its effective use by consultants depends on the ability to estimate accurately the cost of a contract. This skill is covered in detail in Steps 8, 9, and 16 of the proposal-writing process. Read Step 16, Develop Project

Budget and Disclosure Statement, with care because this step is extremely important in setting a fixed fee. Once you have decided to charge a fixed fee, there are many possible contractual arrangements for structuring your fee.

Types of Fixed-Price Contracts

There are several types of fixed-price contracts:

1. The firm fixed-price contract
2. The escalating fixed-price contract
3. The incentive fixed-price contract
4. The performance fixed-price contract
5. The fixed-price contract with redetermination

Firm Fixed-Price Contract. This contract offers a firm, fixed price for specified work and is not subject to change except when the scope or character of the work is changed. All risk is with the consultant who has the greatest opportunity for profit in compensation for his risk.

Escalating Fixed-Price Contract. This contract is similar to the firm fixed-price contract except that it has provisions for upward or downward adjustments of the fee on the basis of predetermined contingencies, such as the cost of living index.

Incentive Fixed-Price Contract. This contract has an "adjustment formula" which is designed to reward the consultant for additional efficiency and penalizes the lack of it. There is a ceiling price below which the consultant gets the extra profit. If the consultant's price goes above the ceiling, the costs are divided according to a predetermined schedule. Both parties might agree that additional expenses are to be borne by the client at a rate of 75% and by the consultant at a rate of 25%, reducing the consultant's profit by that 25%.

Performance Fixed-Price Contract. This contract is the same as a firm fixed-price contract, but it compensates the consultant for special performance. The consultant might get a bonus for bringing the project in early or for some other special achievement.

Fixed-Price Contract with Redetermination. Structured like a firm fixed-price contract, this contract has a provision that allows both the consultant and the client to redetermine or reset the price after the contract has been signed. This contract is best used when the nature of the task is so vague, so uncertain, or so unknown as to make an estimate impossible or almost impossible. At the time the contract is signed, both parties agree on a point in time for redetermination on the basis of their experience with actual costs and expenses. By agreement the parties determine whether the change in price will affect prior work, future work, or both. This kind of contract is usually in the interest of the consultant who is working on some blind or unknown task for which the costs may be much higher than anyone would have conceived. Yet the redetermination may be downward too. If actual costs are a great deal less than anticipated, this contract may be to the advantage of the client.

FIXED FEE PLUS EXPENSES

When the direct expenses are difficult or impossible to foresee the consultant can submit the direct labor charge as a fixed fee, but the client is liable for the direct expenses.

DAILY RATE

Working on a daily-rate basis is safer than submitting a fixed price. Some consultations smack of hidden pitfalls. They are too speculative or too unpredictable for consultants to guarantee either labor or expenses. The client's personality may even lend itself to uncertainty on the part of the consultant. Sometimes a situation just "looks" as if it has surprises in it. You might pad the fixed-price contract you are going to submit. A little padding should not hurt, but a lot may not only dull your competitive edge, but can also border on being unethical.

In daily-rate contracts, consultants submit an estimate of labor and expenses, but they are not responsible for overruns. The clients assume all risk for overruns in both cost areas, and they enjoy all the benefits of underruns.

TIME AND MATERIALS

This contract works exactly like the daily labor contract with a couple of exceptions. One is that the consultant pays for expenses and adds a handling charge, normally at the same rate as the consultant's profit. The consultant then bills the client for the total. The client does not pay the expenses directly. Another is that the clerical support is not built into the daily rates; instead, it is usually charged as an expense. A time and materials contract is a kind of fixed-price contract in that the labor and overhead rates are fixed. What the client winds up paying, however, is far from fixed. Hence this time and materials contract is an incentive for consultants to be anything but efficient—the longer the project takes, the more money they earn.

COST REIMBURSEMENT CONTRACTS

Cost reimbursement contracts focus on costs rather than on fees. In such contracts consultants are reimbursed for the costs that they incur. In the types of the contracts that call for fees—some of them do not—the fees are emphasized less than the costs.

The underlying assumption for all these contracts is that the clients pay all costs or the consultant ceases performance. In this kind of contract consultants act as agents of the client, whereas they act as principals in a fixed-price contract. They run no risk of loss and they do not earn the profit normally associated with fixed-price contracts.

Cost reimbursement contracts are used when the consultation cannot accurately estimate costs and when the consultant's cost accounting system enables clients to monitor the consultant's costs. Clients do not favor these contracts because they have to expend a lot of effort keeping track of the consultant's costs.

The success of these contracts depends on the definition of costs. At the outset, both consultant and client must agree on allowable costs. Perhaps the consultant considers the cost of capital an allowable cost. Perhaps the client does not. Other costs such as automobile transportation might also be disputable. If you enter into a cost-reimbursement contract, define what you mean by cost.

Several different types of cost reimbursement contracts are in use:

1. The cost contract
2. The cost-plus-fixed-fee (CPFF) contract
3. The cost-plus-incentive-fee (CPIF) contract
4. The cost-plus-award-fee (CPAF) contract

The Cost Contract

With this contract the client agrees to reimburse the consultant for all allowable costs, but pays no fee. This type of contract is most widely used when a nonprofit consulting agency can learn technology that will benefit it in the future. Cost sharing is also possible. The client agrees to cover a part of the costs or to share the costs.

Cost-Plus-Fixed-Fee (CPFF) Contract

This type of contract is popular because it is widely used by the federal government. Both the client and the consultant estimate the budget for the project. Usually the consultant does most of the work on developing the budget. Then both parties work out the fee and/or profit for the consultant. There is an incentive for the consultant to save money because the consultant can earn a higher percentage on the costs so that both client and consultant benefit.

In theory the consultant is motivated to keep costs down and thus earn a higher percentage return; in actual practice such is not always the case. Consultants are largely assured of reimbursement for all ''allowable'' costs. They are normally not required to spend funds in excess of the agreed-upon amount, even though the project or consultation has yet to be completed.

Cost-Plus-Incentive-Fee (CPIF) Contract

The CPIF is designed to overcome the low incentive to keep costs down in the CPFF. This contract sets a minimum fee and a maximum fee. Cost overruns can lead to lower fees, sometimes to no fee at all or even a negative fee. The threat of a negative fee is a real incentive! Clients and consultants may also arrange to share costs in some contracts, which lowers the consultant's risk. The overall effect of these contracts is that, if the actual costs turn out to be lower than estimated, the consultant gets a greater fee—up to the maximum. If costs run over the estimate, the fee is smaller, and it may even be reduced to zero if the cost overrun is great enough. In theory the risk for the client should be equal to that for the consultant. In practice each party tries to get as much advantage as possible during contract negotiations. Frequently CPIF contracts involve multiple incentives—one for early completion, another for cost efficiency, and so on.

Cost-Plus-Award-Fee (CPAF) Contract

This fee structure combines elements of the CPFF and the CPIF contracts. The federal government developed this structure to handle the procurement of technical services which may involve unknown costs because they involve new technologies or other elements that are difficult to estimate.

The CPAF differs from the CPIF in that usually an external third party awards the minimum or maximum fee based on an objective evaluation of the consultant's cost efficiency and compliance. The evaluations can be scheduled periodically during the progress of the consultation or at the end of the project. Frequent evaluations are like interim reports in that they give the consultant or consulting firm regular feedback on the progress of the project. This fee structure rewards creativity, quality, and rapid delivery of services.

RETAINERS

Under the various kinds of retainer agreements, the consultant agrees to make his or her services available to the client as need arises. Like the value of the fixed-fee contract, a retainer works only if the consultant is good at estimating. If the consultant underestimates the client's needs, the result is poor cash flow. If the client's needs are greater than anticipated, the consultant may have difficulty in setting aside enough time to properly do the work. The result may be that the client gets poorer quality services or other contracts may suffer.

Usually these agreements establish a minimum level of services with an established rate for work over and above that level.

Such contracts are common in the legal profession and are growing in popularity as arrangements between large corporations and large consulting firms. This type of contract makes sense for the larger client, who often needs various consulting services at a given time. A smaller company may need specialized consulting somewhat regularly. For example, during the start-up period for installing a computer system, a small or medium-sized company may have frequent need for a consultant's services. Such a situation can call for a retainer agreement.

Availability Retainer Agreements

In an availability retainer agreement a consultant is available to the client, usually for a specified level of services. This can take the form of a *time retainer*, in which the consultant performs a specified service on a regular basis, or a *base retainer*, in which the consultant delivers a fixed period of services each month for a fixed fee. With a base retainer the agreement is that time over and above the fixed period will be invoiced at a specified hourly or daily rate.

In a time retainer agreement, the consultant performs a specific activity on a periodic (usually monthly) basis. Occasionally consultants find themselves spending more time with the client than the retainer is worth. Yet they put up with the ''overwork'' because the up-front money is a kind of insurance policy. After a while these arrangements tend to break down because the consultant starts to cut corners and the output suffers. The client then becomes dissatisfied and the relationship stops being a fruitful one.

Making Retainers Work for You

A base retainer is more likely to work if it is a time retainer for a specified scope of work at a specific fee or a base retainer for a specified number of days or clock hours at a specific fee. Suppose that the consultant is to train all new sales personnel about product competition. An analysis by the consultant suggests that anticipated sales, turnover rate, knowledge of new sales personnel, and the like will result in four days of work per month. If the consultant's daily billing rate is $600, the retainer could be set at $2,400 per month.

If the amount of time to be expended is variable in nature, a base retainer will be more effective. Suppose the client's technical staff needs high-level engineering data and resources to meet the requirements of specific customer applications. Both you and the client don't know how much help will be required. You figure your time at $50 per hour and agree to provide the client with 40 hours a month for a fixed amount of $2,000. If the client needs only 30 hours, you still get your $2,000. If the client needs 50 hours in a given month, you will collect $2,500.

With everything clearly specified, clients are well aware of what they are getting and consultants do not feel as though they are being taken advantage of. In this case the retainer is a smart idea.

If you decide that an up-front payment is best for you, getting it generally depends on how well you can exert your will on others. In American business most people expect to pay for services rendered, not for services to be rendered. If you want a retainer, you are cutting across the grain of that tendency. So you must be very firm about your practice.

If you give the impression that you might make an exception, if you seem afraid to lose the client, you will not get your way. Be firm, be insistent. Your only risk is that you will encounter an equally strong-willed client or one whose employer's policy forbids up-front payments.

PERFORMANCE

In any contract when the payment of your fee depends on performance, make sure you and your client both agree on what performance means. A performance contract is not one that says, "If the client is happy, he/she will pay the consultant." Performance has to be something measurable, such as a 10% increase in sales volume, a 4% increase in gross profit, or a 3% decline in personnel turnover. That's the type of performance you can prove in court if need be. The performance-related contract is valuable when there is high-gain potential and it can help overcome client resistance.

High-Gain Potential. In a situation with high-gain potential, you may see that a client will reap substantial and perhaps ongoing financial benefits from the consultation. The performance contract enables you to participate in those benefits. Perhaps the most important thing to remember about performance contracts is that you should not speculate with the client. Do not assume more risk than you have to. Use performance contracts only on sure things.

Almost as important a rule is this: Be very cautious about sharing in profits. At the flick of a pen, profits can be either created or turned into losses. A less-than-honest client could leave you with nothing. Even a perfectly honest client is put into an uncomfortable spot by sharing in profits. To reduce taxes, the client has to show reduced profits. Yet doing so also reduces your fees.

So negotiate for participation in gross sales, gross margin, or some aspect of cost savings. Share in anything that is easily measurable and that is defined in one way by accounting standards.

Client Resistance. Sometimes clients just don't believe that you can do what you say you can. In such cases, offer to work on a performance contract. As soon as you do, the client starts to regard you as someone who is sure enough of success to take a share in the risk. The offer is a very effective way to overcome the uncertainty of a client who is otherwise ready to sign a contract.

Surprisingly, that contract is not likely to be a performance contract—even though you offered one. Client organizations are simply not disposed to deal on a performance basis. From a legal viewpoint, these organizations generally do not have standard performance contracts in the drawer. So either they have to confer with the legal department, which means a weeks-long delay for sure, or they have to hire outside legal help, which means a fairly heavy cash outlay. From an accounting point of view, client organizations could have to make up special procedures for handling your account. Finally, although the people you deal with may be able to approve a check for a flat payment, they may not have the authority to encumber their employers with a performance-related obligation. Getting that authorization may draw more attention to their consulting needs than they care to have. All in all, you're likely to get a contract if you offer to work on a performance basis, but that contract can still be one that puts less risk on you.

You are more likely to offer and get performance contracts with small businesses. You are more likely to be talking with the owner, who can authorize such payments. Small businesses may not have the money available to pay for your services as you deliver work, so making part of the payment dependent on future events makes it easier to pay. It may cost the business more in the long run, but there are increased profits to offset the expense.

Enforcing a Performance Contract. On occasion clients refuse to implement the consultant's recommendations. Although the consultant designs and develops a system for improvement in performance, the client fails to implement it. Or the client implements the plan haphazardly or ineffectively. No savings are realized, no volume increases effected, and so on. As a result the consultant gets no performance fees.

This is a common problem. The solution lies mainly with foresight. A clause in the contract should stipulate that the client is to pay you a certain fee if the plan is not implemented fully and as mutually agreed. With such a clause, you have some protection. Without it, you're just about out of luck.

SUMMARY

Your ability to select the right fee payment structure for a particular consulting project will lead to greater client satisfaction and a higher level of profits for you. Inappropriate fee structures are going to lead to a lower level of services. If you are locked into a long-term contract without a cost reimbursement arrangement, you may have to cut corners on the services you provide just to survive in business. Likewise, if you realize that the contract format you have chosen leaves you with little or no profit, your incentive for performing well is considerably reduced. Knowing how to charge is good for you and for your client.

The fee structure arrangement figures in the proposal process, in which you submit a proposed budget to the client. It is also reflected in the choice of contract, which spells out the payment structure and evaluation procedures, if any. Now that you know how to determine the value of your services and charge for those services, it is time to consider the proposal-writing process.

CHAPTER 3

What a Proposal Does for You

Survey research shows that 95% of all consultations with a dollar value in excess of $5,000 require a proposal and that 70% require that the proposal be submitted in writing. Despite the need for producing an effective written proposal, most consultants are not known for their proposal-writing skills. The reasons for this are clear.

First, consultants tend to approach proposal writing as a technical task. However, the proposal is primarily a marketing tool. A dazzling display of technical knowledge written in specialized language leaves many clients confused and worried that they won't understand what the consultant will do if the project is approved.

Second, consultants tend to disclose too much when they present clients with a proposal. Too much detailed information can make the prospective client self-sufficient and eliminate the need for the consultant's services. If the proposal solves the problem, there isn't any need to retain the consultant's services.

Third, consultants have studied the art of proposal writing from the perspective of general proposal writing. But what applies to a proposal for a major defense contractor to produce tanks may not be true at all for a consulting proposal. A consultant is selling talent, creativity, and specialized knowledge. These benefits aren't sold the same way that manufacturing or construction ability is.

With a different point of view you, as a consultant, can approach proposal writing with the sense of opportunity and creativity that is called for. A good proposal does several positive things.

First, a good proposal sells your services. It is a marketing tool that leaves the prospective client convinced that it is time to retain your services. This happens because a well-written proposal gives you control over defining the problem and sketching out a solution. You can educate and mold the client's opinions and ideas about the project through your proposal.

Second, when you see yourself as being in control of the proposal process, you can avoid disclosing too much about your approach to the client's needs. This happens when you understand that the proposal is a marketing tool and not a research assignment. It does represent research and thought on your part, but the actual work on the client's needs is delivered during the consultation and as part of your final report.

Third, an effective proposal gives you control over fee setting. Part I of this book gave you solid guidelines for understanding your worth and setting a dollar value on your services. The proposal sets out the job you are going to do and states how much that job is going to cost. An effective proposal communicates to the client that you can do the job, you can do it well, and you are worth being paid what you are asking.

Fourth, the written proposal defines you as a reliable member of the business community. A proposal that simply gives technical information shows that you are an expert, but it doesn't show that you understand business. A good written proposal shows your understanding of business through a professional approach to pricing your services and by using language and concepts that the client understands.

Finally, a quality written proposal raises you out of the ranks of amateurs and defines you as a professional consultant. Many consultants start out part time and tend to neglect the need for tight business structure. They may be working for friends or close associates. A well-written proposal is especially important for the beginning consultant because it shows a professional attitude and sets the tone for future consultations.

A quality proposal can be so vital to marketing success that even if your client does not request or require one, you should probably provide it anyway. You may even discover with many clients, particularly the more sophisticated and experienced, that you can collect a fee for the proposal effort. Successful consultants often develop a short or mini-proposal as a marketing piece which proposes a full-scale proposal as the first step in a consultation. The first contract is for needs analysis and proposal development. A follow-on contract would likely be for the work identified as necessary by the proposal.

This part of the book presents a step-by-step approach to writing a proposal for consulting services. Like a cookbook it lists all the ingredients that go into the written proposal. It sets out a graphic representation of each step you must perform to put together a winning proposal. Each step is divided into tasks and every task is illustrated. You are also given strategies to help you make decisions on when to include optional sections in the proposal.

You are given detailed instructions on how to carry out the technical tasks involved in producing a proposal, such as the development of functional flow diagrams, the construction of time lines, budgeting, and so on. Of course, tasks such as an audit evaluation or an analysis of client needs are not directly part of the proposal-writing process. This section covers the actual production of a written proposal and does not delve into the myriad technical procedures that might be part of the consultation.

This section also includes a proposal evaluation questionnaire that you can apply to each proposal you write. At first the evaluation will help you improve the quality of each part of the proposal and make sure that you are including everything that should be there without giving away your services for free. Later the evaluation can keep you from stagnating. If every proposal starts to sound the same as the last, you need a fresh look at the process that begins with an honest and thorough evaluation.

The successful proposal naturally leads to drafting a contract. Part III of the book covers that very important element in successful consulting and you will see how your fee-setting strategy and the proposal give you important input into setting up and writing the contract.

CHAPTER 4

The Proposal-Writing Process

Successful marketing of your services requires that you communicate to the client your complete understanding of his or her needs. This begins when you confer with your client in the initial interview and feed back your perception of the client's needs. Then your awareness and appreciation of the client's perceived needs are expressed in the written proposal.

Some consultants mistakenly conclude that they should simply restate the client's statement of needs. Nothing could be more wrong. The client has sought out the consultant's services, at least in part, to obtain an independent, unbiased, fresh approach to the determination of need. At the same time the client expects to see evidence that the consultant has considered and evaluated the client's perception of the need for a consultation.

The client may be specific or vague about needs. When the client is specific, the role of the consultant is to evaluate the quality of the client's decision making and to accept the need as presented, reject it in its entirety, or accept it in part. The principal difficulty here is that the client's analysis may result in limiting the scope of the search the consultant undertakes.

When the client gives a vague need by saying something like, "I don't know, but somehow we should be more profitable than we are," the consultant has the liberty of approaching the task of need determination with less structure and more imagination. The vague client need usually results in a more protracted and time-consuming analysis of the need.

Usually you determine during the early discussions with your prospective client whether you will submit a written proposal. The client may request it directly or you may offer to submit one for a variety of reasons. You can use this checklist as a guide in deciding whether to submit a written proposal:

Is it strategically prudent to submit a proposal as a way of enhancing the prospects of being awarded this consultation?

Is the project so large and complex that a written proposal will be a valuable guide to both client and consultant?

Will communications be improved between client and consultant by a written proposal?

Will opportunities for future consultations be increased by submitting a written proposal?

Even if you decide not to offer a formal, written proposal, you should go through most of the steps in the proposal-writing process to define and organize the project. By being clear about the purpose and structure of the consultation you can keep costs under control and work more efficiently and effectively.

THE FUNCTIONAL FLOW DIAGRAM (FFD)

Client definition of need is the beginning place for your development of a written proposal. The entire process is presented as a functional flow diagram (FFD). The FFD is a pictorial representation of the activities you will carry out in preparing the proposal. You often include an FFD in your proposals to depict the sequence of activities you will perform for your client.

The FFD is valuable to you, the consultant, as well. Producing a concise diagram of the project helps you to organize your thinking and determine what procedures are necessary to complete the project. It complements the proposal as a guide to internal management procedures. Using the FFD as a guide you can keep costs and labor expenses from getting out of control.

The entire FFD is called the project. It is made up of a series of lines and boxes. A label is attached to each box to represent a major component of the project. The label usually describes one or more activities that may go on during that segment of the project.

> *Example:* In the course of a consulting project, you may be called on to prepare and administer a survey instrument. In the FFD this can be expressed as shown in Figure 4.1.

FIGURE 4.1
Preparing and administering a survey instrument

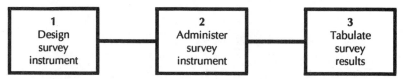

The label in any box of the FFD should begin with an action verb such as *administer, design, compute, analyze, tabulate, determine,* and the like. Every box in your FFD must have an input and an output. In the example above, the input to Box 1 is the requirement for information that gives rise to the whole sequence of activities in the first place. The output of the third box is the survey results. Make sure that every FFD box has both an input and an output.

While you are designing your FFD, you may see a need for additional activities.

> *Example:* You may decide that you need to determine the names of the people to be surveyed in the foregoing example. The result of this activity or step would have to feed into Box 2. (See Figure 4.2.)

Look on the FFD as a working document that guides your development of the project. As you write the proposal, the FFD will probably require modifications. Don't hesitate to make changes. It would be unusual for the first draft to be the same as the one you finally give your client in the proposal.

FIGURE 4.2
Additional activities in administering a survey instrument

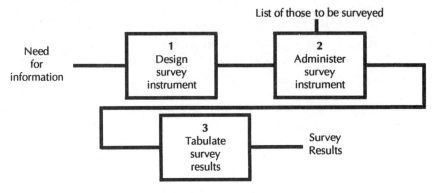

STEP-BY-STEP PROPOSAL WRITING

The FFD of the proposal-writing process, shown on pages 36–37, shows how this development process works. The process begins with the input of an interested prospect.

Steps 1 through 4 relate to gathering information about needs and formulating a statement of objectives based on those needs.

Steps 5 through 10 concern setting up the basic structure of the project, with Steps 8, 9, and 10 enabling you to generate more specific statements of project structure.

- The objective of Step 5 is a translation of the goals in Step 4 into terms that relate to the project. Goals are general directions; objectives are action-oriented statements.
- Step 6 sets down the overall structure of the project based on the objectives.
- Step 7 is the first draft of an outline of procedures for the project.
- The project time line (Step 8) and personnel loading analysis (Step 9) begin to specify how the objectives will actually be met—without revealing exactly what will be done, so as not to give away services.
- Step 10 is a review and modification of the basic project structure.

Steps 11 through 15 set up the structures that communicate to the prospective client that you are responsible and that you can do the job. Each of these steps is clearly related to marketing. You are anticipating possible objections that the client may have and dealing with them before they become serious barriers to your getting the contract.

- The evaluation plan (Step 11) and reporting plan (Step 12) demonstrate that you are accountable for the quality of your work and will communicate with the client.
- The capabilities section (Step 13) and statement of assurances (Step 14) show specifically that you can get the job done and can handle such things as potential legal or liability problems.
- By deciding to include certain appendices and support documents in Step 15, you are providing evidence of your thoroughness and expertise without requiring the client to read these materials. It is a practical reality that most proposals, even successful ones, are never read in their entirety. Some important material is relegated to the appendices simply because it is too technical for the average reader. At the same time you are reassuring the client about your qualifications.

Step 16, developing the project budget and disclosure statement, is one of the cornerstones of a successful proposal. The aim is not merely to come up with a monetary figure. You want to set a fair price while demonstrating that your price represents the cost of getting the project done right. Choosing where to place this information in the proposal and how to present it is very important in terms of your marketing strategy.

Steps 17 and 18 concern the actual writing of the proposal and related documents.

- In Step 17, the abstract and draft letter are constructed.
- The evaluation provided in Step 18 is a review of all aspects of the finished document including its use as a marketing instrument, a guide to project structure, and a review of each section in the proposal.

Steps 19, 20, and 21 relate to the use of the proposal as a marketing tool. A quality delivery and follow-up indicate that you understand the function of the proposal as a marketing instrument. Many

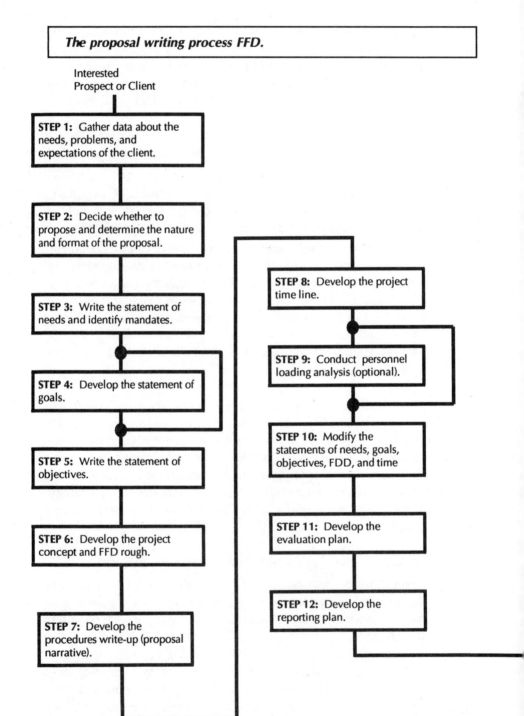

The proposal writing process FFD.

Interested
Prospect or Client

STEP 1: Gather data about the needs, problems, and expectations of the client.

STEP 2: Decide whether to propose and determine the nature and format of the proposal.

STEP 3: Write the statement of needs and identify mandates.

STEP 4: Develop the statement of goals.

STEP 5: Write the statement of objectives.

STEP 6: Develop the project concept and FFD rough.

STEP 7: Develop the procedures write-up (proposal narrative).

STEP 8: Develop the project time line.

STEP 9: Conduct personnel loading analysis (optional).

STEP 10: Modify the statements of needs, goals, objectives, FDD, and time

STEP 11: Develop the evaluation plan.

STEP 12: Develop the reporting plan.

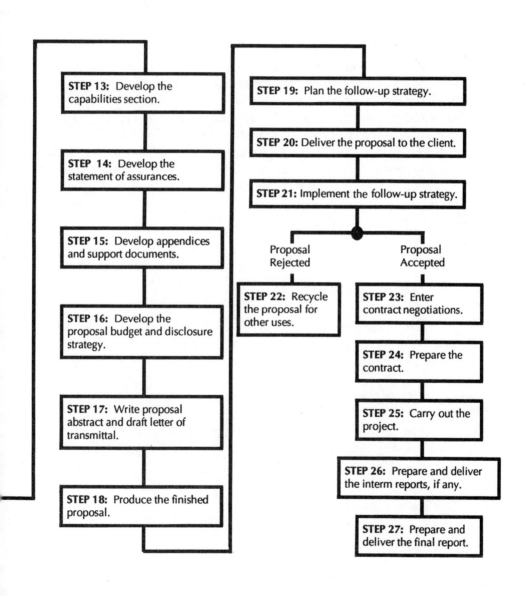

STEP 13: Develop the capabilities section.

STEP 14: Develop the statement of assurances.

STEP 15: Develop appendices and support documents.

STEP 16: Develop the proposal budget and disclosure strategy.

STEP 17: Write proposal abstract and draft letter of transmittal.

STEP 18: Produce the finished proposal.

STEP 19: Plan the follow-up strategy.

STEP 20: Deliver the proposal to the client.

STEP 21: Implement the follow-up strategy.

Proposal Rejected

Proposal Accepted

STEP 22: Recycle the proposal for other uses.

STEP 23: Enter contract negotiations.

STEP 24: Prepare the contract.

STEP 25: Carry out the project.

STEP 26: Prepare and deliver the interm reports, if any.

STEP 27: Prepare and deliver the final report.

consultants just send the proposal to their clients and hope for a sale. In general this practice is not a good sales strategy. It is too easy to file a proposal and forget it. The sections on follow-up show you how to be remembered and have the greatest chance of making a sale.

If the proposal is initially rejected, go on to Step 22 and recycle the proposal for other uses. Your prospect may decide to use your services in the future or others may need your services and you may be able to use the same proposal with modifications. You can also publish articles based on the research involved in setting up the proposal and that can lead to future business.

If the proposal is immediately successful you are ready to move on to contract negotiation (Steps 23 and 24). Here the proposal and your understanding of fee setting combine to guide you in selecting the right contract for the project. Part III of the book, which deals with contracts, looks at the contract as an integral part of the consulting process. Part of keeping your client satisfied lies in the correct use of contracts. Contracts can also be part of your marketing strategy because they give the client reassurance about your professionalism and attention to important details.

The important thing is to see the written proposal in the context of the entire consulting process. Then you can make the written proposal work for you and turn it into an effective marketing tool that helps you produce satisfied clients.

THE FINAL PROPOSAL

Before the step-by-step analysis of the 22 steps for producing a completed proposal and submitting it to your prospective client, it is useful to look at the contents of the final document.

Organization

The overall organization can vary (see Figure 4.3), but the proposal usually contains a:

- front section
- main section
- budget section
- appendix

FIGURE 4.3
Organization of a proposal

Front Section
Title page
Table of contents
Proposal abstract
Statement of assurances (Step 14)
Statement of needs (Step 3)
Statement of goals (optional) (Step 4)
Statement of objectives (Step 5)
Main Section
Functional flow diagram (pages 36–37)
Project time line (Step 8)
Personnel loading analysis (optional, Step 9)
Proposal narrative
Budget Section
Project budget or budget summary (Step 16)
Statement of capabilities (Step 13)
Appendix
Supporting articles
Letters of thanks
Evidence of abilities

The *front section* begins with the title page and includes the:

- table of contents
- proposal abstract
- statement of assurances
- statement of needs
- statement of goals (optional)
- statement of objectives

The front section introduces the project and gives the reader a quick overview. In just a few minutes your client can get a grasp of the essence of your proposed consultation or project.

The *main section* gives the reader a more detailed description of the project. It usually begins with a functional flow diagram (FFD)—the graphic representation of the steps in the project and their order. Then the following items appear:

- project time line
- personnel loading analysis (optional)
- proposal narrative, a written description of the project that defines the project of services you are proposing. It is the verbal description of the FFD

The main section gives a description of the project that is convincing and discloses enough detail to make it believable without giving your services away.

The *budget section* usually follows the main section. This section contains:

- either a detailed project budget or an abbreviated budget summary
- the statement of capabilities

Depending on circumstances, the budget and fee information may be submitted separately.

The appendix, if needed, presents support documents that don't fit in the main body of the proposal. This includes articles that support your approach, as well as letters of thanks and other evidence of your abilities, such as newspaper articles. This is where you include technical articles and information that specifically supports your proposal, but would clutter the main section of the proposal or make it hard to read.

Order of Presentation

The order of presentation may vary. The time line and personnel loading analysis may appear in the budget section and the abstract may be the first element following the title page. The order is largely determined by considerations of clarity and marketing.

This outline is for a formal proposal that you might generate for a large project. A smaller project would call for an abbreviated proposal. Also, a request for proposal might specify the contents and their order. The example proposal in Appendix E doesn't have some of the elements listed above because the format is dictated by a state agency. However, it does demonstrate the considerations of clarity and good marketing that are embodied in the proposal-writing process.

The step-by-step process that follows is designed to produce the elements of the proposal listed above and guide you in arranging them into a convincing and effective document.

STEP 1: *Gather data about the needs, problems, and expectations of the client.*

The objectives of Step 1 are to identify and verify the client's needs and problems. This is probably the most important step in the entire consulting process. If you and the prospective client do not have a shared perception of what the needs and problems are, the project is sure to become mired in miscommunication. The end result will be failure to make a sale or, worse yet, a dissatisfied client.

The tasks in Step 1 are:

- Task 1.1: Evaluate the client's analysis of need.
- Task 1.2: Gather information about the client's needs from the client, client's personnel, customers, vendors, and records.
- Task 1.3: Verify information with the client and request that the client retain your services (optional).
- Task 1.4: List needs in order of priority.
- Task 1.5: Determine any mandates for action.
- Task 1.6: Identify and quantify the adverse impact of failing to address needs.

TASK 1.1: *Evaluate the client's analysis of need.*

Sometimes the client is vague about the reasons for soliciting a consultation. You may have received a casual expression of concerns. In this case you should go on to Task 1.2 and convert those concerns into a list of needs. If the prospective client presents a list of needs to you, you must evaluate the client's analysis to decide whether to accept or reject

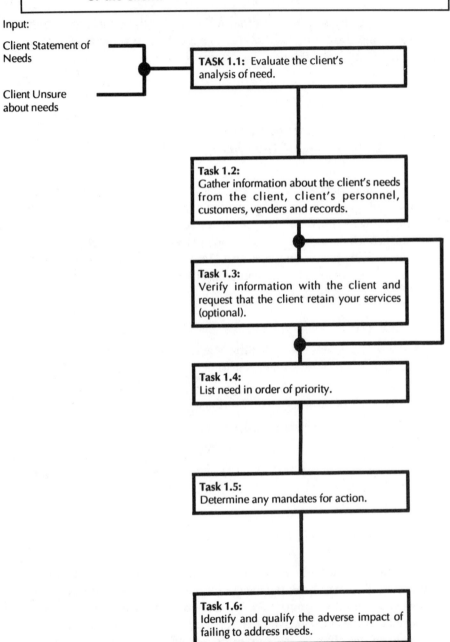

STEP 1: *Gather data about the needs, problems, and expectations of the client.*

Input:

Client Statement of Needs

Client Unsure about needs

TASK 1.1: Evaluate the client's analysis of need.

Task 1.2:
Gather information about the client's needs from the client, client's personnel, customers, venders and records.

Task 1.3:
Verify information with the client and request that the client retain your services (optional).

Task 1.4:
List need in order of priority.

Task 1.5:
Determine any mandates for action.

Task 1.6:
Identify and qualify the adverse impact of failing to address needs.

his or her determination of the needs. The following questions can guide you in evaluating the presented list of needs:

> Does your common sense tell you the client's determination is correct?
>
> Does your personal assessment of the client's intelligence, depth of research and grasp of the situation reinforce his or her determination of needs?
>
> Was the methodology sound?
>
> Is there external, even superficial, evidence that corroborates the client's perception of need?

If you do accept the client's determination of needs, move to Task 1.4. If you reject the client's analysis of needs, or if the client wishes you to identify needs for him or her, move to Task 1.2.

TASK 1.2: *Gather information about the client's needs from the client, client's personnel, customers, vendors, and records.*

You must engage in whatever research, analysis, and information gathering are necessary to identify the client's needs and problems. Use these questions as a guide:

> Do you need to interview the client or any others in the client organization to gather information regarding the need?
>
> Can and should you interview outside individuals such as the client's customers, vendors, or service providers to isolate or clarify problems?
>
> Must you review the client's records and/or procedures to locate the problem?

Dig out all the information necessary to fully understand the need so you can formulate your proposal. Also, consider whether the client has any "hidden needs" that you have not identified. There may be hidden needs that the client does not wish to see formally addressed, but that are very important. Often these hidden needs are the real reason for calling in a consultant, because their sensitive nature prevents members of the client organization from identifying and dealing with them.

> *Example:* John Client may tell you that one of his priority needs is to "review current personnel staffing requirements, procedures, and assignments." By that he may mean that he wishes to put Old Uncle Charlie, who has been with the company for 43 years, out to pasture. However, you are not sure who will have access to your proposal once it is delivered. It might be reviewed by a committee consisting of several executives, including Old Uncle Charlie. Therefore, the need to replace Charlie—and perhaps several other needs—should not be expressly described within the written proposal.

Keep in mind that part of your proposal can be verbal, especially where very sensitive subjects are concerned. You may explain to the client that even though the sensitive areas will not be covered in the written proposal, they will be handled.

Although this instance may seem farfetched, more often than not you will encounter at least one hidden need that must be addressed if you are to fulfill the client's expectations about the project. You may encounter a client who feels some personal embarrassment over a need and therefore hides that need from you. However, to complete Task 1.2, you must test for and ferret out those hidden needs. As a marketing strategy, your grasp of hidden needs and your ability to handle them tactfully is a tremendous advantage. Proper handling of hidden needs can almost guarantee a successful reception for your proposal.

When you believe you understand the client's needs, move on to Task 1.3.

TASK 1.3: *Verify findings with the client and request that the client retain your services (optional).*

You now know what the client's needs are. In some cases you may decide to go on to Task 1.4 and list those needs in priority order. In other cases you may feel the need to verify those needs with the client and form a sound foundation for your consultation. If the client has not already requested a written proposal, it may be appropriate to suggest that your services in developing a proposal be retained at this time.

Use this checklist to be sure you and the client are in agreement about the client's needs:

Does the client agree with your findings?

Can the client, when presented with your findings, point to factual evidence of their existence or their impact on the organization?

Is the client willing to spend organization resources to solve the needs and problems you have identified?

Are the identified needs important enough to have a high priority?

Are there needs of a higher priority which should be addressed? If so, what are they?

Why have these needs not been addressed thus far?

In discussing the client's needs, stress that you and only you have the unique, applicable, acceptable solution to the client's problems. Your aim is to establish a clear connection between the client's needs and your abilities. If the client decides to accept your proposition, he or she may still ask for a written proposal, especially if the project is a large one. Even if the client doesn't request a formal proposal, you should carry out most of the steps to organize and direct your work.

Move on to Task 1.4.

TASK 1.4: *List needs in order of priority.*

Determine which needs must be addressed and resolved first. You may have one set of ideas or priorities and the client may have an entirely different view of what should be done first, second, third, and so on. You must mutually agree on the priority to be assigned to needs/problems and their solutions.

Have you identified any needs that would be less costly to live with than change? By eliminating some needs, you and the client can concentrate on what remains to be done.

Does the client have any "hidden" priorities or problems you have yet to address or discuss? Find out now! By listing priorities, you have the opportunity to meet again with the client and to clarify the true reasons and motives for the consultation through mutual agreement on what has to be done. Make the client collaborate with you in this decision, then move on to Task 1.5.

TASK 1.5: *Determine any mandates for action.*

A mandate for action is usually some basic or widely held belief that adds legitimacy to overcoming problems or pursuing objectives. Establishing a mandate for action adds power to your proposal. Do so whenever and wherever possible.

Mandates for action can include:

- Compliance with existing or expected laws
- Cost effectiveness
- Operational effectiveness
- Profitability
- Creation of synergy
- Avoiding adverse publicity
- Generating positive publicity

The questions below help you to identify and clarify the mandates for your proposal:

> What mandates can you identify within the scope of your present project?
>
> How much pressure is the client experiencing to increase profitability?
>
> Does the client need to reduce or avoid adverse publicity?
>
> Does the client want to increase overall employee health and welfare and thereby increase employees' efficiency?

Whatever the case may be, seek out any and all mandates for action and incorporate them into your proposal and presentation. Once you have determined the mandates that are applicable to your project, move on to Task 1.6.

TASK 1.6: *Identify and quantify the adverse impact of failing to address needs.*

An important part of needs analysis is acquainting the client with the adverse impacts that are likely to result if the identified needs and problems are not attended to. The consultant is well advised to be as dramatic as reasonable in this regard.

Adverse impacts may be stated in terms of undesirable events and results that will affect the client and client organization if the organization fails to respond to the identified needs and problems. Some possible adverse impacts are:

- significant loss of profits
- increase in overhead
- increased employee turnover
- customers deciding to find another supplier

Determine all the adverse impacts of failing to respond to the identified needs and communicate this information directly to your client. Mandates for change are one side of the coin and adverse impacts are the other side. Both you and your client should consider the entire situation before attempting any remedial action.

AT THE CONCLUSION OF EACH STEP . . .

Upon completion of each step, you, the consultant, must test that step and its component parts for validity. Do not omit this test at any point where invalid results would affect the next step. To avoid repetition this point will be addressed only for this step, but be sure to apply it wherever necessary in completing the rest of the steps in the proposal process.

Now that you have determined the client's needs, you must test to determine the validity of each need. Most needs have what is called "face validity." That means that most people in business would agree with the stated need without a mountain of proof that it is worthwhile. For example, the need to establish an inventory control system or the need to increase profitability do not require exhaustive justification.

Now that you have completed your investigation of the client's needs, move on to Step 2.

STEP 2: *Decide whether to propose and determine the nature and format of the proposal.*

The objective of Step 2 is to decide whether to propose and to determine the nature and format of the proposal. Your decision whether

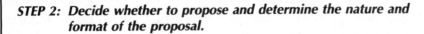

STEP 2: Decide whether to propose and determine the nature and format of the proposal.

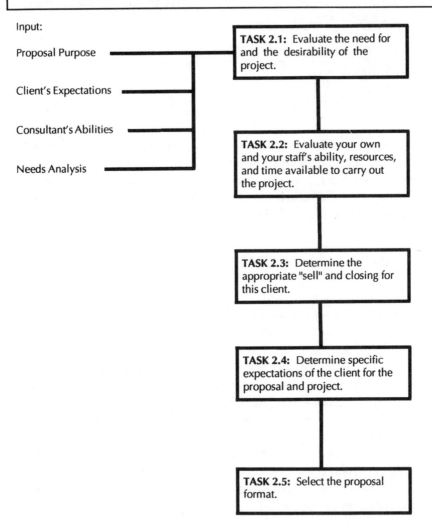

Input:

Proposal Purpose

Client's Expectations

Consultant's Abilities

Needs Analysis

TASK 2.1: Evaluate the need for and the desirability of the project.

TASK 2.2: Evaluate your own and your staff's ability, resources, and time available to carry out the project.

TASK 2.3: Determine the appropriate "sell" and closing for this client.

TASK 2.4: Determine specific expectations of the client for the proposal and project.

TASK 2.5: Select the proposal format.

to propose should be based on the actual need for an intervention and your ability to successfully carry out the consultation. If you decide to propose you need to make intelligent marketing decisions based on the the extent to which the client is convinced of the necessity of intervention. Your choice of format for the proposal is based on your evaluation of the client.

The tasks in Step 2 are:

- Task 2.1: Evaluate the need for and the desirability of the project.
- Task 2.2: Evaluate your own and your staff's ability, resources, and time available to carry out the project.
- Task 2.3: Determine the appropriate "sell" and closing for this client.
- Task 2.4: Determine specific expectations of the client for the proposal and project.
- Task 2.5: Select the proposal format.

TASK 2.1: *Evaluate the need for and the desirability of the project.*

At this point you have limited information on which to decide if you and the client make a viable working combination. The checklist below can help you decide whether to proceed. If one or two of these questions come out negative, undue concern is probably inappropriate. If three or four lean toward the negative, take a very careful look at the desirability of the project. If more than four are negative the project should probably be avoided. The risk of problems down the road is too great.

Do you want this consulting assignment?

Does the client want the project?

Does the client want *you* to perform the consultation?

Have you identified any personality conflicts in your relationship with this prospective client or with the staff of the client organization? If so, how can you overcome the identified problems?

Does the client persist in a set of unrealistic expectations for the consultation?

Has the client made a request that you perform illegal or unethical acts on his or her behalf?

Does the client fail to appreciate the value of the services you will provide?

Have you identified a potential or actual conflict of interest?

Do you perceive that the client will be unable or unwilling to pay your fee?

Once you have completed your evaluation, move on to Task 2.2.

TASK 2.2: *Evaluate your own and your staff's ability, resources, and time available to carry out the project.*

As a professional you want to be sure that you can handle any consultation you undertake. It is frustrating as well as damaging to your reputation to attempt projects that demand abilities or access to personnel that you lack. These questions will help you evaluate your resources for any particular project:

> Is the nature of the work or task you are to provide the client outside your interest, capabilities, or experience?
>
> Do you feel that the technology and strategies you are capable of employing for this client are fully appropriate for the task to be accomplished?
>
> Do you feel that you have sufficient time to complete the client's assignment at the level of quality desired, within schedule? How busy are you?
>
> Is your staff large enough to handle the work load through time scheduling or will you have to hire additional personnel to complete the project on time?
>
> Does your staff (or simply you, as an individual consultant) possess adequate resources and experience to complete the project to your satisfaction?

Many consultants don't have a professional staff and don't hire professional assistance. They get assignments done by subcontracting to other professionals. Clerical help is another matter and most consultants hire the clerical support they need on a full- or part-time basis.

Move on to Task 2.3.

TASK 2.3: *Determine the appropriate "sell" and closing for this client.*

Two important questions must be answered in picking the proper sales approach for your prospective client:

Did the client request the proposal or are you submitting an unsolicited proposal?

What will it take to close this prospective client?

If your services have been sought out by the client, your proposal will communicate to the client your understanding of his or her needs. Your proposal will demonstrate your grasp of the reasons for the consultation.

However, if you seek to *inform* the client of the need for utilizing your services in an unsolicited proposal, you must convince the client of the validity of the needs you have identified and the wisdom of acting on them within the proposal.

Once you have determined the degree of sales/marketing necessary within the proposal, move on to Task 2.4.

TASK 2.4: *Determine specific expectations of the client for the proposal and project.*

You should be able to confirm the client's expectations for the project based on the information you've gathered so far. If you feel unsure about any specifics or expectations, address the problem or question with the client *now*. You can't hope to fulfill his or her expectations or solve problems unless you have completely defined all the specific requirements. Use this checklist to make sure you have covered all the client's expectations of your consultation:

What exactly are the client's expectations for your consultation?

Has the client identified *specific requirements* for your project?

Have you convinced yourself that you are exactly what the client expects of the project?

Do you know what the client expects of you personally?

Once you are certain that you have all the client's expectations completely spelled out and defined, move on to Task 2.5.

TASK 2.5: *Select the proposal format.*

Now you must decide what proposal format will best present the needs of the project and ensure that you will receive the consulting assignment. The situation should indicate to you which format will represent your ideas to best advantage. These questions will guide you in identifying the format that will get the job done.

Has the client sought out your services?

Are you completely finished with the marketing phase and do you have a firm commitment from the client on retaining your services?

Would a brief or detailed proposal be more effective?

Is the client the sole decision maker?

You may want to opt for a letter format, especially where brevity is at premium. A letter proposal is merely a foreshortened version of a full, formal proposal. It may be helpful to consider a letter proposal in terms of a written report to the client which details your findings from the need analysis.

Conversely, does your proposal have to be read and reviewed by a committee of decision makers? If so, you obviously have to continue your marketing efforts within the proposal to convince the committee of the project's necessity. Of course, there is a certain level of marketing in any proposal, if only to reinforce the client's decision to retain your services. It's just a question of degree.

If the level of detail in a formal proposal contributes to the selling of your project, then you should certainly submit one. The situation in which the proposal will be read and the audience who will read it should guide you as to the best format.

To some extent the size, complexity, and level of formality of the client oganization determines the type of proposal. A large, complex organization is used to receiving formal proposals that may contain technical material. A small entrepreneurial organization may be more comfortable with a less formal document. Some organizations are so informal that they accept or even request verbal proposals. Even with a verbal proposal you still need to consider everything covered in this section of the book.

Once you have decided what proposal format best suits your needs, you have completed Step 2. Move on to Step 3.

STEP 3: *Write the statement of needs and identify mandates.*

The objective of Step 3 is to document all statements of need and any accompanying mandates for action. This is an important element in your marketing strategy. If your potential client isn't aware of these needs or is not motivated to respond to them, there is little hope of selling your services.

The tasks in Step 3 are:

- Task 3.1: Write the need statements in order of priority.
- Task 3.2: Test for the client's acceptance.
- Task 3.3: Modify the need statements as necessary.

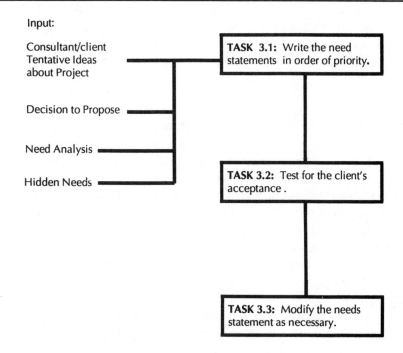

STEP 3: *Write the statement of needs and identify mandates.*

Input:

Consultant/client Tentative Ideas about Project

Decision to Propose

Need Analysis

Hidden Needs

TASK 3.1: Write the need statements in order of priority.

TASK 3.2: Test for the client's acceptance.

TASK 3.3: Modify the needs statement as necessary.

TASK 3.1: *Write the need statements in order of priority.*

In Step 1 you determined needs, verified these needs with the client, and prioritized each. You then determined any mandates for action resulting from the needs identified.

In this task, you formally write each statement of need and its accompanying mandate for action, if any. Describe the problems or their adverse effects in terms that are meaningful *to the client*. Give supporting evidence so the readers of your needs list can independently assess the extent and validity of the needs your consultation is to address. Foster among client personnel a sense of obligation to marshall resources to respond to the needs you have identified.

Make each need statement consistent with the scope of the response you are planning. Make your statements dramatic, compelling, quantified, and able to arouse concern in the reader. The most important item is the bottom line. Clients want to see projected savings or profits before they are willing to put out money for your services. It is persuasive to have quotations or other support material that identifies real savings or increased profits as part of the mandates section.

If you cannot make hard, definite, quantifiable statements based on the input from the first two steps, you may need to perform additional research and analysis to solidify the client's needs.

When your needs statements are clear and firm, move on to Task 3.2.

TASK 3.2: *Test for the client's acceptance.*

Submit all need statements to your client and/or the client's staff so they can evaluate each need statement you write. These tests of each need statement by the people who must live with the results of your consultation reinforce the validity of your determination of needs.

This procedure is most often informal. You don't usually need to present a written list of needs. In discussions with the client and client's staff, you get their understanding about the validity of the needs. This test may have been carried out in Step 1, but it is more often done at this point of the process.

You might also test the need statements on people outside the client organization who work with the organization and may be familiar with problem areas.

Once you have satisfied yourself and your client as to the soundness of your need statements, move on to Task 3.3.

TASK 3.3: *Modify the need statements as necessary.*

In this task you rewrite the need statements based on your testing for client acceptability in Task 3.2. Integrate any feedback you received from the client or client staff so that your need statements reflect both your estimation of the problems you face within the scope of your project *and* the client's ideas, opinions, or input. If necessary, alter your drafted need statements to satisfy both these requirements.

Remember, the statement of needs has a dual communications objective: First, it should enable the reviewers to independently assess the extent and validity of the needs the consultation addresses. Second, it must foster among the client personnel a sense of obligation to marshall resources to respond to the needs you have identified. Convincing clients to retain your services is more difficult if they are unaware of the needs your proposed consultation addresses.

If you have been asked to respond to the needs determined to exist by the client, your task of communication may involve little more than a documentation or formalization of what the client already believes. However, if others in the client organization are not convinced that the identified needs are real, your proposal may be the tool your client employs to:

- build internal commitment among personnel about these needs
- get agreement from friends, associates, or even other consultants that these needs exist or are logical
- serve as a basis for obtaining proposals from other consultants

Even if the client has identified the needs for you, do not take the communication task lightly. It is possible to write an effective statement of needs and still not be selected to carry out the consultation. If the statement of needs is too persuasive, the client may see the problem as more severe than first perceived and feel that it warrants a higher level of organizational concern.

Your statement of need must be consistent with the scope of the response you are planning. A technical response that addresses only part of the need identified is usually viewed as insufficient. Don't paint a big picture and follow up with a little plan of action.

In writing your statement of needs, be certain to describe the problems or adverse effects in terms that are meaningful to the client. It is appropriate and necessary to be both quantitative and dramatic. Avoid the use of soft terms such as "a substantial number," "a high degree," or "a downward trend." Make use of hard, quantifiable statements such as "a 15% decrease in profits will result" or "a 23% increase in sales is projected." This does not mean that you simply convert all soft terms to hard statements. To do so might distort the need. If you are unable to make hard, definite, and quantitative statements, perhaps you need to perform additional research and analysis.

When you are satisfied with the needs and mandates list move on to Step 4.

STEP 4: *Develop the statement of goals.*

The objective of Step 4 is to decide if a statement of goals will be useful for your project and to write specific goal statements if they are necessary. Goals are more abstract than objectives. Goals are broad statements of purpose or intent, usually communicating some value orientation. Goals are never met, you only work toward achieving them. Objectives are specific, more limited in scope, and can be met or exceeded. Some clients respond to statements of goals, others wonder why you bothered to write them down. You have to evaluate the situation.

The tasks in Step 4 are:

- Task 4.1: Decide whether goal statements are necessary.
- Task 4.2: Link needs to the purposes of the client.
- Task 4.3: Write goal statements related to the client's overall purposes.

TASK 4.1: *Decide whether goal statements are necessary.*

You may not require the formal development and inclusion of goal statements for your project. Your client may react to a discussion of

STEP 4: Develop the statement of goals.

Input:

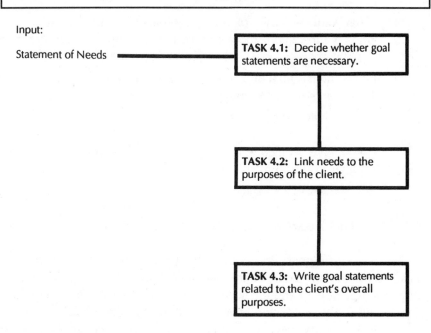

Statement of Needs

TASK 4.1: Decide whether goal statements are necessary.

TASK 4.2: Link needs to the purposes of the client.

TASK 4.3: Write goal statements related to the client's overall purposes.

goals by saying that he or she could care less about long-range goals and as far as your consultation is concerned, is interested only in the design and implementation of an inventory control system. The client's only goal may be increased profitability or decreased overhead.

If you are proposing to the federal government, chances are you will be required to state formal goals. If goals will strengthen and enhance your proposal, include them. If they are clearly not necessary or not required by the client, move on to Step 5. If you decide goal statements are required, the following questions should help you accurately identify the meanings, assumptions, and values embedded in your client's goal statements:

Do the stated goals identified by your client form a foundation for the objectives of the consultation?

Is there clear agreement between you and your client on the goals identified?

Are any of the stated goals unnecessary to the consultation?

Do any of these stated goals hide achievement of the project outcomes?

What values—basic or emerging—underlie the client's stated goals: values about the nature of human beings, about desirable societal characteristics, about lifestyles, about learning?

Is the client's goal an extrapolation of the past or present into the future or is it a new direction?

Is the client's goal the result of faddism?

If you have decided to include goals in your proposal, move onto Task 4.2. Otherwise go on to Step 5.

TASK 4.2: *Link needs to the purposes of the client.*

If specific goals are required for your proposal and project, you must make logical connections or links between the organizational purposes of the client and the needs you have identified. Goals should be clearly tied to the needs you have agreed on with the client.

Relate these needs, in order of their priority, to the overall business and organizational purposes of the client organization.

> *Example:* A client may be facing stiff competition from producers in Latin America. The need might be identified as improved quality control or improved inventory management. The linked goals could be enhancing competitive posture, price reductions, and increasing product acceptability.

Once you have accomplished the link-up between needs and goals, move on to Task 4.3.

TASK 4.3: *Write goal statements related to the client's overall purposes.*

You've determined what goals are necessary to your project and you've linked these goals with their needs. Now write one or more goals statements related to your client's overall purposes for each need statement you drafted in Step 3. Then move on to Step 5.

STEP 5: *Write the statement of objectives.*

The objective of Step 5 is to establish your performance criteria or the objectives for the consultation. The statement of objectives directly addresses and resolves the needs you have identified in the statement of needs. Once these needs are agreed on, it becomes vital for you to establish objectives that will direct your efforts throughout the project. In a performance contract, these objectives will likely be the criteria that will guide your work and serve to gauge your performance. Also, if you have included a statement of goals as part of the proposal, the objectives are steps toward achieving those goals.

The tasks in Step 5 are:

- Task 5.1: Decide how detailed terminal objectives must be.
- Task 5.2: Develop one or more behavior statements for each need or goal.
- Task 5.3: Develop a criterion statement for each behavior statement.
- Task 5.4: Develop a condition statement for each behavior statement.
- Task 5.5: Combine behavior, criterion, and condition statements to form statements of objectives.
- Task 5.6: Decide whether interim and/or audit objectives are required.
- Task 5.7: Repeat Tasks 5.3, 5.4, and 5.5 for each interim and audit objective.

TASK 5.1: *Decide how detailed objectives must be.*

Your statements of objectives must address and resolve the needs you have identified. These objectives guide your work during the course of the project and also serve to measure your performance.

You must be very careful in determining the level of detail of your terminal objectives because you may be held accountable and responsible for meeting the objectives your proposal set for your consultation. Therefore, you must be specific, yet cautious, in establishing the outcomes you will pursue throughout the project.

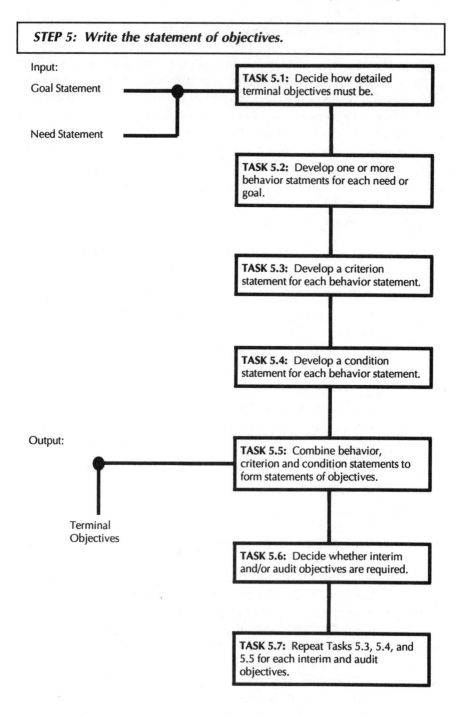

STEP 5: Write the statement of objectives.

Input:

Goal Statement

Need Statement

TASK 5.1: Decide how detailed terminal objectives must be.

TASK 5.2: Develop one or more behavior statments for each need or goal.

TASK 5.3: Develop a criterion statement for each behavior statement.

TASK 5.4: Develop a condition statement for each behavior statement.

Output:

TASK 5.5: Combine behavior, criterion and condition statements to form statements of objectives.

Terminal
Objectives

TASK 5.6: Decide whether interim and/or audit objectives are required.

TASK 5.7: Repeat Tasks 5.3, 5.4, and 5.5 for each interim and audit objectives.

Objectives are based, in part, on client resources and requirements for quality. The Department of Defense, for example, requires accuracy and precision from a consultant and is willing to pay for it. If the city parks department wants to determine how many people used the park system last year to support a grant application, it requires less accuracy and can't afford the level of quality that the DOD can. Does your client want a Pinto or a Cadillac? (See Figure 4.4.)

Never make your objectives more specific than the client requires because your objectives create obligations that you must meet. Use the following questions when considering the level of specificity, detail, and content for your objectives:

How much is enough?

What level of specificity and detail will satisfy the client?

What level of specificity and detail will satisfy the client's staff?

If your objective were to be met, would it complete a plan?

If your objective were to be met, would it be a means or a step toward another objective farther in the future?

Is your objective stated as a general state of affairs?

Is your objective stated as a specific state of affairs?

Can you determine any actual or potential conflicts between stated goals and the proposed objectives?

Is your objective technical? Does it require a certain technology to accomplish?

Is your objective social? Does it require mainly social organization or application?

Is your objective social *and* technical?

Is your objective preventive, inventive, or adaptive?

While asking yourself these questions keep in mind that your objectives must be *specific, definite, measurable,* and *attainable.*

Once you have determined the specificity of your objectives and have considered and agreed with the level of obligation they place on your consultation, move on to Task 5.2.

FIGURE 4.4
Relating terminal objectives to client expectations

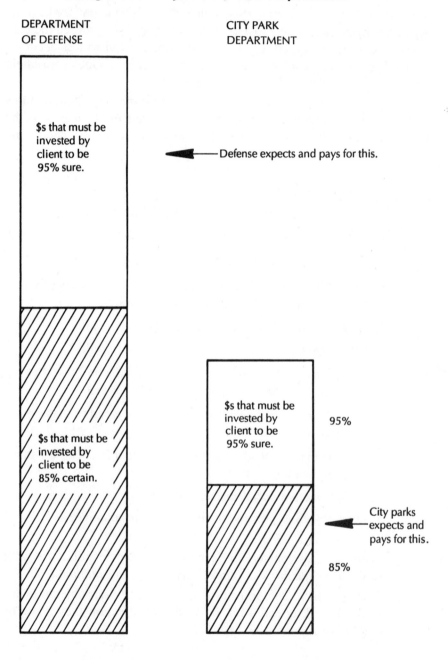

TASK 5.2: *Develop one or more behavior statements for each need or goal.*

In this task you must decide what behavior changes are required to attain your stated objectives. These questions will help to identify possible behavior changes that could or should result from this consultation:

Must client staff or the client alter past behaviors, procedures, or methods to achieve your objectives?

Were those past behaviors responsible for success in the organization and, therefore, are they significantly entrenched in current business dealings?

Can your client and the client's staff realistically be expected to make this behavior change within the scope of your consultation? Within the time frame of your project?

Must you teach them new behaviors?

Have you properly estimated and researched the client organization's ability and willingness to alter past behaviors to achieve the stated objectives?

Are the client and his staff sufficiently convinced of and committed to the objective to work hard enough to attain the altered behaviors?

Once you have determined what you want the client and/or staff to achieve and have developed one or more appropriate behavior statements to resolve each identified need, move on to Task 5.3.

TASK 5.3: *Develop a criterion statement for each behavior statement.*

In this task you develop statements of the criteria for judging the effectiveness of your intervention and success or the failure of the client and the client's staff to attain the proposed behavior changes. Use these questions to guide you in carrying out this task:

Do your criteria permit easy, obvious measurement of your success or failure to attain the desired behaviors?

Do the criteria directly apply to the behavior changes you have determined should be the outcome of the consultation?

Does your client agree with the criteria you have chosen as being appropriate to adequately gauge your performance?

Have you solicited the client's agreement on this point?

If you are submitting an unsolicited proposal, are you able to alter your criteria to meet the client's requirements for measuring the effectiveness of your project?

Once you have reached suitable, appropriate criteria for each behavior statement, move on to Task 5.4.

TASK 5.4: *Develop a condition statement for each behavior statement.*

You have already developed behavior statements and criteria statements. Now you must decide on the conditions under which the behavior changes can be achieved. Two questions are relevant to this task:

Must the desired behavior changes take place in an office environment or under field conditions?

Will the client's staff have to alter their working environment to produce conditions that will facilitate attaining the desired behavior changes?

The conditions under which you expect the client organization to attain the desired behaviors must also be readily attainable or, preferably, already present within the organizational environment.

Determine conditions and move on to Task 5.5.

TASK 5.5: *Combine behavior, criterion, and condition statements to form statements of objectives.*

Now that you've determined *what* you want the client organization to achieve, what the *measure* of achievement will be, and the

conditions under which the achievement must be made, you can combine
the three statements with your drafted objective statements. These final
objective statements list the stated obligations that you are willing to
accept for your consultation. The final objectives give the client a set of
guidelines for your project and the means to determine the effectiveness
of your performance during the consultation. These statements constitute
the terminal objectives of your consultation. Figure 4.5 shows the
terminal form of an objective statement.

After you have drafted your terminal objectives go on to
Task 5.6.

FIGURE 4.5
A typical objective

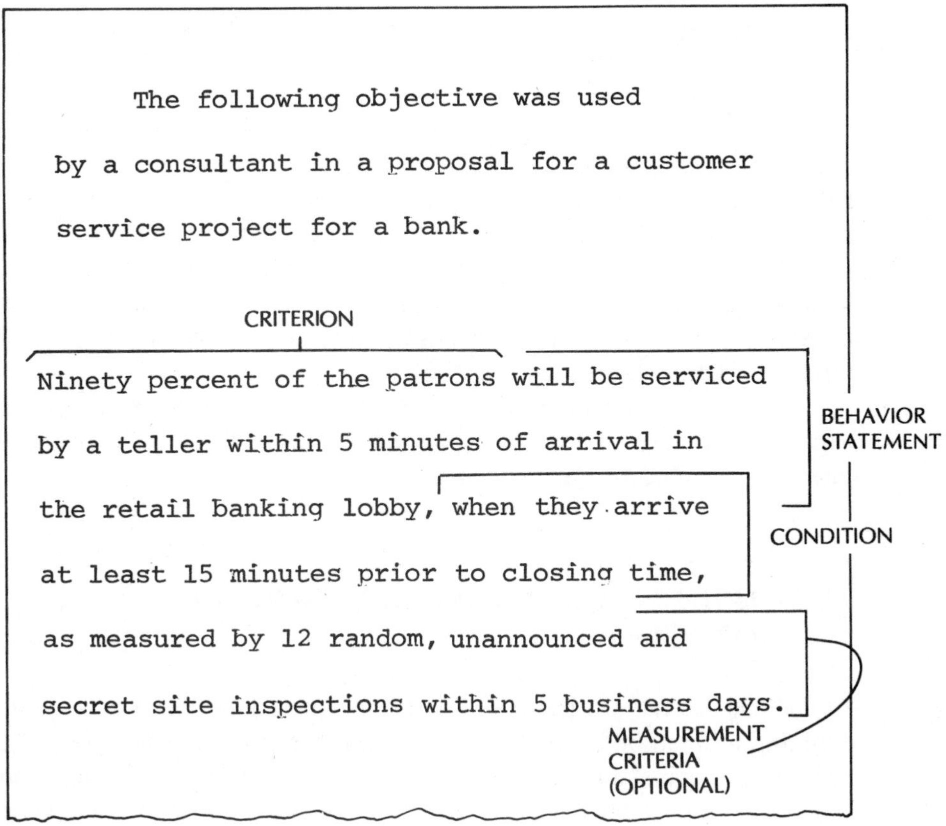

The following objective was used

by a consultant in a proposal for a customer

service project for a bank.

CRITERION

Ninety percent of the patrons will be serviced

by a teller within 5 minutes of arrival in

BEHAVIOR
STATEMENT

the retail banking lobby, when they arrive

CONDITION

at least 15 minutes prior to closing time,

as measured by 12 random, unannounced and

secret site inspections within 5 business days.

MEASUREMENT
CRITERIA
(OPTIONAL)

TASK 5.6: *Decide whether interim and/or audit objectives are required.*

Often the client is interested only in your terminal objectives. But with a lengthy consultation the client may want to gauge your performance during the course of your project and may ask for interim objectives. These are decided on in the same manner that you arrived at your terminal objectives, but they are specifically applicable at certain interim points along the way.

Audit objectives enable the client to evaluate your performance and may be either interim or final or both. As with other optional tasks, include interim and audit objectives only when necessary to fulfill the client's requirements for the consultation. If you determine that they are necessary, go on to Task 5.7.

TASK 5.7: *Repeat Tasks 5.3, 5.4, and 5.5 for each interim and audit objective.*

Your interim and audit objectives are the milestones that tell a client you are making appropriate progress in producing the desired behavior changes. Set up the intervals at which audit objectives will be applied with the client. Then go back to Task 5.2 and develop behavior statements for those changes that should have occurred by the time of the interim audit. Many times you will not specify a complete change in behavior; instead you will list the indications that the behavior is in the process of being altered.

Then go through Tasks 5.3, 5.4, and 5.5 to develop the appropriate criteria and condition statements that will be combined into interim audit objective statements.

UNDERSTANDING THE STATEMENT OF OBJECTIVES

Objectives are not goals. Goals are broad, timeless statements outlining a direction, purpose, or intention. Strictly speaking, goals are never really achieved. Objectives, however, are specific, definite, and capable of being achieved and measured. What you promise to achieve in your statement of objectives should be consistent with the resources you request to complete the task.

Each objective you formulate for your project or consultation must convey to the reader some specific information. Each objective has three components:

First, your objective describes the outcomes you intend to bring about.

> *Example:* Suppose you plan to conduct a training program on internal accounting procedures for your client's staff. Your performance objective outcome could be stated thus:

Each participant in the training shall prepare a line-item budget.

or

Eighty percent of the participants in the training program shall prepare a line-item budget.

> The objective is important because it establishes what you are accountable for. You will find that the second type of statement is often less risky. Suppose that the client organization sends everyone not otherwise busy to the training program, including a group of people incapable of mastering line-item budgets. In that instance, you'll be glad that only eighty percent of the participants were required to prepare a line-item budget.

Second, your objective statements make the outcome measurable. To do this you must establish a scale of values that you will use to gauge the quality of your outcome. The measure could be on a scale of 1 to 100 or from poor to excellent. You may also use numerical measures such as number of defects in product or reduction in the number of inventory errors.

Third, your statement of objectives establishes the level of outcome that you deem adequate in light of the effort and resources being expended to fulfill the consultation or project. To put it bluntly, is there enough bang for the bucks that will be spent on your work? As always, keep in mind that every element in a proposal has a use as a marketing instrument. Choose objectives that are meaningful to the client.

Now that you have set your objectives, move on to Step 6.

STEP 6: *Develop the project concept and FFD rough.*

The objective of Step 6 is to draft a complete functional flow diagram (FFD) to give a complete visualization of the entire project. You must make sure that you produce a sufficiently detailed proposal to convince the client that the objectives will be met—without giving away your services. This delicate balancing act takes skill and an understanding of what it takes to sell a particular prospective client.

The tasks in Step 6 are:

- Task 6.1: Identify all tasks to be carried out within the project.
- Task 6.2: Sequence the tasks to be performed and draw the rough FFD.
- Task 6.3: Modify the tasks to be done and determine the level of detail.

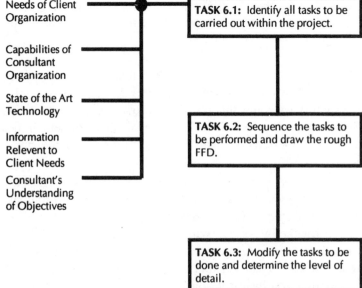

TASK 6.1: *Identify all tasks to be carried out within the project.*

Diagramming each step within your proposed consultation enables you to picture your project, to judge its completeness, and to evaluate your ability to resolve the needs and objectives you have identified. List all the steps in your consultation and move on to Task 6.2.

TASK 6.2: *Sequence the tasks to be performed and draw the rough FFD.*

Your first outline of the sequence of tasks in your proposed consultation is more like a cartoon than a grand painting. Even so, you should carefully consider each step:

> Before you list a task to be performed, have you gathered and analyzed all the information necessary to facilitate that task?
>
> What must be done first, second, third, and so forth?
>
> Does the order you have set follow a logical sequence of steps?

Once you have determined this rough sequence, move on to Task 6.3.

TASK 6.3: *Modify the tasks to be done and determine the level of detail.*

A rough FFD is a working outline of the project. Throughout the consultation you can modify the FFD as the situation and conditions change during the project. The FFD is not carved in stone. It is a practical guide designed to get things done. You may well have to alter it as you grapple with the realities of the consultation.

Consider the following questions as you review your completed rough FFD:

> Does your FFD show how you will solve the client's problems?
>
> Does it graphically illustrate how you will go about fulfilling the client's needs?
>
> Is the client able to see the procedures you will use to make his or her problems go away?

Will your FFD confuse your client?

Will all the readers of your proposal be able to picture your project from your FFD?

Does the level of detail within your FFD allow you to fully visualize the entire project from beginning to end?

Does the flow of tasks make a logical progression through the project?

Does your FFD reflect a level of detail sufficient to provide your client with a complete graphic representation the work you propose?

If so, have you made the FFD and the proposal so detailed that it will be *overly disclosive* to the client?

If you give the client all relevant information and outline all your proposed actions for solving problems in excessive detail, the client may decide to conduct the project without you. You must be certain that you are in control of the level of detail both in the FFD and the entire proposal so that you don't reveal too much.

The process for developing the FFD is described earlier in this chapter on pages 36–37.

Move on to Step 7.

STEP 7: *Develop the procedures write-up (proposal narrative).*

The objective of Step 7 is to draft your complete procedures write-up—the proposal narrative. This written description of the entire project will be included in the proposal. The aim is to communicate the information in the FFD in a written, narrative form.

The tasks in Step 7 are:

- Task 7.1: Describe each function in the FFD.
- Task 7.2: Specify unique, unusual, interesting, or technical approaches for each function.
- Task 7.3: Describe how the client's management will be utilized and kept informed.

STEP 7: *Develop the procedures write-up (proposal narrative).*

Input:

FFD

Project Objectives

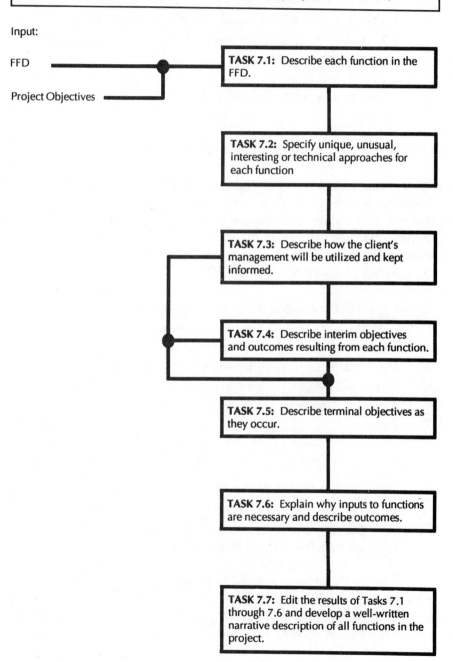

TASK 7.1: Describe each function in the FFD.

TASK 7.2: Specify unique, unusual, interesting or technical approaches for each function

TASK 7.3: Describe how the client's management will be utilized and kept informed.

TASK 7.4: Describe interim objectives and outcomes resulting from each function.

TASK 7.5: Describe terminal objectives as they occur.

TASK 7.6: Explain why inputs to functions are necessary and describe outcomes.

TASK 7.7: Edit the results of Tasks 7.1 through 7.6 and develop a well-written narrative description of all functions in the project.

- Task 7.4: Describe interim objectives and outcomes resulting from each function.
- Task 7.5: Describe terminal objectives as they occur.
- Task 7.6: Explain why inputs to functions are necessary and describe outcomes.
- Task 7.7: Edit the results of Tasks 7.1 through 7.6 and develop a well-written narrative description of all the functions in the project.

TASK 7.1: *Describe each function in the FFD.*

Your completed FFD illustrates those functions you will provide within your consultation that will resolve the identified problems. Describe each function so that your client will understand the necessity for that function and how the outcomes from it contribute to the succeeding tasks within the project. The following questions can be used to evaluate the description of the FFD:

- Have you described each function sufficiently?
- Will your client be able easily to correlate your written descriptions with the same functions on your FFD?
- Are you being careful to avoid giving too much information?
- Do corresponding FFD functions and your written descriptions capture exactly what you propose to do for the client?
- Are you satisfied that the descriptions combine with the FFD functions to give a clear, concise picture of your proposed actions in both written and graphic form?

Move on to Task 7.2.

TASK 7.2: *Specify unique, unusual, interesting, or technical approaches for each function.*

In this section you want to point out those elements of your proposal that set you apart from other possible consultants. What elements in your approach to the client's problems stand out and identify you as the logical choice? Evaluate these elements with the following questions:

What particulars of your approach are unique, unusual, interesting, or sufficiently technical to warrant detailed explanation for your readers?

Will a description of how you will use state-of-the-art techniques enhance your proposal or confuse your client?

If your client is considered a layperson in terms of the techniques you propose to employ to solve his or her problems, have you explained them on a sufficiently simple level to communicate their purpose as well as their advantages?

Address these questions and move on to Task 7.3.

TASK 7.3: *Describe how the client's management will be utilized and kept informed.*

As a consultant you are perceived as an outsider. The client and the client's staff probably have questions about your ability to fit into the organization during your consultation without upsetting routines. The client organization may also have a general suspicion that the consultant will keep people in the dark about what is really going on. Of course, some consultations demand secrecy, but most of the time open communication helps. You need to communicate to the client that you will work comfortably with management and maintain the appropriate level of communication with the client and members of the client organization. Use this checklist to assess your communications procedures:

How will you interact with the client organization's management?

Will you work outside their company management structure or within it?

If you work within the management structure, exactly who will control your activities?

What client personnel will you direct during your project?

How will you communicate needed information to your client and/or management?

What information will client management require to assist you in reaching the outcomes you have set for the consultation?

After answering these concerns, move on to Task 7.4.

TASK 7.4: *Describe interim objectives and outcomes resulting from each function.*

If you have set interim objectives for your consultation, describe them at this point. Demonstrate in writing how they will contribute to achieving your terminal objectives. Move on to Task 7.5.

TASK 7.5: *Describe terminal objectives as they occur.*

Show your client, in writing, exactly what objectives you propose to achieve as a result of your consultation. If you have identified interim objectives, demonstrate how these will lead to achieving terminal objectives. In your description of each terminal objective show the client how its attainment will either alleviate or completely resolve one or more needs or problems.

Tie the entire consultation together by your description of terminal objectives.

Move on to Task 7.6.

TASK 7.6: *Explain why inputs to functions are necessary and describe outcomes.*

Throughout your project each of your functions has inputs and outcomes. You should trace a common thread from one set of inputs through each function to the resulting set of outcomes. Then describe how these outcomes become inputs for the succeeding function.

You must explain this sequence of events so that your client understands the interdependency of all incomes, functions, and outputs. You want your client to understand how all this leads up to the final set of outcomes, which represents your terminal objectives for the entire project. Complete this task and move on to Task 7.7.

TASK 7.7: *Edit the results of Tasks 7.1 through 7.6 and develop a well-written narrative description of all the functions in the project.*

Just as your FFD is a working document, which changes as your grasp of the entire project grows, so too the written narrative is a fluid document. You have built a foundation for the final proposal narrative through each succeeding task within Step 7. Now, you must consider your client's point of view and draft a final, edited, written narrative of all the component functions within your entire project.

Write clear, concise statements that reflect exactly what you propose to do and accomplish at each point in your consultation. Communicate all the information necessary for your client to become convinced of the soundness and timeliness of your proposition.

The written narrative is the final element of the proposal's main section. The purpose of the written narrative is:

- to communicate the outcomes, results, and benefits of the consultation to the reader

- to communicate the procedures and processes to be utilized to achieve the objectives

- to communicate the fact that the client will have the opportunity to manage you, the consultant

The communication of procedures and processes must convince the reader that you can achieve the objectives of the consultation. At the same time your description of procedures must be so general and conceptual or even vague that you do not give your services away for free.

Three kinds of outcomes, results, and benefits need to be communicated to the reader in the written narrative:

1. *Terminal results or benefits.* You will be retained to achieve certain prescribed results or benefits. Often these are specified exactly in your statement of objectives in the proposal's front section. In your written narrative you want to specify the points at which these terminal results and benefits will be achieved.

2. *Enabling results or benefits.* On the road to achieving your terminal results or benefits you will reach certain milestones. These will be accomplishments that are required in order to produce the terminal results. Although enabling results may seem obvious or self-evident to you, they may not be so to your client. Be sure to communicate them to the client: the more the better.

3. *Serendipitous results or benefits.* These are the nice things that happen during the course of the consultation, which you were not asked to achieve and which are not necessary to achieve the terminal results or benefits.

Listing the enabling results or benefits communicates to the client that along the way, while you are carrying out your consultation, there will be evidence of positive results. Suppose you are attempting to determine the image of a manufacturing firm in the eyes of its customers. Some of your enabling results might be: questionnaire designed, survey sample selected, data analysis methods selected, and so forth. Communicating milestone events assures your prospective client that there are checkpoints at which your work can be managed.

Pointing out serendipitous results gives the client the sense that your work will be a wise investment. If you are likely to improve employee morale in the course of conducting a study of job satisfaction, be sure to communicate that fact to the prospective client. Also be certain to communicate to the client that this serendipitous result costs nothing extra. It's just a nice thing that happens. Pointing out serendipitous results helps the client to see that he or she is obtaining more for every dollar invested.

STRATEGIC CONSIDERATIONS

In the proposal's front section, you told the reader what you hope to accomplish. Here, in the proposal narrative, you communicate to the reader that you and only you are the right consulting organization to meet those objectives. The reader should become convinced that the objectives will be accomplished in a cost-effective and efficient fashion. In short, you want to convince the reader that what you propose is superior to alternatives other consultants might offer and superior to what the client could achieve by utilizing internal resources alone.

The proposal narrative is an excellent place to deal with known competition. If you know that other consultants are likely to be submitting proposals against which yours will be judged, tell your reader that you have discarded alternative approaches to the client's needs. Be specific. Tell the client that you considered the obvious approach of doing such and such, but discarded that alternative because it is too costly, too time consuming, or because it requires unreasonably high staff skills, creates adverse side effects, or the like. You must be on solid ground, of course, but your willingness to consider and dismiss alternatives assures your client that you are unwilling to settle for something that will just get by.

Your written narrative should be keyed to your FFD. For each step in your diagram, write up a one- or two-paragraph statement about the activity, which communicates the results discussed above and deals in general and conceptual terms with the procedures to be employed.

How detailed and specific your written narrative should be is a function of two factors:

- how specific you must be to communicate to the reader the type of work that you will be doing, based on the reader's understanding and knowledge of the problem
- the extent of the threat (if any) that your client will take your work and get a free or low-cost consultation.

Once you have completed the written narrative sit back and review it from the standpoint of your prospective client. Be certain that it answers the who, when, where, how, and why of the client's needs. Be sure it flows well and is complete. Also make certain that the written narrative meets the communications objectives discussed above.

Move on to Step 8.

STEP 8: *Develop the project time line.*

The objective of Step 8 is to construct a complete project time line. A time line gives the client an idea of how long the project will take to complete. It is also the first step in determining the fee you will quote.

The tasks in Step 8 are:

- Task 8.1: Draw the time line worksheet.
- Task 8.2: Indicate the completion date.
- Task 8.3: Plot significant milestones.
- Task 8.4: Develop a full project schedule.

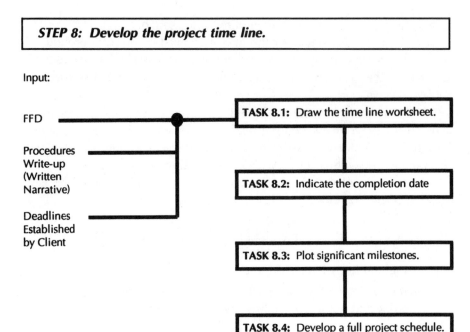

TASK 8.1: *Draw the time line worksheet.*

A time line is an actual line that indicates the dates on which tasks in a consultation will be completed. Draw a line along the top edge of a blank sheet of paper. The left hand end of this line will serve as the point in time when the contract begins. (Assume that you will receive the contract.) To determine the starting date you must calculate how long it will take the client to make a favorable decision. The more complex the organization, the longer it is likely to take for them to get their act together. Our example project is the development and conduct of a training program. (See Figure 4.6.)

By suggesting an early date you may gain an advantage in that you suggest the importance of getting started sooner. It is a good idea to use actual dates, so make assumptions. If you can't make an assumption as to when the contract will be awarded, start your time line on the left end with "Date Contract Awarded" or "Contract Start" as in Figure 4.7

FIGURE 4.6
Initial time line with dates

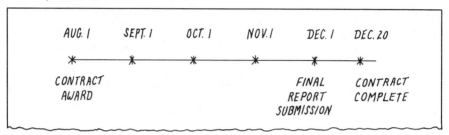

and calculate all other dates in terms of the number of days, weeks, or months following the contract award.

TASK 8.2: *Indicate the completion date.*

The right hand end of your time line will serve to indicate when your contract, project, or consultation will be completed. (See Figures 4.4 and 4.5.)

TASK 8.3: *Plot significant milestones.*

Plot the project milestones by placing an *X* at each specific point between "Contract award" and "Contract completion" when a significant milestone event is planned to occur. In Figure 4.4 we have plotted in the event, "Final report submission," three weeks prior to contract completion.

FIGURE 4.7
Time line expressed in months elapsed

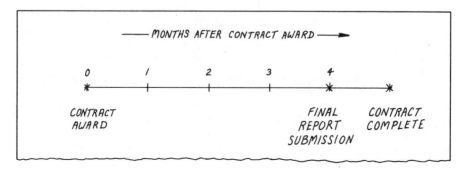

Refer to your FFD and determine the result, benefit, or outcome of each function. This practice helps you identify milestones. For the current example, some of the more obvious milestone events are indicated in Figure 4.8.

It is permissible to have simultaneous events on your time line. Don't be too concerned about having exactly the right amount of time between events, just be sure that you have them in order and that you have left sufficient time for the necessary client reviews and approvals.

TASK 8.4: *Develop a full project schedule.*

You next develop a full project schedule from the time line work completed thus far. This schedule will be included in the proposal document submitted to the prospective client.

First, list vertically on the left hand side of your paper the functions you have developed for the consultation (from your FFD). Next, drop vertical lines from each X on your time line. (See Figure 4.9.) Starting with the first function, shade in the horizontal strip to the right of the function to signify the interval of time during which activities supporting the function will occur. Then go to each succeeding task and shade in the appropriate area to indicate its time interval.

When you have identified on the time line a significant project event corresponding to the completion of a particular function, *do not shade* beyond the point at which the event occurs.

Figure 4.9 should prove helpful in clarifying the details of constructing the project time line.

FIGURE 4.8
Time line with milestone events

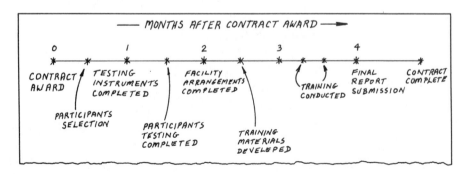

FIGURE 4.9
Full project schedule developed from time line

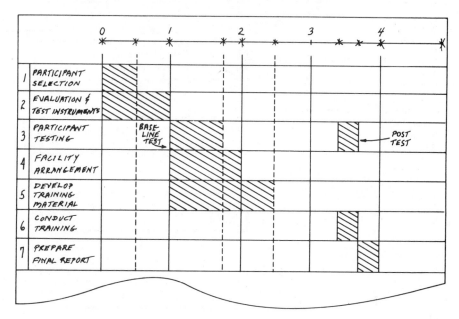

THE VALUE OF A TIME LINE

The time line is a schedule established by you, possibly with your client's help, which identifies when the various milestone events of your project or consultation will be completed. The time line communicates to the client just when the work should be completed. It aids both the consultant and the client in scheduling the availability of resources, staff, and so forth to complete the project within the deadline. Move on to Step 9.

STEP 9: *Conduct personnel loading analysis (optional).*

The objective of Step 9 is to perform a personnel loading analysis to facilitate scheduling and assignment of necessary personnel. This step is optional in the proposal-writing process, but it can be valuable in determining your estimated budget. You need to estimate approximately how many labor days or hours are necessary to complete the project, even if you don't carry out the entire personnel loading analysis at this time.

STEP 9: *Conduct personnel loading analysis (optional).*

Input:

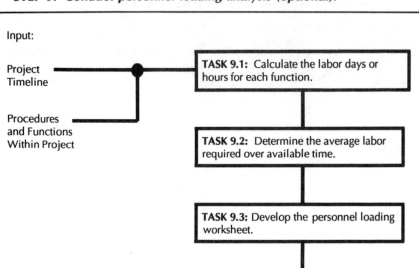

A full personnel loading analysis is typically used only in a large consultation involving a number of personnel. Although it is included in the proposal package only 15–20% of the time, you may find it useful as an internal management tool. You may also want to demonstrate to a client how to engage in personnel loading analysis for greater control of the client's activities.

The main advantage in carrying out a personnel loading analysis is that it helps you guard against designing a consultation that defies management within budget limits.

The tasks in Step 9 are:

- Task 9.1: Calculate the labor days or hours for each function.
- Task 9.2: Determine the average labor required over available time.
- Task 9.3: Develop a personnel loading worksheet.
- Task 9.4: Modify the time line and procedures write-up.

The example in this step is somewhat simplified to clarify the process of conducting a personnel loading analysis. The example assumes that two individuals can do in three days what each could do alone in six days. It also avoids the problem of personnel assignment by assuming that each employee can carry out all assignments. In the real world not all personnel have the same skills and the limited availability of key personnel at crucial times can be a scheduling headache.

To give you the clearest method of completing the personnel loading analysis, the four functional tasks in the FFD have been broken down into six mini-steps. Follow these steps and Figures 4.10 and 4.11 to complete Step 9.

1. In Column 1 of the worksheet list the various functions of your consultation. These should come directly from your FFD.

2. Consider each function and estimate the number of days it would take to complete the function. Enter your estimates in Column 2. In doing this, assume that you can work full time on this activity. Your estimate should be in terms of working days and not calendar time.

3. From your project time line, enter in Column 3 the actual number of days you have allotted for accomplishing each function.

4. Divide each Column 2 figure by the corresponding figure in Column 3 and enter the result in Column 4.

5. Write down the result of Step 4 (full-time equivalent personnel loading—FTE) on your project time line as illustrated.

6. Proceed from the lower left hand corner of your project time line and add up the FTE personnel loading numbers which cross the vertical line above.

In an ideal situation your personnel loading should be essentially constant for the duration of the consultation. If you discover that the loading is not constant, you may wish to rearrange the tasks on your time line to level out this management nightmare. Do this by shifting those functions which have heavy personnel loading forward or backward on the time line to level out the utilization of personnel.

If several consultations are underway in a given organization simultaneously, you may find it beneficial to carry out a joint loading analysis. Doing so highlights periods of time with high or low personnel demand and helps in coordinating projects. Coordinated project planning

FIGURE 4.10
Functional flow diagram for use in constructing personnel loading analysis

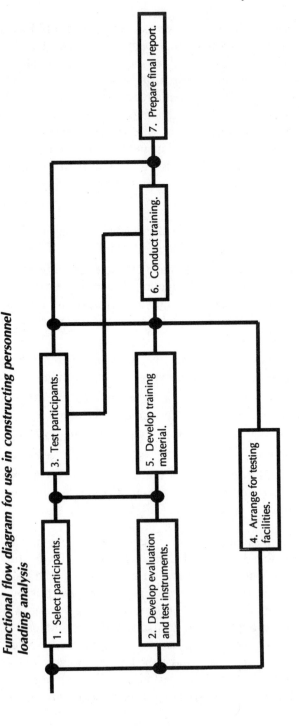

FIGURE 4.11
Personnel loading analysis

FUNCTION NUMBER	FUNCTION	EST. NO. OF DAYS (EFFORT)	TIME ALLOWED TO COMPLETE (DAYS)	LEVEL OF EFFORT (F.T.E.)
1	PARTICIPANT SELECTION	4	10	.4
2	EVALUATION & TEST INSTRUMENTS	1	20	.5
3	PARTICIPANT TESTING	3	20	.15
4	FACILITY MANAGEMENT	3	20	.15
5	DEVELOP TRAINING MATERIAL	22	30	.73
6	CONDUCT TRAINING	15*	5	3
7	PREPARE FINAL REPORT	8	10	.8

* 3 TRAINERS FOR 5 DAYS.

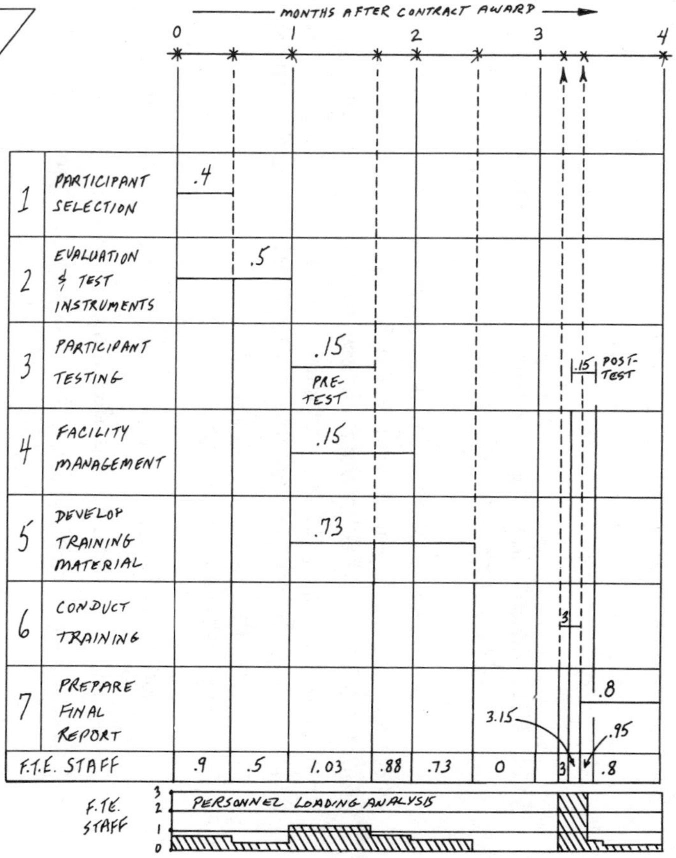

can indicate the appropriate time to schedule vacations or to book small projects to take up the slack. It can also indicate when you need to hire temporary assistance.

Move on to Step 10.

STEP 10: *Modify the statements of needs, goals, objectives, FFD, and time line.*

The objective of Step 10 is to review the project concept as a whole and to modify and rewrite where necessary to integrate the entire project smoothly. This is your chance to make sure that the whole structure fits together. A large, complex project has so many diverse parts that it is easy for mismatches to emerge, especially if there have been several minor alterations during the formative process.

The tasks in Step 10 are:

- Task 10.1: Modify all inputs for conformity and consistency.
- Task 10.2: Rewrite and alter inputs as necessary.
- Task 10.3: Review the fully conceptualized project.

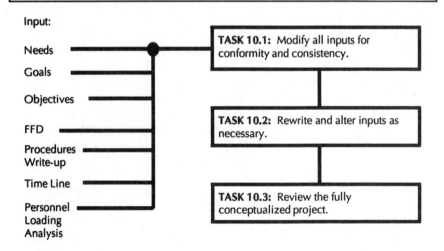

STEP 10: *Modify the statements of needs, goals, objectives, FFD, and time line.*

Input:

Needs
Goals
Objectives
FFD
Procedures Write-up
Time Line
Personnel Loading Analysis

TASK 10.1: Modify all inputs for conformity and consistency.

TASK 10.2: Rewrite and alter inputs as necessary.

TASK 10.3: Review the fully conceptualized project.

TASK 10.1: *Modify all inputs for conformity and consistency.*

With the completion of Step 9, you now have the entire project concept before you. Review the whole plan by looking on the components as pieces of a puzzle. Use the following checklist:

Does everything fit together snugly?

Is there a smooth, ordered flow throughout the project, which reflects your organized approach to solving your client's problem?

Does the completed project vigorously and graphically illustrate your intentions?

Are your procedures easy to grasp?

Is the logic of your procedures clear to your readers?

Put yourself in your client's place and ask what modifications are necessary to make a clearly understandable flow of information throughout your proposal? Move on to Task 10.2.

TASK 10.2: *Rewrite and alter inputs as necessary.*

If, after your review of the entire project, you find any problem areas or confusing or misleading components, rewrite those inputs to integrate them into the whole concept. Move on to Task 10.3.

TASK 10.3: *Review the fully conceptualized project.*

After any alterations and rewrites, review the modified components in relation to your whole proposal. Repeat this modification and review until you smooth your entire concept into final form. Move on to Step 11.

STEP 11: *Develop the evaluation plan.*

The objective of Step 11 is to establish a methodology whereby you can ensure that the project's objectives are met. The aim, in part, is to reassure the client that you are accountable for the outcome of your

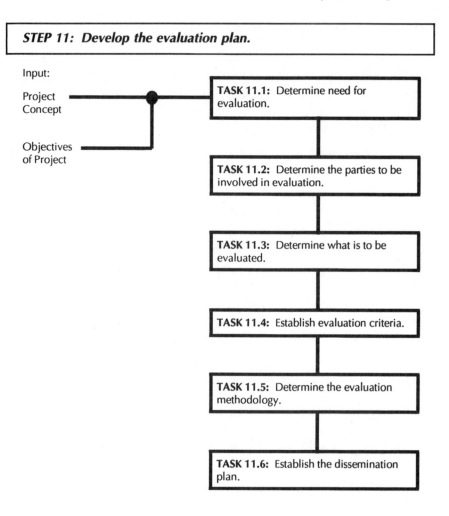

STEP 11: Develop the evaluation plan.

Input:

Project Concept

Objectives of Project

TASK 11.1: Determine need for evaluation.

TASK 11.2: Determine the parties to be involved in evaluation.

TASK 11.3: Determine what is to be evaluated.

TASK 11.4: Establish evaluation criteria.

TASK 11.5: Determine the evaluation methodology.

TASK 11.6: Establish the dissemination plan.

consultation. This is also an opportunity to underline expected results and benefits of the project.

The tasks in Step 11 are:

- Task 11.1: Determine the need for evaluation.

- Task 11.2: Determine the parties to be involved in evaluation.

- Task 11.3: Determine what is to be evaluated.

- Task 11.4: Establish evaluation criteria.

- Task 11.5: Determine the evaluation methodology.
- Task 11.6: Establish the dissemination plan.

TASK 11.1: *Determine the need for evaluation.*

The inputs for this task are the project concept and the project objectives. You can determine whether you need to include an evaluation procedure by answering the following questions:

Will an evaluation procedure make this consultation more attractive to the client?

Does your client require or desire a formal evaluation?

Are the objectives of your consultation obvious, tangible outcomes or are they somewhat more elusive?

Come to agreement with your client on the subject of evaluation of your project. If you decide to include an evaluation, move to Task 11.2.

TASK 11.2: *Determine the parties to be involved in evaluation.*

Others besides yourself may be involved in the evaluation, primarily to assure the client that the project has been satisfactorily completed. The following checklist establishes who should be involved in any evaluation:

Will you evaluate yourself?

Will your client or the client's staff perform the evaluation of your project?

Does the client wish to bring in another consultant to evaluate your work?

Will you have to make any special arrangements or modifications of your proposed project to facilitate proper and complete evaluation?

Once you have made this determination, move on to Task 11.3.

TASK 11.3: *Determine what is to be evaluated.*

Now that you have decided who will take part in the evaluation process, you need to determine what parts of your project will be evaluated. Keep in mind that if several people are involved in the evaluation, some areas will not be checked by everyone. An accountant may look only at the budget or supervisors may evaluate only those outcomes that impact their departments. You can sort out responsibilities with this checklist:

What aspects of your project are to be evaluated?

Will results or outcomes be evaluated?

Will the processes you employed to generate outcomes be evaluated?

Will there be an audit of your budget?

What are your client's feelings on the areas to be evaluated?

Make these determinations and move on to Task 11.4.

TASK 11.4: *Establish evaluation criteria.*

Once you have decided to include an evaluation, determined the parties involved, and determined the subject of the evaluation, you must establish the criteria for that process, using the following guidelines:

Can you evaluate in terms of concrete outcomes?

What yardstick will you employ to determine the effectiveness and completeness of your outcomes?

Will your evaluation generate empirical data?

Will your evaluation generate subjective opinions?

Decide, with your client, how you will judge the project's results and move on to Task 11.5.

TASK 11.5: *Determine the evaluation methodology.*

Based on your criteria for evaluation, now decide what methodology best suits your evaluation. For instance:

Should you perform interviews of client staff?

Should you use testing or procedures analysis to judge the extent of training outcomes and the degree of knowledge imparted to the client organization?

Tailor your methodology to the objectives you must evaluate and move on to Task 11.6.

TASK 11.6: *Establish the dissemination plan.*

Once you have determined what information you will gather and how you will gather it, you must decide on a plan to communicate that information. Two main questions are involved here:

Who needs to know the results and effectiveness of your outcomes?

Do you have to inform only your client or are you treating the client's staff as the recipient of your information?

The number of people who must be informed and the type of information you will impart should guide you in establishing a dissemination plan for your evaluation results.

EVALUATION PLAN AND PROCEDURES

Many consultations require evaluation of the work that is done for the client. This is particularly true when the consultant performs a creative or technical task such as market research, training program design, information system design, and the like. It is also common in all government work.

Describing your evaluation procedures, when required, is important for getting the client to accept your proposal. It provides a check on or measurement of the quality of the consultant's work and the viability of the specific plan and procedures you are proposing. It is a means by which the client can hold you accountable for the expenditure of the client organization's funds.

A properly designed project evaluation plan is like a separate and distinct consultation. Indeed, the evaluation is often given to another consultant to complete. In such cases, the evaluation is called an independent or third-party evaluation. Evaluation is more like a research project than anything else. The wealth of literature on research and experimental design may be of assistance here.

Even if you don't plan to conduct a formal evaluation, you should indicate to your client that an ongoing or in-process evaluation will be conducted. Describe the various activities that will take place. Your client will gain confidence in knowing that a continuous monitoring is underway to assure quality control. Move on to Step 12.

STEP 12: *Develop the reporting plan.*

The objective of Step 12 is to determine the information about your project that will be communicated to your client and the time frame for that communication. Depending on need this can take the form of a simple verbal or written summary or it may call for a formal written final report.

The tasks in Step 12 are:

- Task 12.1: Determine the nature and frequency of reports.
- Task 12.2: Establish the format and style for reports.
- Task 12.3: Communicate the format, frequency, and nature of reports to the client.
- Task 12.4: Modify the time line, FFD, and narrative to include reporting.

TASK 12.1: *Determine the nature and frequency of reports.*

Some form of reporting should be included in your project. The first questions relate to the appropriate frequency for those reports:

> Does your client wish you to include a set of scheduled progress reports within the scope of your consultation?
>
> How often should such reports be made?

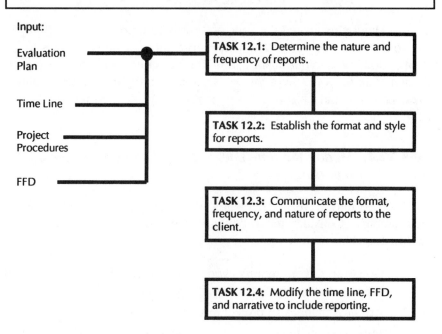

STEP 12: Develop the reporting plan.

Input:

Evaluation Plan

Time Line

Project Procedures

FFD

TASK 12.1: Determine the nature and frequency of reports.

TASK 12.2: Establish the format and style for reports.

TASK 12.3: Communicate the format, frequency, and nature of reports to the client.

TASK 12.4: Modify the time line, FFD, and narrative to include reporting.

At what points within the project should they be made?

What procedures or outcomes is your client particularly interested in?

Once you have established the necessity for reporting to your client and the nature and frequency of those reports, move on to Task 12.2.

TASK 12.2: *Establish the format and style for reports.*

Having established when you will report, you must now decide what form those reports will take.

Is your client satisfied with an informal memo or verbal review?

Does your client need formal, written reports?

Determine what style and format will fulfill the client's requirements suit your needs as well, then move on to Task 12.3.

TASK 12.3: *Communicate the format, frequency, and nature of reports to the client.*

Having evaluated the style and format that best suit your project and your client's needs, you now need to communicate your ideas to the client, along with your justification for selecting that type of report. Demonstrate to your client the integration of outcomes, interim objectives, and terminal objectives in your reporting plan. Move on to Task 12.4.

TASK 12.4: *Modify the time line, FFD, and narrative to include reporting.*

You may have to alter parts of the proposal to meet reporting requirements. Consider the following questions in carrying out these modifications:

How must you modify your time line, FFD, and proposal narrative to include your reporting activities?

Are any changes in project structure required?

Must you evaluate outcomes and report them to your client at certain milestones before you continue with the remainder of the project?

Will your reports necessitate interim decisions from your client before completing the consultation?

Will the style and format of your reporting require alteration of your other proposal and project components?

Once you have modified these sections make sure that your reporting integrates smoothly with the entire project.

REPORTING AND DISSEMINATION PLAN

Many consultations require some type of formal reporting or dissemination of the consultant's work, particularly when the client is a large organization. The smaller client, except in the case of government-supported work, is usually unwilling or unable to pay the cost of a formal final report.

It is in your interest to have the client request some type of final report or dissemination of information about results. These serve as an after-the-fact marketing effort for your skills. Others will read your report and it will serve to generate new opportunities and follow-on business.

The written final report has become commonplace in many consulting situations.

> *Example:* You or your client reproduce 100 copies of the report. Six stay in the client's files, twenty are saved to send out on request, and the balance are distributed to a house mailing list.

You or your client wish to gain benefits from other means of reporting and dissemination that will create greater impact. You may write a paper and have it published as an article or monograph. You may read a paper at a meeting of a professional or trade association. You may develop and present a workshop or training seminar to the client's staff or prepare an audiovisual package, which the client can use with field representatives or branch offices. In some consultations press releases and interviews can be valuable in increasing the client's credibility or visibility. Of course, all of these activities enhance your reputation and are real marketing opportunities.

Your written proposal should specify the nature and extent of the reporting and dissemination plan you will follow. It should also indicate what checks or reviews, if any, your client will have in this process. It may be helpful to your client and to your success in marketing your services to include an outline of the proposed final report in your proposal document. Move on to Step 13.

STEP 13: *Develop the capabilities section.*

The objective of Step 13 is to lend credibility to the consultant's ability to execute the project and to market the consultant's services. This section covers your abilities, the skills of your staff and those you will hire, and your ability to manage the entire project.

The tasks in Step 13 are:

- Task 13.1: Determine what information about capabilities is necessary to sell the project.
- Task 13.2: Draft staff resumes.

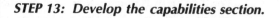

STEP 13: *Develop the capabilities section.*

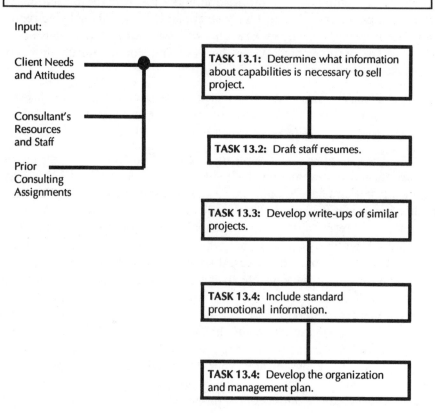

Input:

Client Needs and Attitudes

Consultant's Resources and Staff

Prior Consulting Assignments

TASK 13.1: Determine what information about capabilities is necessary to sell project.

TASK 13.2: Draft staff resumes.

TASK 13.3: Develop write-ups of similar projects.

TASK 13.4: Include standard promotional information.

TASK 13.4: Develop the organization and management plan.

- Task 13.3: Develop write-ups of similar projects.
- Task 13.4: Include standard promotional information.
- Task 13.5: Develop the organization and management plan.

TASK 13.1: *Determine what information about capabilities is necessary to sell the project.*

The capabilities section of the proposal is designed to convince the client that you have the experience, resources, staff, and expertise necessary to make his or her problems go away. Consider these questions:

How much convincing will it take on your part to influence your client's decision to utilize your services?

What information about your past experience can you communicate to this client that will underscore your suitability for this consultation?

Decide how much and what kind of information is needed to sell your client on your abilities to handle the project. Include those components of Tasks 13.2 through 13.5 that will enhance your marketability in your client's eyes.

TASK 13.2: *Draft staff resumes.*

If you will work on this project alone, then your resume is the only one that is relevant. If members of your consulting staff are going to work on parts of the project, you need to develop a set of standard staff resumes. These resumes highlight the past experiences, activities, and education of your staff members as they apply directly to the proposed project. Use the following checklist:

Have you devised a standard format for your staff's resumes?

Have you reviewed these resumes to ensure that only information pertinent to this project is included?

Have you edited staff resumes to delete unnecessary verbiage and inapplicable background information?

Are your staff resumes easy to read?

Is the information formatted so that the client can immediately grasp the applicable experience of your staff members as it relates directly to his or her problems?

CONSULTATION STAFF STATEMENT OF CAPABILITY

The statement of capabilities reassures your potential client that you can successfully complete the project, but it can also have another valuable function. It has become common to place the capabilities statement in the very last section of the written proposal, and for good reason. Placing capabilities last prevents the proposal bid or price from becoming the last section of your written proposal.

The statement of capability usually includes:

- a statement of the consulting firm's approach, resources, talents
- Specific resumes of key personnel who will contribute to the client's project.

Your brochure may often serve as an adequate statement of the consulting organization's capabilities. For individual staff members involved, a resume can help to further inform the client of your expertise.

Staff resumes should be completed in a standard format. This section should not appear as though you ran wild through the files at the last moment to piece together a patchwork of staff capabilities. You must appear as organized within your own firm as you wish to appear to the client throughout your proposal. The last thing you want the client to feel is that you threw together anything you could find to pad the proposal. For this reason development of a standard format is highly desirable. Have staff members prepare their own resumes within the limitations of your standard format. All staff should update their resumes every six months.

Figure 4.12 gives a sample format for staff resumes.

TASK 13.3: *Develop write-ups of similar projects.*

Your ability to demonstrate that you have successfully carried out similar consultations in the past is very helpful in marketing your project. This is primarily a marketing decision that can be made on the basis of this checklist:

> Have you ever performed a consultation in which you solved the same basic problems that you face with this client?
>
> Would a write-up or report of the outcomes of that project enhance your marketability?
>
> Would that write-up convince your present client that you can solve his or her problems because you have faced similar situations successfully in the past?
>
> Would such a report or write-up serve to commit the client organization to your consulting organization?

Include whatever past experiences will build your reputation in the eyes of your client and move on to Task 13.4.

FIGURE 4.12
Sample format for staff resumes

NAME _____

NAME _____

TITLE _____   DEPARTMENT _____

YEARS OF PROFESSIONAL EXPERIENCE (Count College and Graduate School)

EMPLOYER	POSITION	RESPONSIBILITY

ACADEMIC ACHIEVEMENTS:

INSTITUTION	DEGREE	DATES

PUBLICATIONS:

(APPEARED IN)	DATE(S)	PAGES

CURRENT RESPONSIBILITIES: _____
_____
_____

PROJECT EXPERIENCE: _____
_____
_____

HONORS AND AWARDS: _____
_____
_____

TASK 13.4: *Include standard promotional information.*

Including supplemental material like brochures and copies of letters of thanks can add credibility to your proposal, especially if the letters are from firms and executives known to and respected by the client. Ask yourself:

> What promotional brochures do you have available that may serve to convince your client of your suitability for this assignment?

What letters of thanks or congratulations have you received from past clients that would build your present client's confidence in your abilities?

Include whatever information is relevant and helpful. Then move on to Task 13.5.

TASK 13.5: *Develop the organization and management plan.*

You have presented your client with some fine ideas as to how you can address and solve his or her problems. Your suggestions intimate that you can make the problems go away. But how can the client know that your consultation will take your good ideas and employ them systematically to produce solutions?

Your organization and management plan should convince your results-oriented client that you have the organizational and management skills necessary to implement your ideas and bring them to fruition. Review the following questions:

Have you developed an organization and management plan for previous clients?

Will this plan be suitable for your current needs?

If not, what modifications must you make to tailor the plan to this client?

After you have answered these questions, make all appropriate alterations in previous plans so you can use them with this client or produce a completely new plan for this proposal.

VALUE OF THE ORGANIZATION AND MANAGEMENT PLAN

The project organization and management plan is very important because it contains information that enables the reader to assess your qualifications. The management part of the plan is particularly crucial for the larger consulting organization. The prospective client of the larger firm may well feel that those who are proposing the work may have limited, if any involvement in its execution. It must be demonstrated that the consultation will be conducted by individuals who will understand client needs and work harmoniously within the client's administrative structure.

The management and organization plan also serves to demonstrate that the consultant has far more than just good ideas. There are many creative people around, but their ability to produce results may be limited by poor management skills. An effective management plan should put to rest the notion that you may be of one of these people.

The management and organization plan should include:

- a description of the administrative structure of the project, which includes a detailing of any key positions and their associated responsibilities and duties
- a description of the organizational structures that will serve as a connective link between the consultants working on the project and the client's organization (In a larger consulting firm, the linkage between the consulting organization and the specific individuals working on the consultation should also be demonstrated.)
- estimates of the personnel loading that you anticipate in connection with the conduct of the project
- a description of the backgrounds and qualifications of the personnel who will be assigned to the consultation
- a description of any individuals or outside firms you plan to use or work with, including outside consultants, subcontractors, third-party evaluators and job shops.

One of the best means for communicating the project organization is to create an organization chart that shows the lines of authority and responsibility. Such a chart should also show the interrelationships within and between your consulting organization and the client's organization.

Well-written resumes are the best means of communicating the nature and extent of qualifications of the staff assigned to the project. These resumes should differ from the standard job-seeking resume in that each should draw out and embellish those qualities in the background of each staff member that are relevant to the client's needs. Move on to Step 14.

STEP 14: *Develop the statement of assurances.*

The objective of Step 14 is to draft a complete statement of assurances for your client. This statement anticipates possible objections the client may have about liability and responsibility for possible problems arising from the consultation. By anticipating objections you market your proposal more effectively.

Tasks in Step 14 are:

- Task 14.1: Determine the assurances that the client needs.
- Task 14.2: Write the statement for each assurance.
- Task 14.3: Place the statements of assurances in front of the proposal following the abstract.

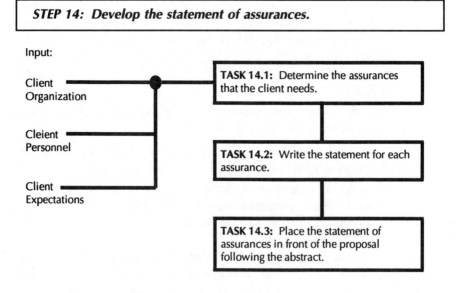

TASK 14.1: *Determine the assurances that the client needs.*

Each client and client organization has different areas of concern. You should make an effort to discover possible sources of concern to your prospective client. Review your client's areas of concern with these questions:

What reassurances do you think your client would like to have in writing as part of your proposal to show that you can and will solve the problems without creating any new fires that must be fought?

During your meetings with your client, have you identified any areas of doubt about your ability to resolve a problem or fill a need?

Has your client voiced any concern over the legalities involved in your consultation?

Has your client mentioned apprehension over your compliance, as one of his subcontractors, with federal regulations to which he or she is subject?

Determine all the apprehensions your client may have regarding your consultation. Identify these areas of anxiety and move on to Task 14.2.

TASK 14.2: *Write the statement for each assurance.*

Reassure your client, in writing, regarding each of the areas of apprehension that you have identified. Ask your client directly if he or she has any questions, problems, anxieties, or apprehensions which you have yet to discuss. Once these are brought to light, write a statement of assurance that addresses and resolves each.

In the statement of assurances you will specify the practices you will employ in this particular consultation to avoid potential problems. It is a professional touch which reduces any anxieties the client may have. It provides a strategic defense against any who might argue against your proposal but who lack substantive reasons as to why your proposal should not be accepted.

The statement of assurances should not contain any startling revelations. It should assure your client that:

- You have produced the most cost-effective approach possible consistent with the client's objectives
- There are no lawsuits or judgments pending against you
- All your costs are true and reasonable estimates and that you have no outstanding proposals which reflect more favorable fees or cost estimates

- You do not discriminate in hiring
- You are self-insured and hold your client blameless and will defend any lawsuits

Your statement of assurances should conclude with the signature of the highest official of your consulting practice and be dated.

Move on to Task 14.3.

TASK 14.3: *Place the statements of assurances in front of the proposal following the abstract.*

The best location for the statement of assurances is directly after your proposal abstract so that it is readily available as your client reviews your finished proposal.

Move on to Step 15.

STEP 15: *Develop appendices and support documents.*

The objective of Step 15 is to provide any necessary favorable support data in the form of appendices and support documents. This information may show that the proposed project is possible, that it has proved effective, and that it is potentially valuable to the client organization.

Tasks in Step 15 are:

- Task 15.1: Determine whether there are nonessential documents that might enhance the proposal.
- Task 15.2: Rewrite the documents or include them, as is, in the appendix to the proposal.
- Task 15.3: Identify the appendices in the table of contents and refer to them in the proposal text, as appropriate.

TASK 15.1: *Determine whether there are nonessential documents that might enhance your proposal.*

As with other phases of the proposal, you want to provide support data and documents without giving away your services. If this information gathering is part of the proposed consultation, then you need only

STEP 15: Develop appendices and support documents.

Input:

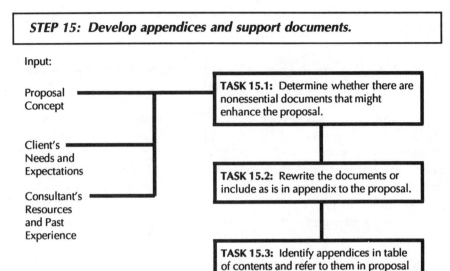

Proposal Concept

Client's Needs and Expectations

Consultant's Resources and Past Experience

TASK 15.1: Determine whether there are nonessential documents that might enhance the proposal.

TASK 15.2: Rewrite the documents or include as is in appendix to the proposal.

TASK 15.3: Identify appendices in table of contents and refer to them in proposal text as appropriate.

indicate that it exists and you have access to it. Evaluate potential inclusions with the following questions:

What materials and documents are available to you that are not essential to your proposal, but would enhance the proposal when it is read?

Have you any previously drafted final reports from past consulting assignments that would demonstrate your level of accomplishment and capabilities to a current client?

Have you any past survey instruments that would be of interest to the readers of this proposal?

Have you published any articles as a result of a past assignment that would impress your readers and enhance your marketability in the present situation?

Have any articles been written about you or your consulting practice that would be useful?

If the prospective client wishes to have another consultant perform the evaluation of your work, would it be advantageous for you to enclose a copy of that consultant's proposal, as an appendix to your document so that the readers could review both proposals together?

Determine which documents you wish to include and move on to Task 15.2.

TASK 15.2: *Rewrite the documents or include them, as is, in the appendix to the proposal.*

Not all documents are useful in their original form. Some are excessively technical or include long sections that are not relevant to your consultation. For these and other reasons you may need to alter the documents before adding them to your proposal. Do you have to rewrite any of the supporting documents you wish to use or can you include them as appendices, as is?

Make any alterations necessary and move on to Task 15.3.

TASK 15.3: *Identify the appendices in the table of contents and refer to them in the proposal text, as appropriate.*

If you do include supporting documents as appendices to your proposal, be sure to list these in your proposal's table of contents. Also, refer to these documents wherever applicable in the text of the proposal. This serves to integrate the appendices into the entire proposal. Move on to Step 16.

STEP 16: *Develop the proposal budget and disclosure strategy.*

The objective of Step 16 is to estimate the project budget and determine the client fee. Any consulting task can be estimated as long as it has definable parameters. Your ability to accurately estimate costs and profit makes it easier to offer a fixed-fee consultation. As noted in the fee-setting section, a fixed-fee project is usually more profitable. It can also be reassuring to the client who knows that there is a lid on costs. A solid budget estimate also helps you control your own costs.

The tasks in Step 16 are:

- Task 16.1: Set up the project budget worksheet.
- Task 16.2: Estimate labor days (hours) for each category of labor.
- Task 16.3: Estimate direct expenses for each project function.

STEP 16: *Develop the proposal budget and disclosure strategy.*

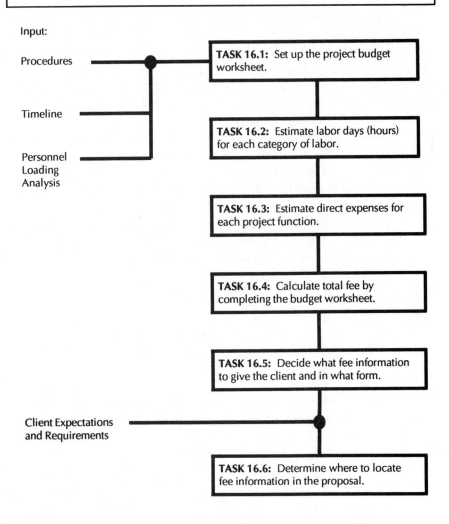

Input:

Procedures

TASK 16.1: Set up the project budget worksheet.

Timeline

TASK 16.2: Estimate labor days (hours) for each category of labor.

Personnel
Loading
Analysis

TASK 16.3: Estimate direct expenses for each project function.

TASK 16.4: Calculate total fee by completing the budget worksheet.

TASK 16.5: Decide what fee information to give the client and in what form.

Client Expectations
and Requirements

TASK 16.6: Determine where to locate fee information in the proposal.

- Task 16.4: Calculate the total fee by completing the budget worksheet.
- Task 16.5: Decide what fee information to give the client and in what form.
- Task 16.6: Determine where to locate fee information in the proposal.

TASK 16.1: *Set up the project budget worksheet.*

To calculate the approximate costs for your proposed project, construct a project budget worksheet (PBW). List all the functions, direct labor costs, and direct expenses for the project. Estimate the number of labor days or hours necessary to complete each function. Be consistent and estimate in terms of labor days or labor hours only. If you mix days and hours it is easy to make mistakes. Then determine the category of labor appropriate for that function.

Use a large sheet of paper for your rough draft of the PBW. Follow the example in Figure 4.13. Divide the page into vertical thirds. The first column is for listing project functions, the second column is for labor costs, and the third is for direct expenses. List each project function by name in chronological order. List the categories of direct labor costs at the head of the second column. Finally, list the direct expense categories in the third column and divide the page into columns and rows so you can cross-index the costs with the functions.

Enter dollar amounts for labor and total direct expenses. Then move on to Task 16.2.

TASK 16.2: *Estimate labor days (hours) for each category of labor.*

In this task you fill in the columns for direct labor rate. Estimate how many labor days it will take by each level of personnel to complete the listed function.

> *Example:* Suppose that the first task is to develop a survey instrument. Will you do part of this yourself at a high level of pay? Can you assign some of the research to a junior level employee? How much clerical work will it take? You might estimate that it will take you 1.5 days to complete your part of the task. You will need .6 days of research by a junior level employee and .4 days of clerical work. Enter these figures in the appropriate space in the row for the first function.

For each function listed you should ask yourself:

What levels of labor are required for this task?

FIGURE 4.13
Project budget worksheet (PBW)

FUNCTION #	FUNCTION NAMES(S)	DIRECT LABOR/RATE						DIRECT EXPENSES						
		High Level: $300/day	Mgmt. Level: $225/day	Jr. Level: $175/day	Clerical: $95/day	Art: $105/day	Staff Analyst: $140/day	Air Fares	Telephone	Xerox	Hotels	Postage	Car Rentals	Misc.
1														
2														
3														
4														
	Total Number of Days													
	Total Labor Costs													
	Total Direct Expenses													

Will this task call for specialized personnel or can a staff member do the same job at a lower rate?

Write down your initial estimates and move on to Task 16.3.

TASK 16.3: *Estimate direct expenses for each project function.*

Your indirect expenses like office rent and utilities are counted as overhead. In this section of the worksheet list those items that are not figured into your basic overhead. Consider such items as:

- Phone
- Air fares

- Xerox
- Hotels

You will probably count your base phone bill as part of your overhead, but long-distance calls for this particular project would be listed as a direct expense. Enter your estimates of the cost for each direct expense and move on to Task 16.4.

TASK 16.4: *Calculate the total fee by completing the budget worksheet.*

To complete your PBW compute the totals for each category. At the base of each direct labor column you will enter the total labor days. Multiply that figure by the labor rate for that category of labor and enter the result in the row for total labor costs. Likewise add up the direct expenses for each category and enter the result in the row for total direct expenses.

It is helpful to transfer your totals and the category headings onto a project budget summary. This is a one page summary of the titles of each category and the figure for that category. Figure 4.14 shows a typical format for a budget summary. The pricing sheet at the end of this step (Figure 4.15) gives you an idea of what a complete budget summary looks like. Complete your budget summary and move on to Task 16.5.

TASK 16.5: *Decide what fee information to give the client and in what form.*

If you feel it would be to your advantage to quote a fixed-price fee without itemizing the contributing costs, you may want to submit only

FIGURE 4.14
Sample format for project budget summary

```
DIRECT LABOR

_____     _____     $6,480
_____     _____     $_____
_____     _____     $_____     $XXXX


OVERHEAD

(          )_____              $XXXXX


DIRECT EXPENSES

_____     $836.
_____     $593.
_____
_____
_____
_____     _____     $XXXXX

SUB-TOTAL                               $XXXXX

PROFIT                                  $XXXXX

TOTAL FIXED PRICE                       $17,960.00
```

the project budget summary. If good marketing calls for giving the client a detailed breakdown of costs, then include the complete budget. After making that decision, go on to the next task.

TASK 16.6: *Determine where to locate fee information in the proposal.*

The fee is often first introduced when the proposal is submitted. Depending on the distribution pattern of the written proposal in the client's organization, you may either include the bid in the proposal itself or put it in a confidential letter, which will accompany your formal proposal as a separate document.

ESTIMATING FOR THE FIXED FEE

Inability to make solid estimates of the labor and direct expenses required for a project keeps many consultants from making a fixed-fee bid. Research has repeatedly demonstrated that the fixed-price contract produces higher profitability than daily/hourly rate contracts. Consultants should never advocate fixed-price contracts if they aren't comfortable or secure in their estimating abilities.

Such discomfort comes from two distinct causes: First, many consultants are not risk takers. They are not really entrepreneurs. Circumstance has put them into business for themselves. They don't like fixed-price contracts because they don't like to take chances. They don't like to make estimates because they might be wrong. This is a matter of entrepreneurial spirit and can't be treated here.

Second, many consultants fear estimating because they don't understand the process. The secret to success in making solid estimates is breaking the project down into its component parts, using the process detailed in this step. At first, to insure peace of mind, the breakdowns need to be very precise and specific. Later, the effort becomes more general and broad.

PADDING THE ESTIMATE

One problem with estimating is the tendency to pad. Fees quoted to clients can be inflated in this manner. Suppose one of your staff members estimates a part of the project. This person asks a second staff member who will carry out a subtask in this area of the project to provide an estimate of the amount of time required for the subtask. Feeling that the second staff member may be "light" in the estimate offered, the first staff member pads it a bit. Then the estimate comes to you and you feel that the first staff member may be "light," so you pad further. This is called the "creeping pad." Before long, what was to have taken 7 working days to accomplish has been increased to 12.

Nothing is wrong with padding estimates to compensate for underestimates by others, but only one person should have the responsibility of padding. If not, you can seriously overprice your services without realizing that you are involved in the creeping pad. And that will make you less competitive.

Move on to Step 17.

FIGURE 4.15
Pricing Sheet

DIRECT LABOR		
Senior professional personnel		
11 Days @ $400	$4,400	
Junior professional personnel		
10 Days @ $250	2,500	
Staff analyst		
5 Days @ $150	750	
Secretarial		
9 Days @ $100	900	
TOTAL DIRECT LABOR		$ 8,550
OVERHEAD (130% of Direct Labor)		11,115
DIRECT EXPENSES		
1. Air fares (3 × $225) (2 × $165)		
(1 × $505)	1,510	
2. Automotive mileage (700 mi.		
× .250)	175	
3. Consultant, R. Londs, Ph.D.		
2 days @ $1,000 per day	2,000	
4. Entertainment	250	
5. Per diem (10 days @ $175)	1,750	
6. Postage	225	
7. Printing and photocopying	600	
8. Rental cars	600	
9. Telephone	250	
10. Miscellaneous	600	
TOTAL DIRECT EXPENSES		$ 7,960
SUBTOTAL		$19,075
PROFIT (20%)		3,815
TOTAL FIXED PRICE		$22,890

STEP 17: *Write the proposal abstract and the draft letter of transmittal.*

The objective of Step 17 is to write the proposal abstract and compose the letter of transmittal. These documents are important because it is likely that they are the only parts of the proposal that will be read thoroughly. For this reason they should be short and to the point while making a good argument for retaining your services.

The tasks in Step 17 are:

- Task 17.1: Write the proposal abstract.
- Task 17.2: Compose the letter of transmittal and title page.

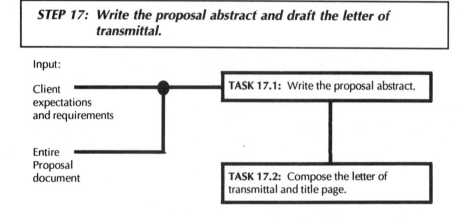

STEP 17: Write the proposal abstract and draft the letter of transmittal.

Input:

Client expectations and requirements

TASK 17.1: Write the proposal abstract.

Entire Proposal document

TASK 17.2: Compose the letter of transmittal and title page.

TASK 17.1: *Write the proposal abstract.*

You've almost completed your entire proposal. The final remaining component is your proposal abstract or summary of the contents of the proposal. Your client or readers may not want to read the entire proposal at the first sitting. They may prefer to move directly to the budget, your procedures, or statements of goals or objectives. You have no way of knowing.

Before readers dive into the middle of your proposal document, they need an overview of the purposes and outcomes of your project. This is the function of the proposal abstract. In one to three pages you summarize your entire project. This introduces the subject of your consultation and gives readers the "big picture" before they focus their attention on any one component.

Be brief! Always remember that your readers are impatient. They may have twenty or more proposals to review. It is far better to give them a general idea of the entire project in the abstract than to kill them with detail. Your objective in the abstract is to summarize and spark interest, not to overwhelm with voluminous facts and figures. Use your procedures and statements of needs, goals, and objectives to encapsulate your project. Make the pill small enough to be swallowed.

The proposal abstract should be written after the proposal is completed. If possible, limit it to one page, single spaced. Words should be selected with great care, as they must communicate more efficiently than the body of the proposal.

An abstract should summarize the proposal document, emphasizing the outcomes, results, and benefits of the proposal and treating procedures to be used in the course of the consultation only in the most general sense. The abstract should not contain any controversy, discussion of the cost of the consultation, or attributes of the consultant.

TASK 17.2: *Compose the letter of transmittal and title page.*

The letter of transmittal formally conveys the proposal document from the consultant to the client organization. The letter should be concise and should precisely specify the contents of the proposal package. Think of the letter of transmittal as the packing slip for your proposal. It should clearly and briefly state the events which have resulted in the proposal being submitted. Mention the preproposal meetings, conferences, letters, and so forth. The aim is to place the proposal in context of the history of your communications with the client.

The letter of transmittal should clearly communicate a high level of commitment. Clients are sensitive to the fact that any other business you have in-house may hinder your efforts on their behalf. Set your client's mind at ease by committing your time, your schedule, and especially your interest to his or her problems. Inform the client that this piece of work is of the highest priority to you and your consulting practice. If you have others working on this proposed consultation, be sure to indicate that you will take steps to maintain total organizational commitment.

The title page of your proposal is the means by which it will be referenced in the client organization. It should contain: the title of the project, the date of submission to the client, the name of the client (and in case the client is an organization, the name of the individual recipient and his or her title), the name of the consulting organization and/or your name and any restrictions.

Make the title short and descriptive. You'll have to live with this title for the duration of the consultation, so avoid cute or overly complex words and words with questionable double meanings. Avoid acronyms because they require constant explanation.

Just as with any other creative document, the title page should hold any restrictions about the distribution of your proposal or its contents to other parties. It may be useful to add the following statement:

> This proposal contains ideas and descriptions which are considered to be of proprietary interest to [name of consultant or consultant organization]. The contents of this proposal are intended for the exclusive review of and consideration by [name of client or client organization]. Redistribution or subsequent disclosure of the materials contained herein is *not* authorized without the express, written consent of [name of consultant or consultant organization].

Move on to Step 18.

STEP 18: *Produce the finished proposal.*

The objective of Step 18 is to prepare the finished proposal for the client. Everything you have done up to this point serves as input. In producing the actual proposal you are bringing your overall conception of the project together and expressing it in a finished document.

The tasks in Step 18 are:

- Task 18.1: Edit for consistency, emphasis, and accuracy.
- Task 18.2: Type and proof.
- Task 18.3: Construct the table of contents, cover, dividers, and binding.

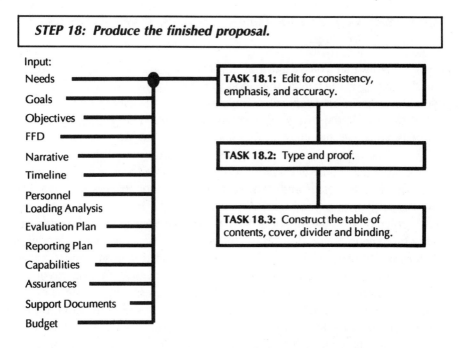

STEP 18: *Produce the finished proposal.*

Input:
Needs
Goals
Objectives
FFD
Narrative
Timeline
Personnel
Loading Analysis
Evaluation Plan
Reporting Plan
Capabilities
Assurances
Support Documents
Budget

TASK 18.1: Edit for consistency, emphasis, and accuracy.

TASK 18.2: Type and proof.

TASK 18.3: Construct the table of contents, cover, divider and binding.

TASK 18.1: *Edit for consistency, emphasis, and accuracy.*

It's obviously pointless to reassure your client in the capabilities section that you have the ability, organization, and management skills necessary for the project if your finished proposal is rife with misspellings and grammatical nightmares. The best proposal in the world would be completely hamstrung by bad grammar and misspelled words.

Take the time now to edit and clear up any of these problems. You'll ensure that your message will be delivered to your client in a clear, crisp manner. Move on to Task 18.2.

TASK 18.2: *Type and proof.*

Once you've edited your proposal, have it typed or type it yourself. When you receive the typed manuscript, proofread it thoroughly to make sure that the text is accurate and free from typographical mistakes. Just as an unedited proposal can destroy a fine presentation, a proposal that hasn't been proofed runs the risk of confusing the reader or even altering the intent of your statements with typos. Run through the typed version with your red pencil, using your original as a guide. Correct and retype as necessary and move on to Task 18.3.

TASK 18.3: *Construct the table of contents, cover, dividers, and binding.*

Now that you've put the proposal into its final, typed form, all that's lacking is the packaging. Don't underestimate the value of the way you showcase your proposal. Think of the brand of beer that you buy. The stuff inside the can is all basically the same. The packaging is what attracts your eye and causes your hand to move to your wallet.

The same is true with the packaging you choose for your proposal. First, construct a table of contents to be located in the front of the text. Make it clear and easily referenced. Your readers may want to skip around within your text. A good table of contents facilitates their easy grasp of your information. Remember that your readers are probably very busy people who don't have the time or patience to wade through a laborious exposition of your ideas. Make the information easy to get to and easy to grasp. Then your proposal will work hard in your favor.

Many see the table of contents as a useless convention. For the proposal, however, nothing could be further from the truth. Look on the table of contents as a road map through your proposal which uses interesting language to involve the reader. Wording such as "problem statement," "anticipated problems," and "alternative solution concepts," arouse reader interest just as newspaper headlines seek to interest the reader.

It is also wise to remember that a proposal doesn't read like a novel. The reader may jump around to gather specific information. A table of contents guides the reader in deciding which parts of the proposal to read.

Dividers can aid your organization of the material presented. If they would be helpful to the readers, use them. The cover and binding should reflect your professional standards without appearing too slick. This decision is another judgement call on your part. Consider what cover and binding will get a positive response from your client and other readers. If you need some outside help with the art work or if you have to generate a significant number of copies, a graphic arts company can typeset and print your proposal copies as well as package your approach to your client in an attractive, appealing cover and binding.

PROPOSAL CHECKLIST

Use this proposal checklist to rate the quality of your finished proposal. Score each of the twelve areas on a scale of 1 to 7, with 7 representing the highest score.

Need Identification

```
1   2   3   4   5   6   7
└───┴───┴───┴───┴───┴───┴──→
```

The proposal clearly states the client's identified needs, showing that all relevant information has been gathered, and communicates those needs in a way that is meaningful to the client.

Goals and Objectives

```
1   2   3   4   5   6   7
└───┴───┴───┴───┴───┴───┴──→
```

The proposal contains statements of general goals and specific objectives. The objectives state the expected results of the project in precise and specific terms based on the initial communication with the client. Specific statements of behavioral changes that are necessary to meet the objectives are included.

Plan

```
1   2   3   4   5   6   7
└───┴───┴───┴───┴───┴───┴──→
```

The proposal presents a specific technical plan for meeting the stated objectives without revealing too much and giving away my services. The plan is presented in the FFD and the proposal narrative. The plan establishes significant milestones, describes communication procedures, and gives an organization and management plan.

Time Line

```
1   2   3   4   5   6   7
└───┴───┴───┴───┴───┴───┴──→
```

The proposal contains a specific time line that shows the sequence of tasks in the project and the approximate times when they will take place.

Evaluation Procedures

1　2　3　4　5　6　7

The proposal specifies how the results of the consultation will be evaluated by defining what will happen and the criteria that will be used to measure results.

Capabilities Section

1　2　3　4　5　6　7

The proposal contains a meaningful statement of capabilities which concentrates on my ability to produce results and bring about changes and accomplishments. Any resumes that are included are rewritten with the current project in mind, eliminating reference to unrelated education and experience.

Statement of Assurances

1　2　3　4　5　6　7

The proposal has a statement of assurances that deals with areas of concern to the client, such as legal liability, ability to successfully complete the project, and adherence to relevant laws and regulations.

Budget Estimate

1　2　3　4　5　6　7

The proposal contains a clear and precise budget estimate that tells the client what my services will cost and what expenses the client will be responsible for. The budget takes the client's resources into account and presents alternatives in level or scope of service when appropriate.

Packaging of Proposal

1　2　3　4　5　6　7

The proposal is attractive and interesting. It reads well and is professionally typed.

Organization of Proposal

```
1  2  3  4  5  6  7
└──┴──┴──┴──┴──┴──┴──→
```

The proposal has a clear table of contents and is organized so that the client can find the information needed with ease.

Communications

```
1  2  3  4  5  6  7
└──┴──┴──┴──┴──┴──┴──→
```

I have provided a comfortable avenue for the client to obtain additional information, if needed.

Marketing

```
1  2  3  4  5  6  7
└──┴──┴──┴──┴──┴──┴──→
```

I have recognized the importance of the proposal in my marketing plan. I have tailored the proposal to the client's point of view as well as that of others who may take part in the decision to retain my services.

Scoring

If your score totals 72–84 you are probably doing just fine. A lower score suggests a need to improve your proposal.

Now that you have completed and evaluated your proposal, move on to Step 19.

STEP 19: *Plan the follow-up strategy.*

The objective of Step 19 is to determine who will deliver your proposal to your client, when it will be delivered, and what follow-up plans you will implement. Some consultants tend to feel that the proposal is finished when it is written. Because it is a marketing tool as much as a document for conveying information, follow-up is a crucial part of the proposal process.

The tasks in Step 19 are:

- Task 19.1: Determine who will deliver the proposal and when.
- Task 19.2: Decide on a follow-up strategy.

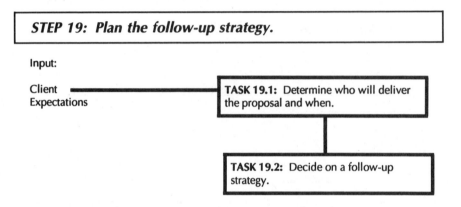

TASK 19.1: *Determine who will deliver the proposal and when.*

The means of delivery depends on the client and on marketing considerations. If you have good communication with the client, you may want to deliver the proposal personally and take advantage of the opportunity to discuss it. You often increase the probability of success if delivery of your proposal is combined with an oral presentation. After you give the verbal presentation, you can leave the written proposal behind for review and further analysis. If your verbal presentation is sufficiently effective, you may receive a verbal acceptance prior to your departure.

When dealing with large organizations it is usually better to have a messenger deliver the proposal or use a delivery service. Sometimes deadlines are a consideration. Don't lose a contract because you miss a deadline. Some considerations are:

> If you are an independent consultant, is it to your advantage to deliver the proposal yourself or do you think that utilizing a messenger would be better?
>
> When must the proposal reach the client?
>
> Do you have a hard deadline to meet?

Decide who will deliver your proposal and when it will be delivered. Then move on to Task 19.2.

TASK 19.2: *Decide on a follow-up strategy.*

Once your client receives your proposal, what next? Some clients should be contacted to discuss the proposal. Others should be left alone to consider it. The questions you should ask about formulating your follow-up strategy are:

How long will you give your client to review your proposal and make a decision?

Will you simply wait for your client to recontact you or have you decided on a set period of time for recontact?

Will you call the client?

Who in the client's organization is your contact person?

Will that individual be the same person you will contact for follow-up?

How will you follow up delivery of your proposal?

Will you recontact your client by telephone? Would it be better to send a telegram? To visit the client in person?

Decide exactly what your course of action will be once your proposal reaches your client and move on to Step 20.

STEP 20: *Deliver the proposal to the client.*

The objective of Step 20 is to deliver your winning proposal to your client in a timely fashion.

The tasks in Step 20 are:

- Task 20.1: Perform the final proposal review and check for completeness.
- Task 20.2: Initiate delivery.

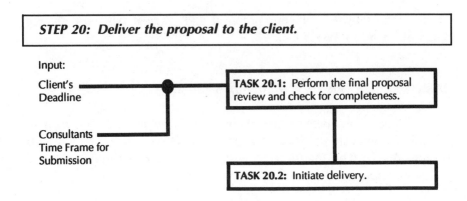

TASK 20.1: *Perform the final proposal review and check for completeness.*

Make sure that all the components are properly positioned within the cover and binding. Carry out a final review:

Is everything complete?

Have you forgotten anything?

TASK 20.2: *Initiate delivery.*

If everything is in place, deliver the proposal. It's finished! Congratulations, you've constructed a vigorous document that reflects your consulting expertise, technical knowledge, and personal style. Good luck!

Move on to Step 21.

STEP 21: *Implement follow-up strategy.*

The objective of Step 21 is to implement your follow-up strategy and get your client's decision on your proposal.

The tasks in Step 21 are:

- Task 21.1: Carry out the follow-up strategy.
- Task 21.2: Obtain the client's decision on the proposal.

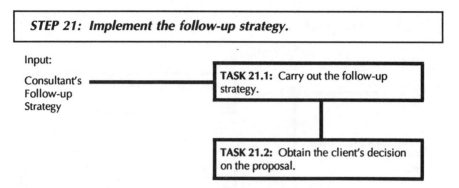

STEP 21: *Implement the follow-up strategy.*

Input:

Consultant's Follow-up Strategy

TASK 21.1: Carry out the follow-up strategy.

TASK 21.2: Obtain the client's decision on the proposal.

TASK 21.1: *Carry out the follow-up strategy.*

Your client has received your proposal. You've waited a suitable length of time for him or her to digest your material. Now you must carry out the follow-up strategy you devised in Step 19 during your follow-up planning.

TASK 21.2: *Obtain the client's decision on the proposal.*

Sometimes you have to contact a potential client to get a decision, even a positive one. Also, some people just don't like to give a refusal, so they avoid contacting you. If your proposal was rejected you need to know it. You also need to find out why it was rejected—if you can get that information.

If your proposal was accepted, move on to the next section and Step 23, Contract Negotiations. If the proposal was rejected, move on to Step 22.

STEP 22: *Recycle the proposal for other uses.*

The objective of Step 22 is to get the maximum possible benefit from your proposal. If it was accepted, you may still have use for it in future solicitations. The same is true if it was rejected. This step lists several other uses for a rejected proposal.

The tasks in Step 22 are:

- Task 22.1: Determine why the proposal was rejected.

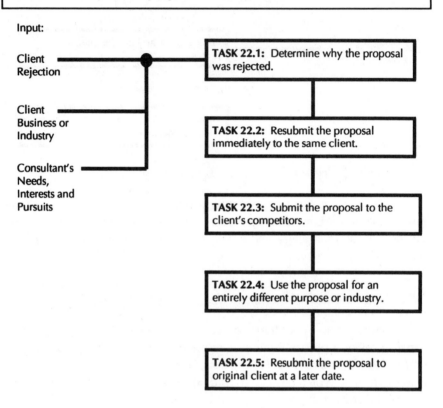

STEP 22: Recycle the proposal for other uses.

Input:

Client
Rejection

Client
Business or
Industry

Consultant's
Needs,
Interests and
Pursuits

TASK 22.1: Determine why the proposal was rejected.

TASK 22.2: Resubmit the proposal immediately to the same client.

TASK 22.3: Submit the proposal to the client's competitors.

TASK 22.4: Use the proposal for an entirely different purpose or industry.

TASK 22.5: Resubmit the proposal to original client at a later date.

- Task 22.2: Resubmit the proposal immediately to the same client.

- Task 22.3: Submit the proposal to the client's competitors.

- Task 22.4: Use the proposal for an entirely different purpose or industry.

- Task 22.5: Resubmit the proposal to the original client at a later date.

TASK 22.1: *Determine why the proposal was rejected.*

Everyone in business fails at one time or another. Successful people fail, too. The difference is that they learn from their failures.

Some of the questions you need to answer about a rejected proposal are:

Why didn't your client offer you the consulting assignment?

Was there some problem with a section of the proposal?

Did the client simply decide that the problems you outlined did not warrant immediate attention?

Use this information to reformulate your proposal and to guide you in writing similar proposals in the future.

TASK 22.2: *Resubmit the proposal immediately to the same client.*

Discover the exact reasons why your proposal was rejected, correct the problem areas, and resubmit the proposal to the same client, immediately.

TASK 22.3: *Submit the proposal to the client's competitors.*

Whatever business your client is in, the chances are that he or she has at least one major competitor, perhaps many. Those companies share similar needs and problems. If your proposal was rejected by your first client because of an internal decision to ignore the problems you outlined, perhaps a competitor will take a more positive view of solving those same problems and meeting similar needs.

Investigate other companies in the same industry that would be likely recipients of such a proposal and submit your proposal to them.

TASK 22.4: *Use the proposal for an entirely different purpose or industry.*

There are many possible applications for a rejected proposal. Sometimes one of these uses can be more valuable to you in the long run than the original contract you were looking for. Consider this question:

Is there a professional journal or magazine that would publish a rewrite of your proposal as an article or monograph?

If you can locate such a publication or if you can employ your proposal as a support document within another proposal package, do so.

Perhaps you can take the proposal to a different company or industry. Ask yourself:

Can I modify the existing proposal to address the needs or problems of another industry?

Carefully consider all these alternative uses of the original proposal document.

TASK 22.5: *Resubmit the proposal to the original client at a later date.*

Your original client may have decided to live with the problems or needs unresolved when you first submitted your proposal. With the passage of time, the client has the opportunity to reflect on the suggestions in your proposal and can also watch the problems and needs you identified.

Have those problems compounded with time?

Are the client's needs more pressing now?

Time can be a valuable ally. You know that the client's problems and needs won't just dry up like evaporating water. If your assessment of those problems and needs was accurate, there is a substantial probability that they will be at least as damaging to the company in the future, if not more so.

Resubmitting your original proposal may just strike the responsive chord that wasn't hit the first time around. Don't neglect to employ this tack. It could result in a lucrative, rewarding consulting assignment.

I've heard it said many times that nothing happens until the client is ready to buy. The consultant who stays around eventually gets the assignment. So be patient and let that hesitant client simmer.

This concludes the proposal-writing section. You won't get a contract every time you submit a proposal, but if you follow the steps outlined in this section you will have plenty of assignments to carry out.

A successful proposal naturally leads to the need to draw up a contract. The next section describes how to handle contracts for consulting projects. A properly drafted contract is the logical sequel to a professional proposal.

CHAPTER 5

Contracts and Your Lawyer

Because a contract is a legal document, you will probably need competent legal advice in drafting one. This section on contracts is not a substitute for your attorney. Rather, it is a tool to help you work with your attorney more effectively and at less cost.

It may seem ludicrous to advise you, a competent consultant, on the importance of using experts. But, as consultants, we tend to forget that we can also be clients. We know that there are expert clients as well as expert consultants. The expert clients (the ''dream'' clients) are those who are thoroughly prepared for their consultations with us. They have their documents ready and have already thought out their questions. They communicate their problems in an organized manner. They get the most from us in the most cost-effective way.

Your attorney will be just as delighted with you if you perform in a similar manner. Like us, lawyers are paid for their time. You can cut your legal fees by at least 50% if you take the trouble to prepare a draft contract and then ask your attorney to evaluate and modify it. Or you can double the cost and ask him or her to draw one up ''from scratch'' without really knowing in detail what it is you are seeking to accomplish.

I have used the following procedure with excellent results. I recommend that you do the same.

STEP 23: *Enter contract negotiations.*

The objective of Step 23 is to complete the preliminary work for drafting a contract. You need to know what the client needs and you need to be aware of what you want to accomplish with the contract. In addition, you need good legal advice to guide you through the process.

The tasks in Step 23 are:

- Task 23.1: Review the needs for the contract.
- Task 23:2: Seek out competent legal counsel.
- Task 23.3: Review the contract strategies.

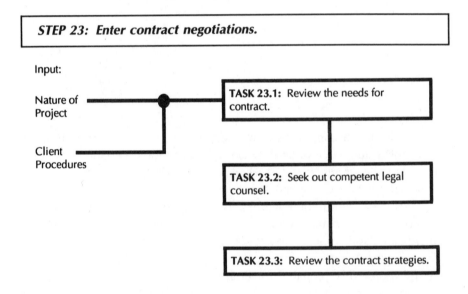

TASK 23.1: *Review the needs for the contract.*

Study the principles in this section. Applying those that best suit your consultation, use the sample contracts in Appendix E. Draft one or more contracts of your own. One may be adequate, but your situation may suggest that you will sometimes need alternative forms.

Your work should be general, designed to serve the circumstances of any situation. As a general document, your contract will lack certain specifics: the description of the consultant's tasks, the description of the client's tasks or responsibilities, the terms and conditions of payment. These will differ for each situation.

When you have completed this step, you should have one or more contract *shells* that express, in general terms, the nature of any contractual agreement for any consulting situation you may become involved in.

TASK 23.2: *Seek out competent legal counsel.*

The best way to find a competent lawyer is through referrals. Your peers are usually more than willing to give you guidance in this matter. When you have found the right person, ask your attorney two questions:

> Is this draft agreement adequate and suitable to protect my interests?
>
> Is there anything that you would add, delete, or change?

If you have done a thorough job of creating your contract shells, your lawyer's work should be minimal.

All that remains is for you to tailor your shell to fit a particular set of circumstances by filling in the specifics. In time, you will come to regard the actual writing of any particular contract as mere routine. This method should clear your mind for something far more essential— *strategic thought.*

TASK 23.3: *Review the contract strategies.*

The successful consultant always employs basic strategies when negotiating a contract with the client in order to achieve six major goals:

- Avoidance of misunderstanding
- Maintenance of working independence and freedom
- Assurance of work
- Assurance of payment
- Avoidance of liability
- Prevention of litigation

It is unfortunate that our society has placed a pejorative coloration on the word "strategy." The purpose and meaning of strategy here is neither to mislead the client nor to be devious. Rather, it is to assure *both* parties that these six goals, which are in your mutual interest, will be reached.

Let's take a good look at each of these goals, because they are important.

AVOIDANCE OF MISUNDERSTANDING

Misunderstanding on the part of the client is derived from *assumptions*. When in doubt, the average client tends to avoid asking the consultant for a full explanation. Instead, the client *assumes* your meaning. If the assumptions disagree with your intent, trouble ensues.

To avoid any misunderstanding and resultant problems, I urge you to spell out everything you intend to do—even the obvious.

Example: Let us assume that a particular project requires the preparation of a questionnaire or survey. You could simply state in the contract that a survey instrument will be designed and implemented. But you should go further and say that your activities in this regard will include:

- Determination of the information requirements
- Design of the survey instrument
- Testing the survey instrument for face validity
- Pilot testing of the survey instrument
- Selection of the sample to be surveyed
- Modification of the survey instrument
- Development of the data analysis scheme

Now we all know that the design and implementation of a survey instrument requires all of the above-listed activities and a great deal more. Listing these activities makes your ultimate fee that much more justifiable, avoids misunderstanding on the part of the client, and allows you freedom and independence in your work.

FREEDOM AND INDEPENDENCE

If you do not specify the tasks in your consultation as I have suggested above, your client may question you in excessive detail about the specifics of your project and/or set down his or her own specifications for it.

Working to conform to the client's list of specifications hampers your freedom and independence in carrying out the project. Your list is obviously comfortable for you. The client's list is a constraint and could ultimately impede your progress. This point is so important that, if a client puts his or her own specifications in the contract, I would strongly advise you to make every attempt to negotiate such a clause out of the document.

Up-front specificity on your part always avoids the client's questions by anticipating them. The fewer questions the client asks in contract negotiation, the more smoothly and quickly you will both reach the dotted line.

ASSURANCE OF WORK

The most dangerous and frequent trap for any consultant is giving away expertise free of charge. This trap awaits consultants at three different junctures in their dealings with clients:

- in the exploratory interview
- in the written proposal
- in the contract

Notice that in the example for specification of activities described on page 132, the consultant wisely stated *what* would be done, not *how* it would be done. Because no contract is signed on the day it is presented, the client could very easily refuse to sign, adopt the methodology of the consultant who was foolish enough to spell it out, and have his or her staff accomplish the project without incurring the expense of a consulting fee.

ASSURANCE OF PAYMENT

You are not a banker, so you should very rarely, if ever, extend credit to the client by billing for the entire amount at the end of the project. A good contract demands a healthy down payment. In most situations, I personally am most comfortable with one-third. This initial installment ensures that regular payments will be forthcoming as soon as your work is in progress. You know that your contract has accomplished assurance of payment if the client owes you no more than 10% of the total fee at project's end.

AVOIDANCE OF LIABILITY

More and more, we in the advice business are being looked upon as doctors. This means that clients are less inclined to allow for honest mistakes. So, like physicians, we shall probably all be insured against malpractice in the next 10 years—a high price to pay for partial safety. The first place for liability prevention is in the original contract. Spell out your responsibilities exactly and include the things you are not responsible for. Spell out those contingencies beyond your control which may cause the project to fail.

PREVENTION OF LITIGATION

There are two primary causes for litigation between consultant and client: the belief on the client's part that work was improperly or incompletely done and failure of the consultant to collect the fee. A well-thought-out, strategically devised contract can go far to avoid either of these primary causes of dissention. Should either or both of these things occur, try to avoid litigation by any and all means. There are a thousand reasons in favor of settling disputes out of court.

Now that you have done the preliminary work, you are ready to go on to the next chapter and Step 24.

CHAPTER 6

Valid Forms of a Contract

Verbal agreements, letters of intent, and written contracts all have legal validity at the outset. Only in litigation does the most specific kind of written document become the form most appreciated by the party who is in the right. Attempting to recall what was said at a meeting in the distant past bears little weight before a judge or an arbitration committee because such evidence is nothing more than hearsay.

A letter of engagement or agreement signed by both parties or even signed only by the client *is an enforceable contract*. In his book *How To Become a Successful Consultant in Your Own Field* (The Consultant's Library, 1985), Hubert Bermont brags that he never signs a contract. He then goes on to say that he requires a letter of intent from the client. Notwithstanding my respect for Mr. Bermont and his accomplishments, I think he plays a cute semantic game with us in this regard. He even tells us that he *sued* a client for *default of contract* based upon the client's *letter of intent—and won!*

What he means is that in his particular practice he does not find it expedient to sign formal contractual agreements with his clients. Rather, he has them sign letters of agreement. All well and good for him. I do not question the validity of a letter of agreement. Indeed, when the occasion calls for one, I sometimes use it myself. There are samples of such letters in Appendix D.

For most consulting projects, however, I advocate a legal contract between consultant and client—the more specific and detailed from the consultant's point of view, the better. Step 24 details how to produce a valid contract.

STEP 24: *Prepare the contract.*

The objective of Step 24 is to prepare a contract that will meet the objectives listed in Step 23 and will hold up in court. This is as important a process as writing a proposal and demands thorough work on the part of the consultant as well as the input of competent legal counsel.

The tasks in Step 24 are:

- Task 24.1: Select the contract form.
- Task 24.2: Designate the contracting parties.
- Task 24.3: Write the contract preamble.
- Task 24.4: Write the basic agreement.
- Task 24.5: State the scope of your services.
- Task 24.6: Determine the method of compensation.
- Task 24.7: Write provisions for the client's protection.
- Task 24.8: Write provisions for the consultant's protection.
- Task 24.9: Assemble the contract.
- Task 24.10: Gather the proper signatures.
- Task 24.11: Amend the contract, if necessary.

TASK 24.1: *Select the contract form.*

Depending on the requirements of your client and the kind of project you will be executing, you may select one of the following three forms of contract:

1. A formal, written contract executed by both parties

STEP 24: *Prepare the contract.*

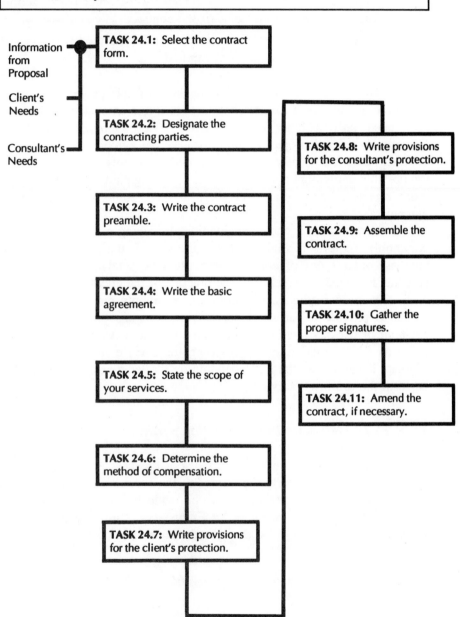

Information from Proposal

Client's Needs

Consultant's Needs

TASK 24.1: Select the contract form.

TASK 24.2: Designate the contracting parties.

TASK 24.3: Write the contract preamble.

TASK 24.4: Write the basic agreement.

TASK 24.5: State the scope of your services.

TASK 24.6: Determine the method of compensation.

TASK 24.7: Write provisions for the client's protection.

TASK 24.8: Write provisions for the consultant's protection.

TASK 24.9: Assemble the contract.

TASK 24.10: Gather the proper signatures.

TASK 24.11: Amend the contract, if necessary.

2. A letter of agreement or a purchase-order type of agreement prepared by one party and accepted by the other party, setting forth the essential elements of the contract

3. A verbal agreement for the services to be rendered with most of the promises and conditions implied

The main consideration is the size of the project. A major consultation calls for a formal contract. For a less extensive project you may need only a letter of agreement or an abbreviated contract. Sometimes a small project needs only a verbal agreement. The verbal contract is the least binding and you should use it only if you can accept the possible unpleasant consequences of not being paid or of having your work rejected. In general, it is best to have some form of written agreement.

Government agencies in situations involving major engagements commonly require formal written contracts. Letter agreements and purchase-order types of contracts can often be safely used where the amounts involved are smaller or the practice of the client is to use such.

Many consultants, like lawyers, commonly make verbal agreements to provide a particular service for compensation based on the per-hour or per-day rate charged by the consultant. An estimate is often made as to the total cost of providing the service involved, but this estimate is subject to change depending on the length of time needed to perform the promised services.

TASK 24.2: *Designate the contracting parties.*

The names, addresses, and types of business entities should be included to identify clearly the parties to the consulting contract. After identifying the parties, reference can be made in the remainder of the form to ''client'' and ''consultant.'' ''Engineers,'' ''insurance analysts,'' or some other term may also describe the consultant.

TASK 24.3: *Write the contract preamble.*

It is common practice to state the underlying background for the agreement or the assumptions on which it is based in a preamble or recitals section. This section is typically the first section of the contract following the designation of the contracting parties. Traditionally, it was customary to use "Whereas" clauses, but the more common form is to make the statement without the use of "Whereas" and to caption the section "Recitals."

Where any preliminary report or agreement has been made, take care to identify it clearly in the recitals. The recitals section may also set forth the authority of the person executing the agreement to legally bind his or her principal.

TASK 24.4: *Write the basic agreement.*

The basic commitment or agreement of the consultant should be set forth. This is where you state exactly what you are going to do during the consultation.

The services you, the consultant, will provide should be set forth in sufficient detail to make clear your undertaking. The services you are to perform should be spelled out in as much detail as possible. Since care is being taken to develop the contract document, it makes little sense to be terse. The best advice is to leave nothing open to question. Enumerate all of the consultation's tasks and major subtasks.

Where the services relate to a particular project or line of work, it should be fully described by means of location and type of work or project involved.

TASK 24.5: *State the scope of your services.*

A detailed statement of the scope and extent of services to be provided is desirable. Where the service provided has a well-defined meaning, a brief statement of the service involved may be sufficient.

If not all the services normally connected with the undertaking are to be provided, you should be protected and the client should understand that only limited services are being provided. The agreement should specifically set forth those services that will be provided, or the general services to be provided, with specific exclusions or limitations concerning those services or areas that will not be covered. Any optional or contingent services should be defined as to scope, showing the party who has the option and the circumstances under which the option may be excercised.

A statement of the detailed scope of the services you are to provide may include office consultations, field investigations and studies based thereon, preparation of reports involving feasibility, economic analysis, cost and designs, assistance in procurement and making contracts with others, supervision of work on the project, inspections, costs, evaluations, and, finally, agreement for assistance in any litigation that arises pursuant to the project.

TASK 24.6: *Determine the method of compensation.*

Setting the method of compensation for your services is essential. Where compensation is based on a charge per time unit, a schedule of these charges should be included, even though based on a standard fee schedule. Maximum and minimum fees should be stated if such are part of the agreement. A maximum figure on reimbursable costs should likewise be included if agreed on.

In cases other than those where a fixed fee is agreed on, clear definitions should be included concerning costs, classifications of consultant personnel, and other terms used to fix the total compensation payable. If payment is to be made on a performance basis, great care must be taken to spell out the performance criteria. The performance criteria should be observable, measurable, evident, and obvious to your client, to you, or to any other party.

The times and conditions of making payment should be set forth in sufficient detail to avoid any misunderstanding. Payments may be made as follows:

- On completion of specified services or portion thereof
- Monthly, either on receipt of an invoice or on the basis of a fixed figure or formula
- In accordance with a schedule set forth, possibly in connection with the rate of completion of work by a third party

Remember that there is a difference between the date a client is invoiced and the date on which payment is made. If this difference is likely to be of critical importance to either party, date of payment rather than date of invoice should be stated within the contract.

TASK 24.7: *Write provisions for the client's protection.*

It is good business practice to include specific guarantees that you will carry out the consultation adequately and without damage to the client. Provisions necessary for the protection of the client are:

1. A time schedule for the completion of your services or a formula for determining such.

2. A requirement for adequate insurance coverage. The client should be adequately protected either by insurance or by a hold-harmless agreement, or both.

3. A provision preventing you and the client from assigning the contract or subcontracting a part of it without the written consent of the other.

4. Although the agreement will normally terminate by provision or implication when your services are fully performed, the client may be given the right to terminate the agreement if your performance is unsatisfactory or if the client has no further need of the service provided, or, in some cases, at any time at the option of the client. A reasonable arrangement for payment of fees in the event of such termination should be provided for.

5. By implication and by specific contract provision, where called for, a requirement may be stated that only competent personnel may perform or continue to perform work for the client. It is not unknown for the client to request the assignment of a specific person or persons to perform the services, with identification of same in the contract. You should note that such a contractual clause limits your flexibility. Avoiding such a clause may be in your interest.

6. Other provisions include requirements that you obtain any approvals required by government agencies, that you maintain adequate records, that you make periodic reports to the client, and that any fee paid for a preliminary report to the client may be applied to the total fee involved for a completed project.

TASK 24.8: *Write provisions for the consultant's protection.*

Of course, the contract will protect your business interests. The agreement should contain some or all of the following provisions to protect your position:

1. Adequate compensation should be provided for in the event you are required to do extra work because of a change in the scope of the assignment or because of a delay caused by the client.

2. In many situations, a provision clearly describing the services you will not provide should be included, especially where the agreement is not standard to the industry.

3. A provision may be included that you may employ persons to assist you in the performance of duties under the agreement.

4. A provision may be included that relieves you of liability where you are unable to perform, or performance is delayed, due to circumstances beyond your control, including those caused by the client.

5. Your performance may be conditioned on receipt of certain information, approvals, and reports from the client on a scheduled basis. To the maximum extent possible, your receipt of information, approvals, and reports as well as any specifications regarding their quality, form, or contents should be spelled out.

TASK 24.9: *Assemble the contract.*

Now that you have written the various parts of the contract, it is time to assemble them into the complete document. The usual components of a formal written contract are the:

- Preamble section
- Project approaches section
- Consultant's tasks section
- Client's tasks section
- Special conditions section
- Payment of consulting fees section

We now review each of these six sections in detail.

1. The Preamble Section

The preamble section of the contract merely sets forth the mutual intention and purpose between you and the client in undertaking the consulting arrangement. A typical preamble shell is as follows:

> This agreement entered into this _____ day of _____, 19xx) by and between _____ (Name of client), hereinafter referred to as the COMPANY and _____ (Name of your organization), hereinafter referred to as the CONSUL-TANT,
> WITNESSETH, whereas the COMPANY and the CONSULTANT are desirous of entering into an agreement for the purpose of _____ (List project goals).

These project goals are general statements of the goals you will accomplish, such as:

- providing assistance to unemployed teenagers through skill training
- upgrading the qualifications of technical staff
- conducting a line of inquiry to determine an effective cure for transportation delays
- creating a more suitable environment for recreational pursuits of our citizens

Naturally, these goals are derived from your statement of goals in the proposal.

2. The Project Approaches Section

This section usually begins with a short statement:

> NOW THEREFORE, it is mutually agreed that: _____
> (List project objectives).

This section typically involves the stipulation of the approach being used in the project. The objectives come from the statement of objectives in the proposal. Unlike the goals section preceding, this section makes direct reference to the means to be employed in accomplishing the project. Typical entries in this section include:

- an orientation program involving 75 new employees will be conducted
- an experimental program involving human subjects, grouped by sex, shall be conducted
- a beautification program shall be undertaken involving the redesign of all track facilities and hiking areas.

Notice that the lack of specificity here is for the protection of you, the consultant.

A particularly useful item to insert here is a reference to the proposal that was written in connection with which this contract is being drawn. Suitable wording for such an insertion is:

> The development and conduct of the project shall be as described in the project prospectus submitted by the CONSULTANT to the COMPANY on _____ (insert date). The relevant descriptions from that document are attached hereto as Attachment A, and thereby incorporated into this document.

3. The Consultant's Tasks Section

In this section of the contract you spell out the specific tasks you will be responsible for. It is customary to preface each numbered paragraph of this section with the phrases:

> The CONSULTANT will . . .

or

> The CONSULTANT shall . . . .

For example, if you are planning to conduct a training program, a typical entry might read:

> 1.0 The CONSULTANT shall design, develop, and/or otherwise prepare in sufficient quantity for participant use, various training

materials which are required to satisfactorily conduct the program sessions as described. Such training materials will include, but are not necessarily limited to:

1.1 Participant Orientation Materials

1.2 Participant Technical Resource Materials

1.3 Program and Agendas, Evaluation Instruments, and the like.

A particularly useful entry in this section provides for your continuing consultation with the COMPANY. For example, consider the following:

The CONSULTANT will regularly consult with the designated COM-PANY personnel for the purpose of monitoring and assessing progress, and to formulate indicated program changes so as to more effectively achieve the program objectives as formulated in Attachment _____ (identifying symbol of the attachment containing the proposal materials.)

If you are required to submit a final report, indicate that fact in this section, too, as follows:

The CONSULTANT will furnish to the COMPANY on or before _____ (insert date on which final report is due) a reproducible copy of the project final report. This report will include program materials and descriptions of all relevant aspects of program activity.

It is important in this section to avoid putting yourself on an accountability path over which you do not have direct control. For example, suppose you are going to prepare a document, certain portions of which are to be supplied to you by the company. Don't put yourself on the hook to deliver the whole report; rather state:

The CONSULTANT shall prepare a document containing all relevant material and results. The CONSULTANT further agrees to incorporate into this report suitable portions of material supplied by the COMPANY as described in Paragraph _____ (paragraph number of CLIENT TASKS section that follows, in which these materials are described).

4. The Client's Tasks

This section of the contract draft is similar to the previous section except that it covers what the client will do. You will find it helpful to require the client to designate one technically cognizant individual to act for him or her in all technical matters pertaining to the contract. In this way, you are assured of a consistent interpretation of the contract terms and language.

It is sometimes useful to require the client to provide your staff with suitable workspace at the company's site. This may also be worded to provide for such unscheduled use of copies, typewriters, and the like as may be required to further improve the effectiveness of the project provided such usage is understood to be on a noninterference basis. All of this will be viewed as reasonable to the client. It provides you with a measure of authority when you need a fast Xerox copy and the client's staff is giving you the run-around about charge codes, authorizations, and so forth.

If you will have need for data, information, or lists that are in the client's possession, write into the contract that such items will be furnished to you. If the client is expected to assist in the administration or support of the project, take care to specify the nature of such assistance. Consider having the client provide facilities and equipment, data processing services, public information services, amenities such as coffee at meetings, and reimbursements to vendors.

Beware of setting up third-party agreements in your contract with the client. They don't work.

> *Example:* Suppose that the client has a project going with organization *X* and the client wants you to incorporate some of *X*'s results in your project. To do this *X* is supposed to give you some of its material. As far as you are concerned, it is the client supplying you with the material, not *X*. You have no formal relationship with *X* and *X* is not obligated to comply with your requests in any way. You must put the servicing of that relationship where it belongs: with the client.

5. The Special Conditions Section

This section may be omitted or it may be substantial. In the other sections you have made many assumptions, whether you realize it or not. For example, you assumed that there wouldn't be civil disorder during your contract term, in which case the problem of maintaining civil obedience with the client's funds doesn't come up. There are contingencies that can and do arise for which the contract should offer guidance.

Example: Consider what happens if the client's funds are cut or withdrawn. It is customary in such a situation to terminate the agreement without creating a financial hardship for the recipient. To accomplish this, a contract termination clause is often used, which provides for a suitable audit of work in progress, after which the client agrees to pay for terminating the work.

Additional areas of possible concern may include: failure or bankruptcy of the client or consultant, an instance of nationwide strike or revolt that makes it impossible to meet contract terms, the results of a man-made or natural disaster that destroys intermediate project accomplishments, the circumstances of fraud or embezzlement leading to insolvency of either party to the contract, and so forth. Your legal advisor may insist on certain protections for you and perhaps for your client in cases such as those described above.

6. The Payment of Consulting Fees Section

This section often begins with the phrase:

In consideration of the satisfactory performance of the CONSULTANT, the COMPANY agrees to reimburse the CONSULTANT on the following basis:

It is important that the wording that follows this phrase be specific. In this section you should spell out the exact terms and conditions that will result in the client providing payment to you.

Example: A $10,000 contract fee could be paid as follows:

Date first mentioned above (date contract is signed)	$1,500
15 August 19xx	$3,000
15 September 19xx	$3,000
15 October 19xx	$1,500
Balance (10%) upon submission of final report	$1,000

In recent years, due largely to tight money conditions and higher interest costs it has become common for the consultant to indicate both the invoice date and the required payment date. Although consultants once commonly relied merely on "trade custom" for the payment of their invoices, the expansion of trade custom from 10 days to 30 days and from 30 days to 90 days generally makes it advisable to specify in the contract the date on which payment is due.

TASK 24.10: *Gather the proper signatures.*

The agreement should be executed by both parties by means of signatures of persons properly authorized to make binding agreements. In regard to corporations, it may be necessary to determine that an officer has been authorized by a resolution of the board of directors—sometimes with a requirement that the signature be attested to—to make such agreements.

In regard to government agencies, statutes and regulations may specify the method and the proper person to execute the agreement. Care should be exercised in determining that proper appropriations have been made to compensate the consultant.

Where the authority of the person signing the agreement is not clear, a certification of the governing body of the organization involved authorizing the person to sign and approve the transaction may be required.

TASK 24.11: *Amend the contract, if necessary.*

In the event of changed circumstances, or if the parties desire to change their agreement, a written amendment of the contract may be in order. If the changes desired are extensive, it is often preferable to completely rewrite the contract as a new document.

THE LETTER OF AGREEMENT

In situations where one party does not wish any written agreement, it may still be possible for the other party to supply persuasive evidence of their agreement by writing a letter. This letter should set forth the essential elements of their verbal agreement and request a reply if it does not accurately reflect the agreement of both parties.

Either you, the consultant, or your client may prepare the letter of agreement. When the client desires to do it, it is possible and often advisable for you to prepare a draft first and submit it to the client for review in advance. The practical impact of this practice is to enable you to retain leadership in contractual matters. Often the precise wording of your draft letter becomes the final wording of the client's letter. Whether the letter is prepared on the client's letterhead or on your own, it will essentially say the same thing.

Four examples of the letter of agreement are included in Appendix D.

THE LETTER OF ENGAGEMENT

In certain situations the engagement is of such limited duration or the time between scheduling an appointment and providing the consulting service is so short that entering into a contract between the parties is impractical. Even so, you may still desire to inform the client of the terms and conditions under which you are willing to provide services. In such cases, you may use the letter of engagement.

Such a letter should contain several features, chief among them are:

1. Acknowledgment of the time and place where the first formal meeting will take place or when work will begin
2. Specification of the purpose of the first meeting and the purpose of the consultation in general
3. An indication of the time or duration that you expect will be involved in the consultation or a statement as to why it is not possible to provide such an estimate
4. A communication as to what the fee will be for the services to be provided or an indication of the basis on which the fee will be charged
5. Specification of the payment arrangements as well as the invoice schedule

In the past, consultants have tended to be satisfied by just telling clients when the invoice will be sent, leaving so-called "trade custom" to govern when payments will be made. With trade custom increasingly turning into 60 to 90 days or more it is a good idea to agree with the client on a more reasonable period of time between invoice date and payment date.

A sample letter of engagement is included in Figure 6.1. Another example of a letter of engagement is included in Appendix D and Appendix E contains several sample contracts.

FIGURE 6.1
Letter of engagement

[letterhead]

[date]

John Q. Doe, President
Doe Industries
1234 Main Street
Anytown, Anystate Zip
Dear Mr. Doe:

This letter will confirm our telephone conversation of this morning. It is my understanding that we will meet for a full day on May 19th at your office for the purpose of developing a proposal for the sale of your widgets to XYZ industries. I will plan to arrive at 8:30 A.M.

Please be advised that the fee for my services is [amount] per day. It is my policy to work on advance retainer basis. Under such an arrangement, my clients deposit with me any sum they wish and I invoice against the retainer that has been deposited. Funds deposited that are not utilized are returned.

Due to the short time between now and the time of our meeting, you may either forward your check for [amount] in advance of our meeting or plan to pay for the services provided at the time of the consultation.

I look forward to working with you next week on what should prove to be a most interesting project.
Sincerely,

(Consultant)

CHAPTER 7

Performance Contracts

Although the use of performance contracts is by no means substantial, it is increasing. Under the terms of a performance contract the consultant is compensated for the quality and/or quantity of services provided. Based on random annual surveys of all consultant fields with responses ranging from 773 to 968 professionals, almost 60% of the nation's consultants said they would work on a performance or contingency fee basis. Consultants were asked the following question:

> Within the last 12 months have you entered into a performance or contingency agreement with your clients, an agreement which resulted in your receiving your fee on the basis of the quality of the result or quantity of results which you created for the clients?

Survey data demonstrate a rather spectacular increase in the rate of performance-based contracts:

Year	Often	Now and Then	Once or Twice	Total Yes
1977	12.3%	16.4%	17.1%	45.8%
1978	12.9	18.2	17.7	48.8

Year	Often	Now and Then	Once or Twice	Total Yes
1979	13.6%	20.1%	18.6%	52.3%
1980	13.4	20.7	20.4	54.5
1981	13.9	21.5	20.3	55.7
1982	14.6	22.4	20.9	57.9
1983	14.9	21.8	21.3	58.0
1984	15.1	22.6	22.1	59.8
1985	14.7	23.1	21.5	59.3
1986	14.9	24.3	22.9	62.1
1987	15.2	25.7	32.2	64.1

This trend is interesting in light of traditional consulting values. It has been a tradition, largely among established professionals, that work on a contingency or performance basis is unethical. Those who share this attitude believe that the consultant is or should be like a surgeon, who sells time and effort and does not guarantee results.

This trend among consultants toward performance-based contracts may well be a largely American phenomenon. Consider the following data from both Britain and Canada for the years 1979–1981. The following question was asked both British and Canadian consultants:

Do you ever perform services on a contingency fee basis for your clients?

In a survey of 212 British consultants and 303 Canadian consultants the "yes" response was as follows:

Year	British	Canadian
1979	10.6%	17.2%
1980	10.4%	17.4%
1981	11.0%	17.8%

The fact that the incidence of performance-based consulting is less in Britain than it is in the United States is certainly not surprising. Britain is a far more traditional society than ours. The small percentage of Canadians working on a contingency basis is, frankly, more difficult to understand. Canadian consulting practice is far closer to the practices in the United States than to the mother country.

Even more surprising is the lack of growth in the trend toward contingency and performance arrangements by consultants in Canada and

Britain. Although the data between the United States and the Canadian and British study are not directly comparable, they suggest a fundamental difference in attitude toward fee setting.

There is no doubt that the practice of consulting in the United States is far more entrepreneurial in its orientation than elsewhere. Respondents to the 1982 survey in the United States shed some light on the rationale behind the growth in the number of consultants working on a performance-contract basis and the changing attitude toward the respectability of the performance arrangement.

The 887 respondents to the 1982 survey were asked how they viewed their professional peers who engaged in providing services under a performance or contingency agreement.

Among those who "often" engaged in the practice, a not surprising 88.5% found the practice to be ethical and appropriate in almost every condition or situation.

Among those who "now and then" engaged in the practice, a total of 55.4% held this attitude, but a total of 98.2% found such arrangements to be ethical and appropriate under "many" of the situations they faced as a consultant for their clients.

Among those who never engaged in such contingency or performance arrangements with their clients, a startling 41.1% said that they did not necessarily find such arrangements unethical or inappropriate. More than 35% of the respondents mentioned the fact that lawyers engage in such activity with their clients as a basis for accepting performance-based fee setting.

Over time the traditional anticontingency attitude of the nation's consultants seems to be eroding because of their observation that their peers are engaged in such activity and that other professionals, with whom they identify, engage in such activity on a fairly regular basis. On a practical level, these attitudes may be changing because the consultants who make use of these arrangements have found them to be satisfactory both financially and operationally.

The following question was asked of respondents to both the 1981 and 1982 surveys:

> Do you find such arrangements (performance and contingency) to be satisfactory financially? That is, are they sufficiently satisfactory that you will continue to seek out contingency and performance arrangements with your clients in the future?

The results are revealing:

	1981	*1982*
Respondents who do engage in such arrangements	67.3%	71.1%
Respondents who engage in such arrangements "often"	80.5%	82.4%

Despite the increasing popularity of performance contracts indicated above, if you are considering the possibility of working on a contingency or performance arrangement with your client, there are several questions you really need to ask yourself before making a commitment to do so:

1. In working with the client, will I be able to identify hard, tangible, measurable criteria, which will clearly and unmistakably indicate that the performance has been completed and that the performance or contingency fee is due and payable?

2. Will the client be willing to provide me with operational and managerial control over the resources that will enable me to produce the outcomes and results necessary to deliver the hard, tangible, manageable, and observable phenomena that are required for the performance fee to be paid? On the other hand, will the client be in a position to alter, change, modify, or otherwise have such control as to render my contributions ineffective, with the result that I will be unable to achieve the result that will produce the contingency or performance fee?

3. Am I willing to receive my entire compensation through the means of a contingency or performance fee or shall I insist on some base fee (daily, hourly, fixed dollar amount) together with an incentive or performance fee to be based on measurable or observable results? If I am working on a performance basis only what provisions can be made to provide me with advances to cover costs and living expenses while awaiting the determination of results/achievement of performance? If I have made arrangements for advances against future performance, am I willing to provide the means for repayment of such advances in the event that the project performance is not achieved?

4. Since I am entering into a risk arrangement with my client, have
I been adequately compensated under the performance or contingency fee arrangement, for my time and technology as well as for
the additional risk I will be undertaking compared to a nonrisk fee
for the consulting assignment?

There are basically two situations that give rise to your proposing
a performance or contingency arrangement with the client. The first and
most obvious, of course, is that you see yourself as providing a service
that would result in a substantial economic benefit for the client—perhaps
the creation of a substantial positive cash flow or profit for the client. It
might be that you will greatly reduce a certain expense the client is
incurring.

The second situation results when you see the performance-based
proposal as a way of overcoming the sales resistance the client projects.
That is, you do not foresee a substantial economic gain, but you believe
that offering a performance contract is a possible way to overcome the
concern that the client obviously has about your ability to accomplish the
task set forth. In this situation the performance contract becomes a
method of alleviating the client's fears. In this case, the proposal to work
on a performance basis often serves to "win the client over." Even
though the client elects not to work on a performance basis (perhaps
because the client is unwilling to give up control of the resources that will
create the performance or result) your willingness to work this way may
reduce the anxiety the client is experiencing about your ability or
know-how.

A performance-based contract may specify that all fees will be
based on performance or it may allow for expenses and indicate a bonus
if certain objectives are accomplished. The clauses that define payment in
either case must be carefully worded. If you are using the sample
agreements contained in the appendices, you will have to modify the
terms and conditions of payment to reflect inclusion of the performance
clauses.

CONCLUSION

You now have all the necessary tools to construct a solid
consultant/client contract. I cannot, however, leave this subject without a
few important warnings.

First, if for any reasons, you feel or know that the project is not "doable," that the client is involved in something unethical, or that you may not be able to collect your fee, back away from the deal altogether. However, if you feel that you must take this project on for reasons of personal greed or whatever, eliminate airtight contractual clauses that prevent you from escaping without breach further down the line.

Second, remember to have your attorney check all your work. An incorrect or omitted word or phrase can make all the legal difference in the world.

Finally, if you forget everything else in this book, remember this: *Stay out of court!* If you have to litigate, you have already lost.

PART IV

Reporting and Fee Collecting

CHAPTER 8

Interim and Progress Reports

The client can easily become worried about the progress you are making during a long consultation. An effective consultation often depends on cooperation between the client and consultant in a spirit of teamwork. Interim and progress reports reassure the client that you are delivering high-quality service and improve the quality of communication through improved feedback. This can benefit the outcome of the project and enhance the marketability of your services by increasing client satisfaction.

Effective interim reports add to the consultation's overall success and provide an ongoing account of the progress toward the client's goals and objectives. From the client's point of view the interim report serves as a check-up. This check-up enables you to make the necessary adjustments if the project is not proceeding as planned and increases the chances that the consultation will be successful and the client satisfied.

For you, the consultant, the interim report serves to document the progress that has been made and provides an opportunity for feedback from the client. This improves ongoing planning and scheduling.

This chapter helps you determine whether the time, effort, and expense of the interim report is worthwhile. But the interim report doesn't have to be a time-consuming chore if you follow the steps listed below.

By using the appropriate elements of your proposal you can quickly outline your interim reports. Then you combine this outline with evidence about the progress of the consultation. Careful planning from the beginning will enable you to take full advantage of this effective form of communication with your client.

WHAT IS AN INTERIM REPORT?

An interim report is any report delivered to the client before the final report. Usually interim reports are given at regular intervals, such as once a month. A progress report is usually given when specific milestones are reached. In this chapter the term interim report refers to both interim and progress reports. The interim report generally describes:

- The work completed to date
- Benefits derived from the completed work
- Upcoming activities or phases in the consultation
- Discussions, decisions, and recommendations essential to the project's success

The primary purpose for writing an interim report is to let the reader know how the project is progressing. These reports can also supplement oral discussions with the client and presentations.

Interim reports can be long narrative pieces, containing visual or graphic material, memos, and letters. Or they may be short progress reports. The longer, fully documented reports are generally required as part of government contracts, which often stipulate that reports will be issued at the completion of each significant milestone. Long reports are also appropriate in situations where large capital expenditures are involved.

Short reports of three to five pages are used in the majority of remaining cases. In a 1984 study of the interim reporting activities of 144 consultants, the following data were collected with respect to the most recently completed consulting assignment:

Number providing at least one interim report	102
Number providing a progress report at least monthly	81
Average number of typewritten pages (8½ × 11)	3.8

Over 70% of the consultants surveyed provided one or more interim reports. This high percentage underlines the value of these reports. On the other hand, most of these reports were very short—about four pages in length. It takes relatively little effort to produce interim reports in comparison to the considerable benefit they can have for both you and your client.

STEP 25: *Carry out the project.*

In the FFD diagram at the beginning of Chapter 5 the step following contract preparation is Step 25, the actual execution of the project. Of course, this depends on your expertise in your specialization. The next step deals with preparing and delivering interim reports.

STEP 26: *Prepare and deliver the interim reports, if any.*

The objective of Step 26 is to determine whether to submit interim reports and then to set up and deliver such reports. An understanding of the difference between final and interim reports should guide you in settling on format and delivery schedule.

The tasks in Step 26 are:

- Task 26.1: Decide whether to submit interim reports.
- Task 26.2: Organize and determine the content of the interim reports.
- Task 26.3: Prepare and submit the interim reports. .

TASK 26.1: *Decide whether to submit interim reports.*

At this point you may want to review Step 12 in the proposal-writing process. It is useful to determine whether to submit such reports when you prepare the initial proposal. Sometimes the value of interim reports becomes obvious later, when you begin the project. To guide you in this decision consider some of the important benefits to the client:

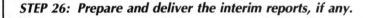

STEP 26: *Prepare and deliver the interim reports, if any.*

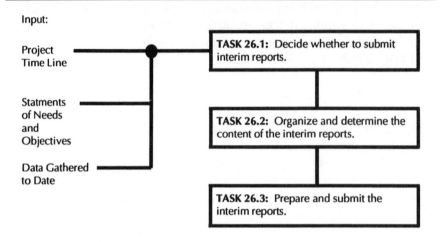

Input:

Project
Time Line

TASK 26.1: Decide whether to submit interim reports.

Statments
of Needs
and
Objectives

TASK 26.2: Organize and determine the content of the interim reports.

Data Gathered
to Date

TASK 26.3: Prepare and submit the interim reports.

- The client will appreciate being kept informed, which is especially important when personal contact between client and consultant is limited.

- The client will have a sense of control over the project by being able to oversee the work.

- The client will be satisfied that your work is making progress toward the mutually established goals.

- The decision maker will have better information when reporting to superiors.

- Regular communication increases client involvement, acceptance, and gratitude.

- The client can be encouraged to utilize your services in the future as he or she learns more about your methods, findings, and recommendations.

- In the event that a dispute arises, reports provide written proof of what has been said and done.

Even though your client may not perceive a need for interim reports, you should be alert to the advantages such reports will provide. It may be that the client is not sufficiently sensitive to the politics of his or her organization and fail to realize that the pressure from higher levels of authority will be better managed by careful documentation of the consultant's work. Successful consultants are sensitive to both the expressed and unspoken needs of their clients and take steps to insure that all needs are met as fully as practicable.

You, too, derive many benefits from interim reports:

- Writing interim reports forces you to discipline yourself throughout the project.
- Interim reports can act as procedural guides and continuing references throughout the project.
- The process of writing the report can help you find procedural problems that can impede the progress of the consultation.

As in all areas of consulting, your decision regarding interim reports should first and foremost reflect the needs of your client. Keep in mind that a satisfied client is your best marketing tool. Also remember that you often have to point out to the client that you are doing quality work.

TASK 26.2: *Organize and determine the content of the interim reports.*

Many of your clients, particularly government and large organizations, provide you with a preestablished format for interim reports. If the client has no preference for the format, it is up to you to decide what to include.

The exact structure depends on the project's requirements and the client's needs. In most cases an interim report that parallels the initial proposal and your execution of the project plan will reinforce the process in the client's mind.

A lengthy, formal interim report may well include all or most of the following:

1. *Table of contents.* This is advisable except in very short reports. The table of contents allows the reader to visualize the report's content and organization. It also permits readers with limited time to find necessary information quickly and scan needed data.
2. *Summary or abstract.* This is also referred to as an executive summary or report. It is often included at the beginning of the report. Sometimes the client does not read the entire report, so

the summary or abstract should provide a logical, overall guide to the report's structure. It is particularly useful when more than one individual in the client organization will be reading the report. Some will have a need for detailed information; others, such as those in positions of higher authority, may need only summary data.

3. *Project background.* This is a short history of the project, which helps the reader place the project in perspective.

4. *Objective and scope.* This section highlights the project's purpose and its limits. Your findings and recommendations are directly related to this section.

5. *Data-gathering methodology.* Because your methods influence the results, it is important to describe your data-gathering methods as clearly as possible. Be sure to gear your language to your reader.

6. *Analysis and synthesis.* This section presents the relevant data gathered to date concerning the project and gives a preliminary interpretation of the data.

7. *Findings and conclusions.* This section identifies what has been learned to date in carrying out the project in relation to the identified objectives.

8. *Recommendations.* These should correspond to both the project's objectives and to your findings. You identify what needs to be done to achieve those objectives.

9. *Projected or realized benefits.* This section highlights the benefits achieved thus far in the project. It also lists those that can be achieved through your recommendations.

10. *Implementation guide.* This section considers implementation methods.

11. *Appendices.* These include necessary charts, exhibits, tables, correspondence, and analyses.

The report should contain pertinent main ideas and topics, some of which will have subdivisions. A formal system of numbered or lettered headings and subheadings is helpful in setting up the report's structure and can guide you in determining priorities and genuine topic divisions. This formal system promotes the orderly organization of the report, economizes the layout, and avoids repetition.

A chronological narrative is the most popular organization. Events that have taken place are reported in the order of their occurrence. However, the report's contents need to be arranged in the sequence that will best enhance its nature and purpose. Therefore, progress toward the project's goals determines the structure of the report and the information included.

Many progress reports are not as comprehensive as the formal report. The needs of the client and your own purposes are the determining factors in setting up the report's format. It is quite common for a consultant to prepare a shorter report for management, even in the form of a memorandum of a few pages' length, which is divided into the following subclassifications:

- Activities undertaken to date
- Accomplishments and results to date
- Problems and difficulties encountered to date
- Activities to be undertaken in the next reporting period
- Accomplishments and results expected in the next reporting period
- Difficulties anticipated in the next reporting period

Some consultants are reluctant to identify and report on difficulties that may hinder achievment of the desired results. But including difficulties in your reports is a good idea. By doing this you make the client a part of the consultation. This section can make the client aware of the specific steps that he or she can take to reduce the impact of these problems. Asking for the client's assistance is not a negative reflection on your abilities. Remember, the consultation is a cooperative, not an adversarial effort. You and your client are working together to achieve a result and enlisting the client's support is often a vital aspect of a successful consultation.

After deciding on the organization of the report you need to determine the contents of the report. The essence of an interim report is news. Therefore, the report should include:

- Facts discovered for the first time
- Newly discovered significance of little-known facts

- Newly found connections between known effects and hitherto unknown causes
- Substantial departures from the initial proposal or contract and their rationale
- Interim decisions that shape or alter the project
- Recommendations and their justification

Three important considerations regarding content can help you determine the appropriate level of detail:

1. *Objective of the consulting project.* If the project is designed to reach a specific goal, you may need only to report on progress, problems, and other factors that demonstrate effective use of the client's resources and that document progress toward general goals or specific objectives. If the objective of the project is to develop a system or methodology or to design something new, it is likely that the client will want considerable detail. If much of your work consists of making decisions and acting on them on a regular basis, the client will probably want full details.

2. *Client's technical level.* The client who is a technical expert or professional in your own field generally requires far less detail. If you are writing a report for someone whose field is completely different, all terms should be explained in detail.

3. *Objective of the report itself.* Reports that are more or less routine require little detail since they are read for the immediate information provided. Reports that are the objective of the project or the end product of the project require much more detail.

TASK 26.3: *Prepare and submit the interim reports.*

The report itself must look professional in every respect. The cover and binding, if there is one, should be visually pleasing to give a good first impression. It is a good idea to develop your own standard format for presentation and binding. Use one that distinguishes your reports but still accommodates regular filing and control. Allow a generous binding margin on the typed page. Use only high-quality paper with an impeccably typed double space on a well-adjusted machine. All proofreading and subsequent marks and corrections should have been made prior to the final presentation copy. Use margins and indentations to ease reading and create the impression of a calm presentation. All graphs, charts, and diagrams should be well drawn and reproduced at the same quality level as the text.

The production schedule is also important. Schedule time to type, proofread, and correct the report. Be sure to add copying and binding time as well.

Finally, reread the interim report before it leaves your office. Look for spelling errors, misplaced pages, and miscellaneous marks. Have your editor do the same. The report should go to the client only after this final check and approval has been completed.

There are a number of ways to present and distribute an interim report. If at all possible, face-to-face presentation is preferable. At that time all questions can be answered and points clarified. In large companies and government agencies interim reports are often sent to designated people without face-to-face contact. When these procedures are required, it is in your best interest to follow them to the letter. When dealing with clients who have no set procedure, you are best guided by the client's needs and your own professional judgment.

Report distribution is determined by client needs and specifications. Although it may be beneficial, from your standpoint, to provide wide report distribution, the practice must be defined by the client's instructions. Sometimes reports contain confidential information that requires limited dissemination.

A review of the client's objectives should indicate the distribution. If you have any doubt, discuss the issue directly rather than make a decision on your own.

COMMON MISTAKES IN PREPARING AND SUBMITTING REPORTS

Consultants typically make a number of errors that render interim reports less effective than they could be. Some of these errors are substantive, but most involve report style and can easily be corrected. The following list describes how to avoid some of the more common errors.

1. Estimate the percentage of the project completed by measuring work accomplished rather than proportion of time or money expended. To do this you must find some external measure to mark progress. Choose something totally objective and unrelated to the time or money spent.

2. Only results count. Don't confuse effort with importance by giving emphasis to events that do not represent or contribute to progress.

3. Avoid the tendency to use text for all presentations except numerical data. Graphs, charts, and other visual aids help significantly to get your point across.

4. Avoid jargon and codes. They are inappropriate for communicating, especially when they are used to surround your profession with a mystique as an explanation for lack of results.

5. Do not make unsupported claims. Report only facts and data based on demonstrable facts. Avoid hyperbole and superlatives.

6. Do not make the assumption that your professional reputation and image will make your client accept anything contained in your reports on your authority alone. Even in cases where you are reporting conclusions drawn from logical analyses, always present the facts objectively.

TIPS FOR IMPRESSIVE INTERIM REPORTS

The format and technique you use for the interim report can also enhance your client's positive reaction. Use the following checklist:

Make sure you have enough to write about. Outline the general content. If an area lacks sufficient depth, gather enough *limited* detail to flesh it out.

Use a neat, organized format.

Use documentation carefully. Add a bibliography at the end, if needed.

Use a personalized style. Avoid the passive voice. Don't say, "The business has increased 15% during the period of my consulting assignment," when you can say, "Your business has increased . . ."

Keep the report as brief as possible. Limit each topic to one page, if possible. This forces you to write concisely and prevent the reader from becoming confused.

Vary sentence length, but keep them short (20 words or less). Avoid complex sentences and long, technical words. Remember to adjust your terminology to the reader.

Emphasize major points with format. Use indentations, underlining, asterisks, bullets, or capital letters.

Use statistics judiciously. Figures tend to call attention to themselves. Decide when absolute values have more significance than percentages, and vice versa. When quoting figures from other sources, be exact. When estimating, consider the order of accuracy and round off.

Keep every item in the report relevant. Avoid giving the impression of padding.

Meet your deadlines!

Look at each interim report as an opportunity to show progress on the assignment, as well as a chance to make a case for additional time, personnel, or cooperation, if needed.

USING THE INTERIM REPORT TO INCREASE YOUR EFFECTIVENESS

The interim report can increase your effectiveness as a consultant in three different areas:

1. *Success of the project.* A well-written, professional-looking report shows how well you perform and how organized you are. As a permanent record, it leaves a permanent impression.
2. *Implementation of recommendations.* Making recommendations that are relatively easy to achieve and within the decision maker's capabilities increases the possibility of successful implementation and future assignments.
3. *Additional consulting business.* Use the recommendations section as a preliminary proposal for additional consulting. If appropri-

ate, encourage widespread distribution of the report within the client's organization.

The interim report is an effective way to keep a long and complex consultation on track. At the same time it creates a positive connection between you and the client that can lead to favorable acceptance of the final report.

CHAPTER 9

Writing and Submitting the Final Report

For some clients your final report is the most important element of the consulting project. Most professional consultants and sophisticated clients realize that it is the actual results obtained, or even the process used to obtain the results, that determine the true benefit of the consultant's work. Documenting your results can leave a lasting impression. A final report serves as a determination of how well you have performed and how effective you have been.

The success of a consulting project depends on your ability as a consultant to do what the client has requested within or close to the time frame and budget set at the beginning of the project. However, the success of the project is also dependent on your ability to communicate effectively what has occurred. If the client doesn't fully understand what you have done, the consulting project has not been successfully delivered.

STEP 27: *Prepare and deliver the final report.*

The objective of this step is to decide whether to submit a final report and to set its structure and content. The final report is an important element in more than half of all consulting projects. But unless you consider its value and structure, it will be a disappointment to you and to your client.

The tasks in Step 27 are:

- Task 27.1: Decide whether to prepare the final report
- Task 27.2: Select the appropriate type of report
- Task 27.3: Set the structure and content of the final report
- Task 27.4: Decide on the style of the final report
- Task 27.5: Prepare, present, and distribute the final report

TASK 27.1 *Decide whether to prepare the final report.*

Review Step 12. As with interim reports, it is best to determine whether to submit a final report when you submit the initial proposal. Occasionally you will need to review the need for a final report as the consultation proceeds. The decision to write a final report should be based on the benefits of such a report for both you and your client. If these benefits are worth the time and effort involved in preparing the report, you would be well advised to write one. If not, the presentation of a verbal report is recommended. The best question you can ask yourself in this regard is:

Is writing a final report the most productive use of my time?

The professional consultant has a responsibility to expend time in ways that are in the best interest of the client. It is your responsibility to help the client determine whether a formal final report or other documentation is needed.

POTENTIAL BENEFITS OF THE FINAL REPORT

In deciding whether the preparation of a final report represents the most productive use of your time, the following potential benefits should be considered:

Potential benefits for the client include:

- The report provides written evidence that the assignment has been carried out. It shows that the consultation has been delivered and indicates the successful achievement of the client's objectives.

STEP 27: Prepare and deliver the final report.

Input:

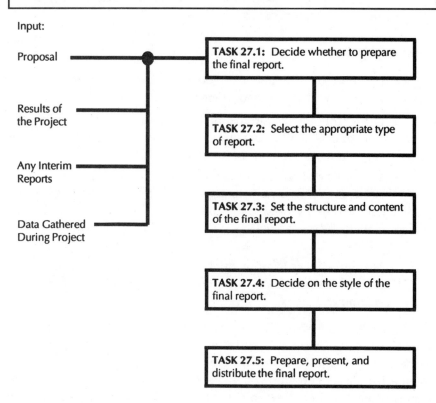

Proposal ——————————●—————— **TASK 27.1:** Decide whether to prepare the final report.

Results of
the Project ————

Any Interim
Reports ————

Data Gathered
During Project ————

TASK 27.2: Select the appropriate type of report.

TASK 27.3: Set the structure and content of the final report.

TASK 27.4: Decide on the style of the final report.

TASK 27.5: Prepare, present, and distribute the final report.

- The report formally documents your conclusions and recommendations. This can help the client make decisions, carry out long-term planning, and take advantage of future opportunities to implement your recommendations.

- Your report is often the only systematic presentation of the data, analysis, and findings that resulted from your consultation. As a result the report can serve as a guide for further study, analysis, and research.

- The dissemination of the report may produce a "spread effect" throughout the organization for the consultant's ideas. In case the management or administration changes, the ideas and results of your consulting project can continue to be implemented and to benefit your client.

- The dissemination of your report demonstrates to upper management and to the client's colleagues the wisdom of having retained your consulting services.

Potential benefits to you, the consultant, include:

- The report is a reminder of your contributions and increases the probability of repeat and referral business.
- The report may lead to the implementation of your ideas in other departments and/or organizations. This can lead the client to retain your services at a future date.
- The quality of the consultation is often judged by the quality of the report. This is particularly true when third persons who were not directly involved in the consultation will be in the position of making recommendations on your findings or evaluating your efforts.
- The effectiveness of communication in the report may well determine whether the client chooses to carry out your ideas and recommendations.

If the final report is not mandated and if it appears valuable to your client, you may wish to market it as part of your consulting package. Market the benefits that the final report will provide *to your client*. Emphasize those benefits you believe your potential client is most interested in. It is important to note here that the client is to be charged, either directly or indirectly, for all of the time you spend in preparing and presenting the final report. If the client can't afford the report and wants to reduce the overall fee, you can offer a simple verbal report as a means of decreasing the cost of the entire contract.

TASK 27.2: *Select the appropriate type of report.*

There are three general types of final reports.

1. technical reports
2. reports for executives
3. reports for publication

Each is described below in the following paragraphs.

The technical report is prepared for someone who requires detailed information about the procedures and results of the consultation. The reader of this type of report is usually someone with operational, technical, or middle management responsibility in the client organization. Besides giving detailed evidence that the project has been effective, this type of report helps the client with future decision making and long-range planning. It may lead to further analysis and study. The technical report is beneficial to the consultant because the in-depth treatment shows the reader the specific accomplishments and detailed methodology of the consultation. This can be a convincing argument for retaining the consultant's services again at a future date.

The report for executives is designed to inform the reader of the crucial elements and findings of the consultation. It is usually intended for top-level decision makers, such as CEOs and board members. These executives look forward to getting some strong guidance for decision making, as well as some demonstrated results that indicate the wisdom of having retained the consultant. Reports for executives are aimed both at giving a broad overview of the consulting project and providing information that can serve as the basis of decision making in the client organization.

The report for publication is the type of report that most consultants prefer to make whenever possible. It disseminates for an external audience the results and processes used during the consultation. It is frequently recommended to clients for two reasons:

- The marketing advantage of a report for publication can be considerable, particularly when readers are likely to be potential clients themselves or when they may come in contact with potential clients.
- Although the report for publication requires greater creativity on the part of the consultant, it is often the easiest to write. This is due to the relative absence of technical jargon, detailed explanations, and specific applications and recommendations, which the other types of report require.

In choosing which type of report to submit consider the foregoing points concerning the *report for publication*.

A given reporting effort often combines two or all three of these types. The most frequent combination is of an executive and a technical report. The executive report is prepared for top management and the technical report is for middle management who will be specifically charged with implementing the consultant's findings. In addition, this type of combined report may be prepared for a party of interest, such as an outside auditor or evaluator. The information required by such external parties will likely differ from the needs of those within the client organization.

> *Example:* Those who have provided the funds for the project may be interested in the way the funds were expended and whether the terms of the contract were met. Those within the client organization may have a need for more specific procedural data which will guide changes in approach or procedure.

Such a dual reporting approach allows high-level and external decision makers to concentrate on major issues without being distracted by details. The more specific and detailed information is available to those who need it. This detailed information may be provided in a separate document or as an appendix to the executive report.

The report for publication may be combined with either a technical report or a report for executives. In either case, a report aimed at broadened readership both within and outside the client organization is accomplished by information specifically intended for the client or for those within the client organization who will assess the consultation.

When deciding which type of report to suggest to your client, concentrate only on what is in the best interest of the client.

> *Example:* If a report for publication is much more beneficial for you than for your client, do *not* try to sell such a report. As a responsible and professional consultant, meeting the needs of your client is always your first consideration. By avoiding superfluous or unnecessary items that add to the cost of a consultation you enhance your reputation for producing practical, no-nonsense approaches to problems. This attitude will lead to more business in the future.

TASK 27.3: *Set the structure and content of the final report.*

Some clients have their own standard format for the organization and content of the report. In this case, many of the decisions have already been made for you. Generally, though, your client gives you only overall guidelines for the final report or has no preference at all. In these cases you must rely on your own best judgment in determining how to organize your final report and what to include in it.

In making these decisions, look again at the type of report you are writing and your reader's expectations. The reader of a *technical report* is likely to possess technical expertise or to need specific, detailed information. In writing a technical report include enough information for the client to carry on with a degree of self-sufficiency without giving away valuable data and techniques that may reduce the demand for your services in the future. You want to solve the client's stated problems, not set him up in the consulting business.

The reader of the *executive report* is usually an upper-level manager or a board member. These readers usually want only the grand design of the consultation and well-formulated, specific conclusions and recommendations. The reader of this type of report should be able to implement your results in decision making, long-range planning, and in the future operation of the client organization.

The *report for publication* requires that you first determine the expectations of your readers as well as the precise communications objectives of the client. It is only in this way that you can write a report that is in the best interests of the client, as well as serve your own best interests.

Regardless of the type of report, all final written reports should include the following:

1. A statement of the goals and objectives of the consultation. These goals and objectives should be stated in terms that are as specific, measurable, and objective as possible.

2. An account of the events which occurred during the project. The emphasis here is on those events that occurred during the project—those events that helped to achieve the project's goals and objectives. Interesting but superfluous events should receive minimal discussion or be excluded entirely. Parts of the project that took a good deal of time and attention but were unproductive should also be left out, unless they are important because they represent unproductive avenues that should be avoided in the future.

3. A discussion of the problems encountered and how they were overcome or resolved. It is best to be honest about any difficulties

encountered that make the achievement of the project's objectives difficult. If such difficulties are minimized or glossed over,
your integrity as a consultant may be jeopardized. It is also
important to discuss these problems so the client organization can
deal with them if they appear while the organization is implementing your recommendations or if they recur in the future.

4. An examination of the results of the consulting project. This
   should be tied directly to the stated goals and objectives of the
   consultation, explaining to what extent these were achieved. Full
   explanations should be given as to why certain goals were
   successfully met and why other goals and objectives were not
   met.

5. Conclusions and recommendations for further implementation
   and/or study. Again, these should be an outgrowth of the goals
   and objectives of the project and the extent to which they were
   achieved.

There are a number of different ways in which the final report can
be organized. In a 1983 research study I conducted that involved over 300
consultants, I discovered the following organizational formats used in
order of priority:

1. chronological or historical
2. reverse chronological
3. general to specific
4. greater importance to lesser importance
5. scientific

In the last type of format, hypotheses are presented and followed by
supporting and refuting data. Finally the conclusions are given.

TASK 27.4: *Decide on the style of the final report.*

There are a number of factors to consider in determining the most
effective writing style for your final report. The following suggestions
represent the most important ones:

1. The report should be useful. Besides serving as a reminder of

your contribution as a consultant, the report should be written to be used as a resource, rather than another volume to collect dust. Its use as a resource is a particularly crucial consideration if you have written a technical report.

2. The report should effectively communicate information to the reader. Use a clear, direct, and concise style that leaves the reader no room for misinterpretation or misunderstanding.

3. Make the report come alive. While you are writing, keep in mind the elements of the consulting project that make it exciting, interesting, and fun. By focusing on those aspects of the project and the accompanying feelings, excitement and interest will come across in the words you are writing. Another way to make the report come alive is to ask yourself, "If I were the reader, what would make me read every word in this report?" Answer your question and write accordingly.

4. The successful report is written so that it encourages the reader to take the appropriate recommended actions.

5. The presentation of findings in the final report should fit the decision-making style of the client. If the decision maker needs only the facts necessary to support a foregone conclusion, just provide the bare facts. If the decision maker is relying on you to make the appropriate suggestions and recommendations, you may want to include more detailed information and more in-depth argument. If you aren't aware of that person's decision-making style, ask the decision maker what is needed in the final report.

6. Keep the broader audience for your report in mind. Make your writing consistent with their interests and level of understanding regarding the consultation.

TASK 27.5: *Prepare, present, and distribute the final report.*

How your final report is presented and distributed depends on what is best for your client. A face-to-face presentation of the final written report is generally best for several reasons. First, you can give explanations and answers immediately. This reduces the chances of misunderstandings and misinterpretations. Second, you can find out first-hand how the decision maker reacts to the report and choose how to respond and/or make plans for future action. Third, you enhance your image as a consultant by taking the time and trouble to appear in person with your completed report. Finally, a direct presentation enables you to make the report "come alive." This adds to the perception that the consulting project has been effective and successful.

If at all possible, suggest that you present the final written report in person. Sometimes it is not possible to make an in-person presentation. In those cases where it will be read by outside evaluators, even the suggestion that you personally present the written report could be viewed as inappropriate. You should be guided by your own professional judgment and by your understanding of your client's best interests.

Distribution of your final written report should be guided by the potential benefits to your client. Your client may wish to keep a *technical report* out of circulation because of the nature of its content. The decision maker may want to make copies available to those in the organization who will implement the recommendations or who will further analyze and research the findings.

Your client may favor a wide distribution of the report within the organization or field because of the favorable light cast by the project's success. The visibility of such a report may make the decision maker more visible to his superiors and increase his or her chances for promotion. This is particularly true with respect to a *report for executives* or a combination of a technical report with an executive report that is tailored to an upper managerial audience.

In distributing or selecting a publication vehicle for a *report for publication,* it is wise to keep the client's needs in mind. If you do this, your client will have further evidence that you have acted in his or her best interests, even though publishing the report is clearly to your benefit as well. This consideration will enhance your reputation with the client and with others; it may also lead to additional consulting contracts with the client and referral business based on favorable recommendations about the professional nature of your approach.

MAKING THE REPORT EFFECTIVE

By following certain guidelines and by avoiding common errors your final written report can have maximum impact. Some of the pointers below are similar to those given for the interim report. The difference is in your perspective. You have finished the project and are reviewing what has happened. Any further steps have to be carried out by the client. The following suggestions can help to make the final report as effective as possible:

1. **Keep your audience in mind.** The content of your report should be consistent with the needs and expectations of your readers.

2. Be aware of the reading level of your audience and use a vocabulary that is consistent with that level.

3. Be aware of the level of technical expertise of the reader and match the content of your writing to that level. Avoid terminology that does not add meaning to what you are trying to communicate. Avoid jargon whenever possible. The reader is interested in understanding what you have done, not in watching you show off by using words that are beyond his or her comprehension.

4. Your report should be as well written as possible—lucid, accurate, informative, complete, and constructive in its approach. At the same time, the tenor of the report should be dignified and objective.

5. Use simple, direct language and clear, concise writing. Avoid the use of qualifiers, superlatives, and hyperbole. Don't equivocate. State your position in a direct and forthright manner.

6. Communicate in terms that are meaningful and practical. It is acceptable to include theory and speculation in your report. However, such material must be consistent with the purpose of the report and must be tied to concrete facts, findings, and recommendations.

7. Preserve the credibility of your report with scrupulous care. Avoid errors of fact or method at all costs. Such mistakes can damage your professional consulting skills and your reputation.

8. Back up all of your statements with facts and supporting evidence. Don't make the common mistake of assuming that your professional reputation or image will make the client accept everything you say on your authority alone.

9. Use the active voice in your writing.

10. Put necessary supporting data in the appendices. Don't clutter up the report.

11. If mistakes were made, admit them. Describe what happened and emphasize the corrective action that was taken. The reader will

respect a consultant who takes responsibility for errors made and will easily recognize and discard one who won't own up to such mistakes.

12. Don't confuse effort with importance in determining the content of your report. Only those events or functions that contributed to the progress of the consultation should be emphasized.

13. Remember, only results count. No one cares about the storms you met at sea; they ask only if you brought the ship home.

AVOID PROCRASTINATION IN FINAL REPORT WRITING

No realistic piece on final report writing would be complete without addressing the fact that almost every consultant dislikes writing final reports. Here are several suggestions that may help you avoid the procrastination that can accompany this task:

1. Make the decision to write a final report as early in the consulting project as you can. If at all possible, include the possibility of a final report in the initial proposal to the client. This will prepare you psychologically for writing the final report.

2. Begin the report as soon as possible. If you have written a comprehensive proposal, much of it can be included in the final report, with necessary revisions and the addition of conclusions and recommendations. Keeping an ongoing written account of the progress of the consultation can provide much of the body of the report and help you remember the high points of the project. Interim reports are very useful in this regard. Starting early keeps you from becoming overwhelmed by having to start the final report from scratch at the conclusion of the project.

3. Set aside time to write the final report. If you have blocked out the time in advance, it is less likely that you will schedule in more desirable consulting activities during that time.

4. Learn to use dictating equipment. For many it is a much more efficient way to write. You can become proficient in its use in much less time than you would think.

5. Delegate as much of the report-writing task as you possibly can

without sacrificing quality. As consultants, many of us have a great deal of difficulty delegating any task to our colleagues or subordinates. However, keep in mind that one of your associates may genuinely *like* doing this kind of work. You could be doing yourself and that person a big favor by providing him or her with such an opportunity.

6. Arrange to delay full and final payment for the consulting project until the final report has been completed and delivered. Many clients require this anyway. But if your client does not, you can set up the payment schedule so that the funds due motivate you to deal with procrastination.

7. Reward yourself when the report is completed. Like most self-motivated people, you are probably satisfied with intrinsic rewards, such as knowing that you have produced an excellent final report. But it won't hurt you to plan something nice, like a weekend get-away, on its conclusion.

The decision to prepare a written final report should not be taken lightly. If you find that the expense involved for the client is worth the benefits the client will realize from a final report, then you certainly should recommend one.

Final report writing is quite common. In the 1983 research study of over 300 consultants, the following question was asked relative to the last consulting contract/project undertaken:

Did you prepare a final written report detailing the findings, conclusions, methodologies and/or recommendations relative to the consulting project or assignment?

Yes	63.4%
No	36.6%
If yes, was the report prepared at the request of the client, an external party, or at your suggestion?	
At the request of the client	59.2%
At the suggestion of the consultant	22.4%
At the request of an external party	6.7%
Jointly requested/suggested by client and consultant	8.1%
Not sure who requested or suggested	3.6%

Those who prepared final reports were asked to indicate the length of their final reports in terms of the number of double-spaced typed pages the report contained:

Fewer than 5 such pages	9.8%
5 to 10 such pages	21.2%
11 to 20 such pages	32.5%
21 to 30 such pages	24.4%
31 or more such pages	12.1%

Finally, for those who prepared final written reports, it was determined that 23.7% presented their reports in person, providing a verbal summary or presentation of the final report to one or more representatives of the client.

These research results underscore the value of a final report. A professional consultant knows the potential benefits of the final report to the client and to the success of the project. The FFD given at the beginning of the proposal-writing Section outlines the natural progression from the beginning of a project to the submission of a final report. By understanding and using this structure you can become a more effective and successful consultant.

CHAPTER 10

Fee Collecting

Collecting your fees is the last topic covered here, but it should not be the last thing you think about. As in any business, consultants sometimes have trouble collecting their fees. A number of precautions can help you avoid this problem, and several tactics can help solve difficulties when they occur.

Determining the payment schedule for your services depends on the kind of contract you establish with your client and the structure of the project. Sometimes the payment schedule is tied to the submission of interim and final reports, especially if these reports are linked to milestone achievements in the consultation.

Sometimes the structure of the payment schedule is arbitrary and set up for the mutual convenience of the client and consultant. Monthly or quarterly billing may be appropriate for a long-term project or for a retainer situation. In any case the arrangement should be clearly laid out between client and consultant. This is usually done in the contract or the letter of agreement.

A GOOD CONTRACT

With an adequate, point-for-point contract in hand, you and your clients know just where you stand. A written contract is usually enough to make your obligations more legal in your clients' minds. For small billings, a wave of the contract is usually enough to shake the payment loose.

When large fees are involved, litigation may become necessary. If so, a detailed contract is invaluable. A contract with an arbitration clause might get you your money *and* keep you out of court.

The type of contractual relationship and the way you plan to charge for your fees and expenses should be taken into account during the marketing stage and certainly by the time you are ready to develop and negotiate the contract. If you will be using a fixed-price contract, the contract should state the precise dates and amounts of all invoices that will be submitted to the client.

You may also wish to include the terms of payment in the contract. Use clauses like, "All invoices submitted will be paid in the net amount within 30 days following receipt of the invoice by [client's name]."

If you are working with the client on a daily or hourly rate (time and materials) contract, you should state the frequency with which invoices will be submitted and you may also indicate the terms and conditions for payment. The contract should specify how expense reimbursement will be handled during the consulting assignment and provisions for prepayment of expenses should be noted, if necessary.

Taking the time to deal with the issue of the invoice at the time of contract negotiation serves to inform your client that payment of your fee is an important consideration that requires attention on the part of both parties. It also serves to set expectations clearly and to improve communication between client and consultant.

DECIDE WHEN INVOICES WILL BE SENT TO THE CLIENT

Invoice schedules are important just as the payment dates for the charges are important. When you send and receive payment of your invoice has important consequences for the management of your practice. The invoice may be sent at periodic times as agreed to by you and the client or you may time the sending of an invoice to coincide with certain milestone events that will occur during the course of your consultation.

In either case consider an often-used practice—*accelerated invoicing*— the practice of causing the client to assume that the early activities in the course of the consultation are more involved, detailed, and time consuming than the later tasks. This justifies asking for a greater part of the fee or budget during the earlier stages of the consultation.

The Wording of the Invoice

With a fixed-price contract, more than one invoice is usually submitted. In most cases a schedule for invoices has been established and written into the contract. The invoice normally includes the following information:

- *Name, address, and telephone number* of the consultant
- *Person and client organization* who will receive the invoice
- *Date* of the invoice
- *Period of time* or description of tasks the invoice covers
- *Invoice number,* if any
- *Terms and conditions* of payment
- *Name of person* to contact in the event of questions
- *Signature* of authorized agent, if desired

Daily or hourly rate contracts require the above information in addition to a description of the time expended on behalf of the client and a listing of expenses.

MUTUAL UNDERSTANDING

There is no substitute for having a good head-to-head understanding with clients. No contract and no agreement can substitute for it. If you and the client cannot see eye-to-eye up front, then your contract is going to run into trouble at some time in the future. So make sure that you and the client both look at the written contract in the same way. A strong mutual understanding can be an important asset when collecting the fee.

PROGRESS PAYMENTS

Most clients are willing to pay on a progress basis, either at prescribed intervals or after a percentage of the work is completed. So don't be afraid to ask for progress payments. If you can arrange accelerated progress payments, you can always be working on the client's money. The payments are larger up front and smaller at the end. The earlier payments cover the work already performed and part of the remaining work. This arrangement helps your cash flow and requires only a little ingenuity in dividing up the invoices.

Even if you do not ask for progress payments, you should ask for payment of sizable expenses in advance. Perhaps you had to have something printed, or maybe you needed to lease a piece of equipment. If these costs aren't covered as they occur, you are effectively lending the client money without charging interest.

WITHHOLDING OUTPUT OR RESOURCES

Sometimes a client has withheld payment in the past or otherwise seems likely to do so. In such a case you might consider withholding the results or product of your service. One accountant I know holds his client's books until he is paid. He even writes out the checks and has the clients sign them!

FACTORING

Occasionally you do business with large, solvent organizations that pay—but pay slowly. The money is coming, but your cash flow needs an injection right away. Factoring is sometimes a handy solution. With clients like IBM or the New York Board of Education, a bank will usually advance you a percentage of your accounts receivable. This approach won't work if you are consulting with relatively small or unknown clients.

Once work is billed to the client, bring the invoice to your bank and ask the officer to advance a percentage of it. Typically you can get up to two-thirds of the invoice amount right away and pay it back with interest when the check comes in. You might even ask the client to let you put the bill in a little early so that you can get it factored.

COLLECTION PROCEEDING

Ultimately you may have to resort to collection proceedings. Collection agents are not usually suitable for collection of consulting fees. They charge a lot and all they can do is send out a series of letters, each one a little more threatening than the last. When they run out of letters, nothing happens.

Instead of a collection agency, you have to use your ingenuity. Somewhere in the organization is a spot that you can touch to embarrass or hurt the one holding up your money. Find that spot. Sit down, diagnose the organization, and determine who can make life uncomfortable for the culprit client. Don't be vindictive. Being vengeful could cost you business in the future, not to mention referrals. Find that sensitive spot.

A FEW LAST WORDS ON FEES

Some consultants feel that by submitting a low-ball estimate on the first assignment from a client they can "buy some business." Their rationale is that they will work their way into the good graces of the client and eventually make back their losses on the low estimate. The fact is that they don't buy any worthwhile business that way. Your client will be eager to tell everyone what great work you do for such low prices. Getting rid of that image may take a long time.

ON-THE-SPOT ESTIMATES

Telling clients your hourly or daily rate is one thing. Quoting a whole job on the spot is quite another, even if you know right away. Ascertain the client's needs, think about the job, do an estimate of your own if necessary, and then submit a reasoned estimate. Clients will be more impressed with a considered estimate than with a snap judgment.

INCREASING FEES

Increasing fees is necessary and expected, since prices are always on the increase. Keep in mind that your increases should not occur too frequently. You don't want to create the impression that every time your client turns around your fees are up again. Limit your increases to once or twice a year at most. Your increases should be substantial enough to last six to twelve months.

Informing regular clients by letter about 90 days in advance of a fee increase gives ample notice for client planning and spurs those thinking about making use of your services to get down to business now rather than later. When informing clients that fees will be increased, provide a letter with a justification of why fees are being raised. Point out all of the factors that have given rise to increased costs: rent, utilities, secretarial assistance, increased self-employment taxes, and so on.

Now that you know how to set your fees and get what you are worth; you are ready to determine how to charge for a particular project. The following appendices cover your options with regard to charging for a project and to setting up a fee structure that will generate maximum income.

APPENDICES

APPENDIX A

Current Consulting Fees

In setting your fees, it is useful to know what others in your field are charging. The findings in this appendix resulted from the 16th semiannual study of the economics of the consulting and training profession conducted by the Professional Consultant & Seminar Business Report in March, 1988. The survey focused on fees and incomes of 7,003 consulting firms. The data reported have been determined to be significant at the .05 level.

The median daily billing rate for the nation's consultants as a whole reached an all time high of $929 per day. Pretax (after business expenses) income averaged $91,102.

Slightly more than 45% of the consultants surveyed increased their fees during the previous 12 months by at least 10% and almost all consultants (93.1%) increased their fees to some extent. Listed below are the median daily billing rates for consultants by field of specialty for the United States and Canada. The Canadian figures were converted into U.S. dollars at the exchange rate applicable as of March 31, 1988.

Of course, in setting your fees you need to take the level of your expertise and time as a consultant into consideration. A beginning consultant usually charges less than those with more experience. These are average figures, so those with more experience and a greater reputation can charge more than the figures listed above. There are also regional variations depending on local cost of living and level of overhead. Nevertheless, these figures can serve as a valuable guide for fee-setting.

Daily Billing Rates
(As of March 31, 1988)

	$		$		$
All Consultants	929	Executive Search	859	Personnel/HRD	769
Accounting	912	Export/Import	967	Production	883
Advertising	1001	Fashion/Beauty	546	Psychological Services	637
Agriculture	629	Finance	993	Public Relations	752
Aerospace	1023	Franchise	902	Publishing	786
Arts & Culture	644	Fund Raising	711	Purchasing .	844
Banking	922	Grantsmanship	628	Quality Control	982
Broadcast	872	Graphics and Printing		Real Estate	686
Business Acquisition/		Trades	655	Records Management	595
Sales	846	Health Care	1024	Recreation	611
Chemical	923	Hotel/Restaurant/Club	724	Research	
Communications	682	Insurance	707	& Development	1043
Construction	850	International Business	980	Retail	807
Data Processing	926	Investment Advisory	821	Scientific	1097
Dental/Medical	1049	Management	933	Security	708
Design (Industrial)	788	Marketing	939	Statistical	719
Economics	899	Municipal Government	691	Telecommunications	872
Education	682	New Business Ventures	789	Traffic/Transportation	758
Engineering	1086	Packaging	818	Training	790
Estate Planning	869	Pension	842	Travel	634

Average (Mean) Annual Income of Consultants
After Business Expenses and Before Income Tax (For the 12 Months Ending March 31, 1988)

	$		$		$
All Consultants	91,102	Executive Search	95,988	Personnel/HRD	68,126
Accounting	95,098	Export/Import	90,142	Production	89,052
Advertising	93,323	Fashion/Beauty	57,505	Psychological Services	80,907
Agriculture	66,622	Finance	97,689	Public Relations	69,199
Aerospace	93,274	Franchise	87,755	Publishing	79,727
Arts & Culture	54,285	Fund Raising	69,213	Purchasing	81,144
Banking	85,234	Grantsmanship	58,984	Quality Control	87,863
Broadcast	86,990	Graphics and Printing		Real Estate	81,650
Business Acquisition/		Trades	70,418	Records Management	79,668
Sales	96,299	Health Care	97,977	Recreation	63,235
Chemical	85,887	Hotel/Restaurant/Club	70,445	Research &	
Communications	64,721	Insurance	68,461	Development	106,143
Construction	84,236	International Business	94,332	Retail	72,936
Data Processing	81,008	Investment Advisory	98,826	Scientific	108,774
Dental/Medical	92,985	Management	91,222	Security	80,244
Design (Industrial)	66,776	Marketing	90,465	Statistical	78,198
Economics	90,654	Municipal Government	69,078	Telecommunications	89,543
Education	58,430	New Business Ventures	70,120	Traffic/Transportation	76,200
Engineering	96,311	Packaging	85,556	Training	75,733
Estate Planning	82,237	Pension	85,003	Travel	71,993

APPENDIX B

Sample Letter Proposals

This section contains two proposals in letter form. Such proposals lack the strict organization and structure of a formal proposal, but they must be carefully written to cover major points and answer questions that the client might have. In a letter, brevity is the key to success. Every word and phrase must be chosen with care to have the maximum effect.

The first example is a brief proposal, containing an outline of the steps and goals in the project and a skeletal time line. The fees are listed on a fixed-fee basis and there is a provision for charging for direct expenses and excess time spent on the project. Flexibility is introduced by giving the client a range of choices in retaining the consultant's services for all or part of the proposed project.

The second example is a letter that combines a proposal and a contract. This letter proposal/contract gets right to the heart of the matter and dispenses with legal formalities. Nevertheless, it constitutes a binding legal contract if accepted by the client. Usually it is better to keep the proposal and the contract separate, but sometimes this approach is appropriate and useful.

SAMPLE PROPOSAL

Date

Name
Company
Address
City/State/Zip

Dear

I enjoyed our telephone conversation of _____. AAA has an excellent marketing opportunity for its video seminars as public seminar programs and this letter is designed to serve as a proposal to define the steps which I believe should be undertaken to evaluate and capitalize on the marketing potential. When we spoke, I had only received the video introduction, leader guide, and participant materials for _____. Following our conversation, I received your letter of _____ and enclosures. The enclosures were particularly beneficial in the preparation of this proposal and I apologize for taking your time on the telephone to answer questions which were handled by the enclosures.

Name
Company
Date
Page 2

In my estimation, the decision of how to distribute should be based upon a recognition that AAA brings to the market for distributors a significant and very valuable asset. Accordingly, the analysis of options should carefully determine the market value of the programs to ensure that the full profit potential be realized. Careful attention needs to be given to potential outside distributors relative to such factors as:

> Market experience and capability;
> Financial viability and resources;
> Importance of the AAA opportunity to their business; and
> Credibility and capability to perform at a high level.

I believe that the following steps should be undertaken to evaluate and capitalize upon the marketing (as public seminars) of AAA seminars in general and _____ , specifically:

1. Determine the relative advantages and disadvantages of self-distribution in comparison to obtaining one or more established distributors.

This step would include a competitive analysis of distributors, a determination of their marketing capabilities and their financial viability/future plans. It would also include an estimation of expenses and revenues (a pro forma) for self-distribution and would evaluate various self-distribution models such as licensing, franchising, and establishing an independent dealer network. Particular attention would be paid to operating practices and distribution models of successful and less than successful operating practices and distribution systems of established seminar companies including such organizations as ... Further, the evaluation would concentrate on emerging learning methods which may, in time, prove more efficient and effective than live seminars and the consequences which such technological changes might have on AAA programs in general and _____ in particular.

2. Identify and select potential outside distributors.

Step 2 would build on the work already accomplished in Step 1 and would serve to identify those organizations which might serve as a suitable distributor for AAA programs as public seminars in general and _____ specifically. The result of this activity would be to identify a list of candidate organizations which might be solicited by AAA for that purpose. It is anticipated that such candidates would include established seminar providers as well as other organizations not currently involved in the seminar business with strong, related marketing capabilities who would be in a position to serve as a viable distributor.

3. Establish requirements for performance by outside distributors.

This step would establish minimum requirements which distributors would have to meet to be acceptable to AAA and would be based on marketing and financial information gained about providers in general and candidate distributors as a result of the analysis undertaken in steps 1 and 2, above. It is anticipated that such requirements would be quite specific about the nature and extent of marketing effort to be provided by potential distributors to ensure that distributions proposals submitted in the future by such candidates could be adequately evaluated relative to self-distribution options.

4. Structure offering package to outside distributors.

On the basis of minimum requirements for distributors established as a result of the completion of Step 3, and the determination of the profit potential for self-distribution

Name
Company
Date
Page 3

determined as a part of Step 1, the specific offer(s)/proposal(s) to be made to potential distributors would be developed.

5. Solicit outside distributors.
Offer(s)/proposal(s) developed in Step 4 would be forwarded to candidate distributors.

6. Review outside distributors responses.
Responses received from interested distributors would be reviewed and acceptable respondents would be interviewed and evaluated.

7. Decide upon method of distribution/select outside distributor(s).
Acceptable distributor offers/proposals (as modified as a result of Step 6), would be evaluated and compared to self-distribution options and a final decision would be made with respect to the distribution for _____ , specifically and perhaps for other AAA programs as well.
I believe that the above activities can be accomplished as quickly as follows:

FEBRUARY 16–MARCH 6, 1987
     1. Determine the relative advantages and disadvantages of self-distribution in comparison to obtaining one or more established distributors.

MARCH 2–MARCH 13, 1987
     2. Identify and select potential outside distributors.

MARCH 9–MARCH 20, 1987
     3. Establish requirements for performance by outside distributors.

MARCH 9–MARCH 20, 1987
     4. Structure offering package to outside distributors.

MARCH–MARCH 27, 1987
     5. Solicit outside distributors.

MARCH 30–APRIL 17, 1987
     6. Review outside distributor responses.

APRIL 13–APRIL 24, 1987
     7. Decide upon method of distribution/select outside distributor(s).

I would be please to provide my services in connection with the above to AAA on either a per-hour fee basis or on a fixed fee plus expenses basis, as you determine to be in your best interest. Listed below, is my estimate of the hours which I would anticipate would be required on my part to complete the above activities. Also, please find the fixed fee which would be charged for the completion of each activity. If it is your preference to work on an hourly fee basis, the charge would be _____ dollars ($XXX) per hour.

1. Determine the relative advantages and disadvantages of self-distribution in comparison to obtaining one or more established distributors.
          Estimated number of hours 30–40
          Fixed fee charge................................ $_____

Name
Company
Date
Page 4

2. Indentify and select potential outside distributors.
        Estimated number of hours 12–20
        Fixed fee charge. . . . .$____

3. Establish requirements for performance by outside distributors.
        Estimated number of hours 10–15
        Fixed fee charge. . . . .$____
4. Structure offering package to outside distributors.
        Estimated number of hours 14–19
        Fixed fee charge. . . . .$____

5. Solicit outside distributors.
        Estimated number of hours 01–04
        Fixed fee charge. . . . .$____

6. Review outside distributors responses.
        Estimated number of hours 10–30
        Fixed fee charge. . . . .$____

7. Decide upon method of distribution/select outside distributor(s).
        Estimated number of hours 15–25
        Fixed fee charge. . . . .$____

In addition to the above, AAA would be charged for direct expenses incurred for travel
and non-routine communications, if any. The above estimates are based upon a total
meeting time with you or others you might designate in amount equal to 15 hours.
Should it become necessary to meet for a duration or frequency in excess of 15 hours,
additional meeting time would be billed at $XXX per hour. There would be no charge
for the first 25 hours of travel time, if any.

There is no requirement on my part for AAA to contract for all of the services
indicated above. I you prefer, they can be taken one at a time and you could reach a
decision at each stage as to the wisdom of further retention of my services. In the
event that you were to find it advisable to contract for all or several of the services
outlined, please understand that AAA would be provided with the right to terminate
my services at any time during the course of the consultation.

I am hopeful that the above information is sufficient to meet you requirements. If I
may provide further information please don't hesitate to let me know.

I look forward to the prospect of working with you on this very challenging project.

Personal regards,

_____

SAMPLE LETTER PROPOSAL/CONTRACT

Pursuant to our conversation of September 24, 1980, the following is the proposal of _____ (hereinafter referred to as the CONSULT-ANT) for establishing and operating a recruiting effort designed to acquire the services of a minimum of 5 qualified software engineers for   (hereinafter referred to as (the CLIENT):

PROPOSAL

1. Scope. The plan involves the consultant assisting the client with a thorough preparation of the positive aspects of living and working in Phoenix, Arizona: recruiting, interviewing, screening, and qualifying candidates; conducting personal interviews when applicable; establishing "prime candidate" status; presenting candidates for final approval; assisting in closing negotiations with successful candidates; and establishing start dates.

2. Plan & Requirements. The consultant will develop a portfolio which will present all that the client and the area have to offer in a positive way.

We will require a plant visitation. While there, we will require scheduled meetings with key personnel.

You should have prepared

a. Complete job descriptions for current recruiting assignments;
b. A complete statement of relocation policy or assistance program, as well as any contractual requirements in connection with these policies; and
c. A comprehensive explanation of wage, salary increases, benefits, and advancement programs and schedule, as it applies or is required for the recruiting assignment.

3. Charges & Terms. To accomplish all of the above, the consultant will require a retainer in the amount of $5,000 per month for each of the 2 months covered hereby and a like amount for each renewal month. The amount paid as a monthly retainer shall be applied against the service charge, as set forth below. For example, the service charge for the hire of an engineer is $9,000; therefore, the amount owed by the client will be $9,000 minus $5,000.

The recruitment cost for the hiring of software engineers each at an average salary of $30.00 per our regular service charge schedule (copy attached) would be $9,000. However, our quantity discount to you will reduce this amount.

The schedule is as follows:

Should you hire:

1 — 2 Engineers	Standard Charge per Engineer
3 — 5 Engineers	15% Discount per Engineer
6 — 8 Engineers	20% Discount per Engineer
9 or more Engineers	25% Discount per Engineer

In addition to the professional service charge, we will expect the client to reimburse the consultant for reasonable and preapproved expenses incurred in the course of this assignment.

Should the client terminate any of its employees hired through the consultant as a result of this assignment within the first 90 days of employment, the consultant will make every effort to replace them at no additional charge to the client.

4. Term of Agreement and Cancellations. This proposal will be in effect for a period of 60 calendar days from the date of receipt of the retainer and signed confirmation by the client. The consultant agrees to present to the client a minimum

of 8 qualified and prescreened software engineers during the period of the proposal, otherwise a pro-rated portion of the retainer will be refunded to the client.

At the conclusion of said 60 days, the proposal may be renewed or extended by mutual agreement of the parties hereto.

5. The client retains the right of first refusal to all candidates recruited during the period of the proposal. At the conclusion of the agreement, all candidates recruited by the consultant and not employed by the client or in the process of being employed by the client become the property of the consultant.

6. Consultant shall not, during the term of this agreement or afterward use or disclose to the client's detriment any confidential information whatsoever OB-TAINED from or through the client as a result of work done pursuant to this agreement, nor display for any purpose any drawing, letter, report, or any copy or reproduction thereof belonging to or pertaining to the client without written authorization from the client, unless such drawing, letter, or report has been previously published by the client. The term confidential information used in this subparagraph shall mean any device, process, method, or technique originated by or peculiarly within the knowledge of the client, and its representatives, employees, and those in privy with it, which is not available to the public and is subject to protection as property under recognized principles.

7. The consultant shall not divulge without the permission of the client the terms and conditions of this agreement.

Either of the parties hereto may cancel this agreement on thirty (30) days written notice.

If the above set forth proposal is in accordance with your understanding of our agreement, please sign and return the enclosed copy of this proposal, along with the first month's retainer, to our office.

By_____

By_____

Dated_____

APPENDIX C

Sample Formal Proposal

The formal, written proposal in this appendix displays the important features of a good proposal, even though it is structured according to the requirements of a government agency. The proposal is directed to the California Department of Education and has to follow the format dictated by the department.

Common elements such as a table of contents are omitted because the organization of the proposal is laid out on forms that the department of education supplies. Despite this restriction, the consulting organization presents the main points of the proposed project in the first few pages by giving quick overviews that are more fully developed in the following pages.

The summary sections are carefully worded to give the main advantages of the project as quickly as possible. By reading only four or five pages, an administrator can get an overview of the project.

The strategic organization of the cost of alternative approaches stands out as an example of guiding and forming the reader's opinions. The gold-plated option comes first. This approach takes care of every different district in a unique way. But it is obviously too expensive and unnecessarily complex. Then comes the silver project. This is a good choice, but it takes too much time from the busy schedules of the district administrators.

The third choice is presented as a solid combination of effective action and fiscal conservatism. It is less expensive than the silver program, but not so much less as to be cheap. It is obviously the best investment because it gets results without bankrupting the state's educational training budget.

The material that follows in the opening section deals with the actual structure of the project. There is a schedule of activities and an evaluation procedure. Note that nothing is given away. After reading this material, an administrator would have a general idea of the structure of the project without actually learning any of the specifics.

It might seem that Attachment 1, "Determination of Need," gives away the vocational education survey, but the project is not intended to survey needs, it is designed to train and change attitudes. The survey instrument only measures results; it does not produce them. If this were a proposal for conducting a survey, then it would be poor strategy to include the survey instrument because the department could carry out the survey by using the form that was given in the proposal.

Attachment 4 gives much more detail about the proposed project—or at least it seems to. All the right phrases and ideals are expressed, but there is little actual content. As with the initial outline of project activities, the reader gets a general idea of what will be done without learning any specifics.

Attachment 5 describes the qualifications of the consulting organization by describing its purpose and operations, by giving the background of its officers and personnel, and by listing some of the projects it has carried out. Obviously, the programs that are described are related to education and vocational training. The projects described demonstrate the resources and capabilities of the consulting organization as related to vocational education and support the values that educational administrators are likely to share.

Despite the constraints imposed on format and organization by the department of education, this proposal is carefully constructed to show that:

- The project will meet the requirements of the department.
- The project is worthwhile.
- The project is the best one possible for the investment.
- There will be quality control.
- The organization has the necessary resources.
- The organization has carried out similar projects.

All this is done without giving a detailed description of the actual project. After all, the aim of a proposal is to demonstrate that the consulting firm can carry out the project, not actually to begin it.

At the same time the functional flow diagram for the project is presented and can serve as a guide to both the department and the consulting firm. Likewise the evaluation procedure will enable all involved to assess the results of the intervention, which will be summarized in the final report.

It is well worth investing some time in reading and studying this proposal. It demonstrates how the guidelines in the section on writing a proposal can be elegantly and presuasively applied in an actual written document.

CALIFORNIA STATE DEPARTMENT OF EDUCATION VOCATIONAL EDUCATION SECTION		
	1. Project Number:	
	2. Date Funded:	
ABSTRACT		
3. TITLE OF PROJECT A STATEWIDE CONSORTIUM TO CONDUCT INSERVICE TRAINING		
TYPE OF PROJECT		
4. PROGRAM CODE AND TITLE	5. SUBPROGRAM CODE	
PROJECT DIRECTOR		
6. NAME	7. POSITION	8. INSTITUTION OR AGENCY
9. STREET OR DEPARTMENT	10. CITY	11. STATE / 12. ZIP CODE
13. OFFICE TELEPHONE / AREA CODE / NUMBER / EXTENSION	14. HOME TELEPHONE / AREA CODE / NUMBER	
15. NAME OF APPLICANT INSTITUTION OR AGENCY		

1.0 BRIEF DESCRIPTION

Write a brief description (not to exceed 500 words) of the proposed project such as might be used in a brochure or by the Educational Resources Information Center (ERIC). Include sufficient detail to provide prospective participants with necessary infomation as to the project's focus and major components. (If necessary, continue on reverse.)

Based upon an identified and documented common need for career and vocational education professional staff development a consortium of 19 California County Offices of Education was formed. This program provides inservice training activities for 674 participants through the provision of six four-hour workshops and three three-hour orientation and key administrator training activities. Six pre-workshop learning packages provide orientation information passing and skill development practice exercises. This program:

- Serves the inservice professional development needs of career and vocational education personnel in local districts of 19 counties.

- Utilizes demonstrated and proven inservice training approaches, procedures and materials.

- Is founded upon the desire to improve the effectiveness and strengthen the accountability of vocational education delivery systems in the participating counties.
- Involves over 650 participants including secondary level teachers, counselors, administrators, cooperative and work-experience education coordinators and other personnel related to the delivery of career and vocational education (e.g., special educators, community college personnel, media specialists).
- Is conducted at 19 locations within the state.
- Provides 51 participant training hours including 27 participant group workshop contact hours to each of 541 participants and 6 hours of special training for an additional 133 participants.
- Utilizes structured, interactive, problem solving small group workshops rather than formalized lectures and presentations. Workshops are led by expert trainers who facilitate learning and exercise problem solution by drawing upon the experience of participants.
- Makes optimal use of supporting, individualized learning packages containing training, resource and orientation materials.
- Provides long-term district resource capability through trained personnel and potential widespread dissemination of learning packages.
- Provides for the orientation and involvement of key district decision makers (e.g., superintendent, principals).
- Utilizes in-process quality control to assure maximum program effectiveness.
- Includes impact evaluation to document program achievements.
- Is delivered at a per-participant hour cost of less than $4.25 of federal funds.

CALIFORNIA STATE DEPARTMENT OF EDUCATION
VOCATIONAL EDUCATION SECTION

PROJECT APPLICATION

1.1 TITLE OF PROJECT

TO SERVE (SEC. 553(a))

TEACHERS X TEACHER EDUCATORS ___ ADMINISTRATORS X SUPERVISORS X

COORDINATORS X OTHER ___ (Specify) _____

THROUGH TRAINING___ RETRAINING ___

TYPE OF ACTIVITY (SEC. 553(b))

INDUSTRY EXCHANGE___ IN SERVICE EDUCATION X SHORT-TERM INSTITUTE___

OPERATING DATES___TO___   NUMBER TO BE SERVED___

FUNDS REQUESTED

1.2 DETERMINATION OF NEED

The need for this project was determined and validated as a result of the following activities:

1. It was determined from the results of a successful predecessor project (   ) that a similar project would be of benefit to (a) those individuals within districts participating in the predecessor project who did not themselves participate and (b) those individuals from districts which had not participated in the predecessor project.
2. An identification was made of specific applicable aspects and results of the predecessor project toward improved regional vocational education delivery and accountability.
3. Next, an identification of those County Offices of Education representing participating districts which are experiencing a similar need for delivery system improvement was undertaken by means of a survey administered to County Coordinators of Vocational Education. Of all county offices surveyed, 19 were determined to have a significant level of need for the same or sufficiently similar delivery system improvement and a willingness to reduce the impact of unfavorable regional problems to form a consortium of counties for the purpose of providing district professional staff development activities under the auspices of a single large program.

The survey instrument which enabled the identification of the 19 counties is contained as Exhibit 1 in Attachment 1 to this document. The summary of responses from the 19 county offices is presented as Exhibit 2, Attachment 1. Individual responses from each of the county offices with respect to the priorities of project training objectives will be found in Attachment 2.

1.3 ACTIVITY OBJECTIVES

The overriding purpose of all project objectives and activities is to create for students a more responsive system of vocational education delivery within each of the 19 participating counties. This purpose is accomplished by conducting a program of professional vocational education staff development at each location which responds to the specific needs for such staff development at that location. This project has specific objectives at what might be identified at two levels: an overall set of objective(s) at the consortium level, and a specific set of objectives at the individual county program level.

OVERALL OBJECTIVES (DESCRIPTIVE)

Overall project objectives are the following:

1. To foster among key district decision makers including board members, superintendents and principals the understanding of and commitment to the improvement of the established regional mechanisms of career and vocational education delivery.
2. To foster the long term impact upon career and vocational education programs in the participating districts of improved personnel and program articulation, responsiveness to student needs, and demands of those job markets into which students seek to enter.
3. To seek to disseminate techniques which will enable district staff to become more accountable with respect to the operation of those components of the vocational education delivery system which are (historically) least measurable.
4. To foster the adoption of vocational program development which permits more effective articulation with collateral district efforts to implement a total and comprehensive career education approach.
5. To foster the acquisition (by participating district staff) of specific skills to improve their ability to present more effective programs of vocational instruction. Specific skill objectives include:

5.1 Upgrade teacher and counselor skills in identifying student needs and insuring that vocational education programs are positively influenced to better meet these needs.

5.2 Upgrade teacher and counselor skills in identifying the specific job performance requirements of employers, in the local education agency's job market, to insure that vocational education programs adequately prepare students to satisfy employer entry level skill demands.

5.3 Upgrade teacher skills in specifying appropriate learner performance objectives and to cause the setting of such objectives in such a way as to positively impact curriculum design to insure that students receive relevant instruction.

5.4 Upgrade teacher, counselor and administrator skills to modify vocational education programs to insure that vocational education opportunity is made available to handicapped students who elect participation in such programs.

5.5 Upgrade teacher, counselor and administrator skills which serve to improve articulation between the vocational education delivery system and the source(s) of labor market demand (employers) to insure that employers have high confidence in the "products" of vocational education.

5.6 Improve teacher, counselor and administrator skills in appropriate modification of vocational education delivery to provide further assurance that vocational education provides opportunity for and serves the needs of the disadvantaged student.

5.7 Provide incentives among teachers, counselors and administrators for improving information dissemination and articulation, leading to the improved regional delivery of career and vocational education thereby insuring more effective and uniform achievement of career and vocational education program goals and objectives.

SPECIAL SESSION OBJECTIVES (DESCRIPTIVE)

At each institution, two special sessions are planned for key decision makers at the district level. Participation includes but is not limited to board members, superintendents and principals. These special sessions have the following objectives.

Pre-Program Session
To foster an understanding of the region's career and vocational education delivery system, the impact it creates, and the resources which are available in the region to meet the demand for vocational education, and the role of professional development in maximizing the district's rate of return on career and vocational education investment.

Post-Program Session
To foster knowledge and understanding of the most optimal allocation of newly developed manpower resources to meet the district's commitment to provide effective and responsive career and vocational education programs.

1.4 RELATED TO STATE PRIORITY(IES)
This project directly responds to state priorities which have been established for professional vocational education staff development programs which qualify for consideration for support from EPDA, Part F. Specific priorities for which a direct program response is provided include:

1. Increasing the Effectiveness of Teaching for Disadvantaged and Handicapped
   Directly responded to by training session objectives 5.3 and 5.5 , with additional response to this priority offered by training session objectives 5.1, 5.2 and 5.7.

2. Updating Administrative and Supervisory Skills
   Directly responded to by the training objective for the key district decision maker sessions. In addition, reinforcement of relevant administrator skills is accomplished in individual (main) session components including such skills as: planning, scheduling, forecasting.

A STATEWIDE CONSORTIUM TO CONDUCT INSERVICE TRAINING
SUMMARY OF HOST LOCATIONS, NUMBER OF PARTICIPANTS
AND TRAINING OBJECTIVES

TRAINING HOST LOCATION	NUMBER OF PARTICIPANTS	OBJECTIVES						
		5.1	5.2	5.3	5.4	5.5	5.6	5.7
— County	57	X	X	X		X	X	X
— County	43	X	X	X	X	X	X	
— County	22	X	X	X	X	X	X	
— County	22	X	X	X	X		X	X
— County	32	X	X	X	X	X	X	
— County	22	X	X	X	X	X	X	
— County	32	X	X	X	X	X	X	
— County	32	X	X	X	X	X	X	
— County	77	X	X	X	X	X	X	
— County	32	X	X	X	X		X	X
— County	32	X	X	X	X	X	X	
— County	32	X	X	X	X		X	X
— County	32	X	X	X	X	X	X	
— County	32	X	X	X	X		X	X
— County	32	X	X	X	X	X	X	
— County	17	X	X	X	X		X	X
— County	42	X	X	X	X	X	X	
— County	32	X	X	X		X	X	X
— County	32	X	X	X	X	X	X	

3. Orienting Non-Vocational Education Personnel to Vocational Education
   Approximately 40% of the consortium host locations have indicated a desire to involve non-vocational education personnel in the inservice training activities. An even greater emphasis is given to this non-vocational educator orientation by the key district decision maker personnel training sessions.

4. Improving Instructional Effectiveness
   This priority is responded to directly by each of the training session objectives which are listed in section 1.3. The term instructional effectiveness is interpreted in a broader sense than simply teaching effectiveness. For example, training session modules 1,2,4, and 6, are designed to enhance the overall relevancy of programs offered. This will have the ultimate impact of improving instructional effectiveness through the mechanism of creating a more meaningful and responsive learning environment for the students served.

1.5 ANALYSIS OF ALTERNATIVES
Describe at least three alternative ways that were considered when planning this proposed program.

DESCRIPTION OF ALTERNATIVES FOR ATTAINING　　　　　　　　APPROXIMATE
THE ACTIVITY'S OBJECTIVES　　　　　　　　　　　　　　　　　　　COST

(A) Individual District Programs.
This alternative would provide that each county office submit an individual project designed to meet its six priority areas of need through the use of structured workshop activities and supporting materials development for information passing, orientation and practice exercises. This alternative would produce 19 distinct training projects serving a total of 674 participants. This alternative would involve a modification of materials used in the successful predecessor project. Training activities would consist of 51 hours of training, including 27 contact hours for 541 participants and 6 contact hours for 133 participants. The training would take place in the context of small work groups led by expert trainers who facilitate learning and exercise problem solution by drawing upon the expertise and experience of participants rather than lecturing in the formal sense. This alternative requires the provision for released time and substitute reimbursement for 327 of the 674 participants.   TOTAL $450,000.00

(B) Consortium Program Utilizing Workshop Training Activities Only.
This alternative would provide for a consortium of 19 County Offices pooling their individual requirements for career and vocational education professional staff development and utilizing materials developed for the predecessor program. These materials would be in the form of six 8-hour structured workshops, plus special sessions for key district decision makers, to combine information passing, practice exercises and orientation as well as the application of small work group activities led by expert trainers as described in Alternative (A), above. This alternative requires the provision of six days of released time and substitute reimbursement for 325 of the 674 participants.   TOTAL $192,112.00

(C) Consortium Program Utilizing Workshops and Learning Packages.
This alternative, proposed in this project application, provides for a consortium of 19 County Offices of Education to provide inservice professional development activities for 674 participants through the provision of six four-hour workshops and pre-workshop learning packages designed to provide necessary orientation, information passing, and practice prior to actual workshop conduct. An additional three-hour orientation session and two three-hour key district administrator sessions result in a total of 51 training and 27 contact hours for 541 participants and 6 contact hours for 133 participants. The three-hour orientation session is conducted prior to participant enrollment in the program. The workshop component of the training activity is utilized only for activities that may best meet or are required to meet the training objectives in that specific training means format. The learning packages are utilized for activities that do not require a workshop atmosphere. This highly cost-effective method for training development has a record of demonstrated learning effectiveness and requires limited release time and substitute reimbursement. This alternative also provides for two special workshop sessions (in addition to the six four-hour workshop sessions) for key district decision makers and an orientation session for other participants. Alternative (C) utilizes a modification of existing materials from the successful predecessor project. Workshop activities take place in the context of small work groups led by expert trainers who facilitate learning and exercise problem solution by drawing upon the expertise and experience of participants rather than lecturing in the formal sense. Monthly newletters are provided to all participants to assist attitude development and communicate information about program conduct. The learning packages will be made available at cost to educators through out the state to promote widespread information dissemination and long-term resource capability.   TOTAL $122,906.00

1.6 JUSTIFICATION FOR SELECTED ALTERNATIVE LETTER C
Alternative C has been selected on the basis of the following:

• There exists a high degree of certainty that its means are effective and sufficient for meeting the project objectives.

- It is the most cost effective satisfactory means for meeting the project objectives, in terms of development and conduct costs as well as the cost of substitute reimbursement for released time.
- The training activities, including both the learning packages and the workshops, are tailored to meet the specific and distinct needs of local district personnel in each of the 19 counties participating.

1.7 DESCRIPTION OF ACTIVITIES

The implementation of this project is described in terms of a series of interrelated activities. These activities are broadly classified into eight categories as follows:

Activity 1—Finalize Enabling Agreements
Activity 2—Finalize Conduct/Logistics Plans
Activity 3—Conduct Participant Selection/Orientation
Activity 4—Implement Evaluation Design
Activity 5—Implement Quality Control Procedures
Activity 6—Format Training Materials
Activity 7—Conduct Training
Activity 8—Submit Project Report

The interrelationship between these project activities is described (schematically) in Attachment 3, Exhibit 1. The time phased relationships of these activities are presented in Attachment 3, Exhibit 2. Each individual activity is further broken down into a series of discrete tasks to be accomplished. An expanded description of the project at the task level is presented in Attachment 4.

1.8 TIME SCHEDULE FOR ACTIVITIES

The project is conceived and developed for presentation during the period January-–May 1973, and September–December 1973. The specific dates for scheduled completion of individual project activities are shown in the schedule chart of Attachment 3, Exhibit 2. A tentative schedule of session conduct dates is presented in Attachment 3, Exhibit 3.

1.9 PREPLANNING ACTIVITIES

Preplanning activities have taken place in preparing this application. In addition, extensive preplanning at each training session location is planned involving County Office host coordination staff, district staff, participants, and State Department of Education officials. The chronology of preplanning activities prior to submitting this application have included:

Spring
- Informal meetings with prospective host coordinators to determine the need for program development
- Preparation and distribution of need survey instrument to assess and verify program need
- Preliminary discussion of project feasibility with cognizant State Department of Education personnel.

Summer
- Analysis of need survey data
- Meetings with prospective host directors to establish criteria for proposed consortium membership
- Development of descriptive program materials for distribution to prospective project consortium members.

Fall
- Informal meetings with prospective host directors to modify preliminary program approaches
- Preparation and distribution of expanded program descriptions incorporating suggested modifications

- Meeting of all prospective host coordinators (and cognizant State Department staff) to critique and regionalize program approach.

Winter

- Distribution and critique of results of the meeting of consortium host directors
- Assembly of relevant data and program constraint information for each consortium member
- Preliminary development of project application
- Distribution, review and modification of project application
- Endorsement and commitment of consortium members to project submission.

Additional preplanning activities are scheduled subsequent to project approval. These are described more fully in the expanded project description presented in Attachment 4.

2.0 EVALUATION

Evaluation will comprise two distinct undertakings:

1. An impact evaluation conducted by an independent, third-party evaluator which will be designed to determine the extent to which the project objectives have been met and provide diagnosis to permit recommendations for future projects.
2. An ongoing assessment of participant knowledge and skill acquistion and a determination of participant attitude and acceptance of training strategies and methods employed, for the purpose of altering project activities to insure maximum participant learning.

A diagram depicting the interrelationship of these two evaluation activities will be found on Page 207.

The independent, third-party impact evaluation which is described in greater detail in Activity 4 of the expanded activities description (Attachment 4) provides for the selection of an individual or organization on the basis of prior experience, technical capability, references and cost. The evaluation team is required to interact according to a specified schedule with the project development staff. This will assure the collection of adequate measures of impact data not only subsequent to training, but also prior to and during the training process as well. The evaluated activity and the results will be made part of the final report.

Based on experience, the ongoing assessment or quality control of the project activities is essential for the purpose of making necessary changes to enhance participant learning and the motivation to learn. This will permit the achievement of the full benefit of the coordinated instructional systems approach utilized in the development and conduct of the project. The details of this ongoing assessment or quality control are provided in Attachment 4, page 215. This assessment includes, but is not limited to:

- Baseline testing to determine entering participant skill, knowledge and attitude levels
- Periodic testing to determine extent of participant acquisition of skills and knowledge necessary to meet objectives
- Post-session participant attitudinal survey to determine appropriateness of training strategy and methods selection
- Technical briefings for training conduct staff to insure that the training conduct strategies are appropriate for the purpose and intent of materials
- Logistical and interpersonal briefings for training conduct staff to insure that training activities make due accomodation for interpersonal and logistical advantages and difficulties
- Formal and informal reporting procedures involving the participant, host directors and training staff.

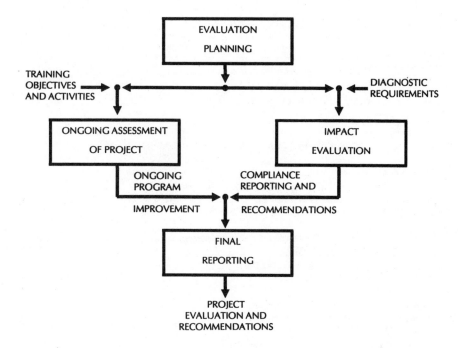

ATTACHMENT I

DETERMINATION OF NEED

EXHIBIT 1—Vocational Education Survey

NOTE: All data received by _____ will be treated as confidential.

THE FOLLOWING ARE STATEMENTS RELATING TO THE IMPACT OF VOCATIONAL EDUCATION PROGRAMMING. BASED UPON PERSONAL KNOWLEDGE OF YOUR AREA, REACT TO EACH STATEMENT ON THE SCALE PROVIDED.

STATEMENT OF IMPACT	STRONGLY AGREE				STRONGLY DISAGREE
1. Adequate justification is provided for vocational education program expenditures.	1	2	3	4	5
2. Instructional program design includes specification of meaningful learner objectives.	1	2	3	4	5
3. There is evidence suggesting that vocational education could better respond to the needs of students.	1	2	3	4	5
4. There is evidence suggesting that vocational education could better respond to the needs of employers comprising our job market.	1	2	3	4	5
5. The majority of vocational education graduates are securing employment relevant to their courses of instruction.	1	2	3	4	5
6. Relevant vocational education programs are available, which are responsive to the specific needs of the handicapped student.	1	2	3	4	5
8. Employers comprising our job market have high confidence in our understanding of their entry level requirements.	1	2	3	4	5
9. Vocational education personnel have communication skills which contribute significantly to the accomplishment of program goals and objectives.	1	2	3	4	5
10. Openings exist in fields for which our students have been trained, but our trained students remain unemployed.	1	2	3	4	5

11. Students completing our vocational education programs, who go on to community college:
    a. Find community college training redundant
    b. Find they are inadequately prepared
    c. Do well in community college
    d. Often change their program in community college
12. Vocational education students:
    a. Enter vocational education on the advice of a counselor
    b. Enter vocational education without adequate guidance from a counselor
    c. Experience a higher-than-usual drop-out rate
    d. Change programs at a rate higher than normal

PLEASE COMPLETE THE FOLLOWING ITEMS: (Approximate figures may be used.)

13. Number of vocational education personnel employed in your area:
    Instructors, with Teaching Credential _____
    Instructors, without Teaching Credential _____
    Counselors _____
    Work Experience Coordinators _____
    Aides _____
    Administrators _____
    Other _____ (Describe____
    _____)
14. The units for which you are responsible: (Secondary Schools, Community Colleges, Training Centers, etc.)

    A._____ C._____

    B._____ D._____
15. Student enrollment in vocational education programs:

    Secondary_____ Community College_____

    Other_____ (Describe_____)

              a. Handicapped _____(%)   b. Disadvantaged _____(%)
16. Number of personnel who could participate in a training program at any one time. _____
17. Number of the above for whom substitutes would be required.
18. Current daily rate for substitutes. $_____
19. Best day(s) of the week for training programs: _____
    _____
              a. Best time of year: _____
20. Most likely city in which to hold a training program for your area:
    _____
21. Are training facilities available to you in that city?
    _____ Yes   _____ No
22. Would participants in your area be permitted to accept university credit for inservice training program completion?
    _____ Yes   _____ No
NAME _____ TITLE _____
REPRESENTING _____
ADDRESS _____ TELEPHONE ( ) _____

EXHIBIT 2—Summary Results of Training Need Analyses

INSERVICE TRAINING PROGRAM OBJECTIVES

NUMBER OF FOR WHICH	5.1	5.1 & 5.2	5.1 through 5.3	5.1 through 5.4	5.1 through 5.5	5.1 through 5.6	5.1 through 5.7
100% of top priority district staff training need is met	3	5	10	11	16	17	19
At least 50% of top priority district staff training needs are met	6	15	18	18	19	19	19
100% of second priority district staff training need is met (in addition to top priority need)	0	0	2	6	8	12	19
At least 50% of second priority district staff training needs are met (in addition to top priority need)	0	2	4	12	13	16	19

Attachment 2

CONSORTIUM COUNTY REGION DATA SHEET

MAP CODE NO._____

_____

_____

_____CALIFORNIA_____

NAME/TITLE OF COUNTY COORDINATOR _____ Director, Regional
                                                                                              Occupation Programs

_11__ Number of districts offering educational programs for grades 9–14

13,227 Number of students enrolled in educational programs for grades 9–14

STUDENT CHARACTERISTICS

Ethnic distribution by percentage:

_2.7_ Black or Negro   _-_ American Indian

_8.3_ Spanish Surnamed American   86.6 Anglo American

                              2.4 Other

Demographic characteistics by percentage:

_18.6_ Economically Disadvantaged   16.6 Bilingual

_40.0_ Migrant   7.0 Handicapped (Physical,

                              .05 Gifted   Mental)

Residence distribution by percentage:

_50.0_ Central City   _____ Suburban

_25.5_ Other Urban   24.5 Rural

REQUIRED TRAINING MODULES AS IDENTIFIED FROM NEED ANALYSIS

MODULE PURPOSE   PRIORITY

	1st	2nd	3rd	NOT RANKED
1. Identifying student needs	X			
2. Identifying specific job performance requirements for local areas	X			
3. Specifying learner objectives and applying objectives to curricular design	X			
4. Modifying programs to respond to needs of the handicapped			X	
5. Improving articulation between educational programs and employers		X		
6. Modifying programs to respond to needs of the disadvantaged				
7. Improve teacher/counselor/administrator communication to achieve vocational education program goals and objectives			X	

COUNTY OFFICE _____ MAP CODE NO. _____

UNIFIED DISTRICTS	ENROLLMENT	NUMBER OF CAMPUSES
— Unified	421	1
— Unified	105	1
— Joint Unified	258	1
— Unified	176	1
— Unified	375	1
— Unified	2293	2
— Joint Unified	2165	2
TOTAL	5793	9
HIGH SCHOOL DISTRICTS		
— Joint Union High	204	1
— High	368	1
— High	929	1
TOTAL		
COMMUNITY COLLEGE DISTRICTS		
— Community College	5891	1
TOTAL	5891	1
COUNTY OPERATED SCHOOLS		
— County	42	1
— County	—	2
— County	—	3
TOTAL	42	6

ATTACHMENT 3

FLOW CHART AND SCHEDULES

EXHIBIT 1 — Schematic Program Flow Chart

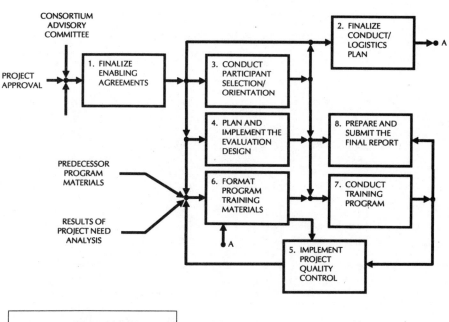

EXHIBIT 2 — Schedule of Project Activities

PROJECT ACTIVITY	JAN.	FEB.	MAR.	APR.	MAY	JUNE	JULY	AUG.	SEPT.	OCT.	NOV.	DEC.	JAN.	FEB.
1. FINALIZE ENABLING AGREEMENTS	++++													
2. FINALIZE CONDUCT/ LOGISTICS PLAN	++						++							
3. CONDUCT PARTICIPANT SELECTION/ORIENTATION	++++	++++						++++	++++					
4. PLAN AND IMPLEMENT EVALUATION DESIGN	++++	++++												
5. IMPLEMENT PROJECT QUALITY CONTROL		++++	++++	++++	++++	++				++++	++++	++++	++++	++
6. FORMAT PROGRAM TRAINING MATERIALS	++++	++++												
7. CONDUCT TRAINING PROGRAM			++++	++++	++++	++				++++	++++	++++	++	
8. PREPARE AND SUBMIT FINAL REPORT													++	++++
INTERIM REPORTING			++			++			++					
PARTICIPANT NEWSLETTER			+	+	+	+		+	+	+	+	+	+	+

EXHIBIT 3 — Tentative Training Schedule

LOCATION									
	2/13	3/5	3/19	3/19	4/9	4/9	5/7	5/7	5/28
	2/13	3/5	3/19	3/19	4/9	4/9	5/7	5/7	5/28
	2/14	3/6	3/20	3/20	4/10	4/10	5/8	5/8	5/29
	2/15	3/7	3/21	3/22	4/11	4/12	5/9	5/10	5/31
	2/16	3/8	3/26	3/26	4/16	4/16	5/14	5/14	6/1
	2/20	3/9	3/27	3/27	4/17	4/17	5/15	5/15	6/4
	2/21	3/12	3/28	3/29	4/18	4/19	5/16	5/17	6/5
	2/22	3/13	3/30	3/30	4/20	4/20	5/18	5/18	6/6
	2/23	3/14	4/2	4/2	4/30	4/30	5/21	5/21	6/7
	2/26	3/15	4/4	4/5	5/2	5/3	5/23	5/24	6/8
	9/17	10/1	10/15	10/15	11/5	11/5	11/26	11/26	1/7
	9/18	10/2	10/16	10/16	11/6	11/6	11/27	11/27	1/8
	9/19	10/3	10/17	10/17	11/7	11/7	11/28	11/28	1/9
	9/20	10/4	10/18	10/19	11/8	11/9	11/29	11/30	1/10
	9/21	10/5	10/22	10/23	11/12	11/13	12/3	12/3	1/14
	9/24	10/8	10/24	10/25	11/14	11/15	12/4	12/5	1/15
	9/25	10/9	10/26	10/26	11/16	11/16	12/6	12/6	1/16
	9/26	10/10	10/29	10/30	11/19	11/20	12/10	12/11	1/17
	9/27	10/11	10/31	11/1	11/21	11/22	12/12	12/13	1/18

ATTACHMENT 4

EXPANDED ACTIVITY DESCRIPTION

Each of the eight basic project activities listed in Section 1.7 is subdivided into distinct tasks. This attachment to the project application includes a detailed description of the scope of effort assigned to individual project tasks.

ACTIVITY 1—FINALIZE ENABLING AGREEMENTS
(Percent of Total Project Effort = 1)

Two main tasks comprise this activity. First, it is necessary to execute a joint powers agreement between participating consortium members. Second, it is necessary to execute enabling subcontract agreements with the program development and conduct agency, _____ , and the independent third-party evaluation team. The joint powers agreement will be executed for each consortium member by the project fiscal agent, in this case acting on behalf of all consortium members. Such a joint powers agreement is conventional and stipulates the provision of training facilities and participants at the host location, and also stimulates the terms and conditions of district reimbursement procedures for substitute payments and any other allowable expenses. A joint powers agreement similar to the one to be used is included as Attachment 5, Exhibit 1, to indicate the form and content typically prescribed.

Program development, conduct and evaluation subcontracts will be developed in consultation with County Counsel (for subsequent Board approval) by the project fiscal agent. Such contracts follow standard form and are expected to present no difficulty.

ACTIVITY 2—FINALIZE CONDUCT/LOGISTICS PLAN
(Percent of Total Project Effort = 1)

Included in this project application is a preliminary session conduct schedule. This preliminary schedule is subject to modification pending adjustments made to accommodate individual district constraints that may arise. Individual site visitations are scheduled with project staff at each consortium host location for the purpose of determining the suitability of proposed training sites, arranging for logistics, distributing promotional literature, and finalizing participant eligibility/ selection criteria. An important consideration during this activity will be to coordinate the distribution and analysis of participant baseline data collection instruments with participating county offices and districts. Discussions will be held to assist in further structuring the format of the special administrator's introductory workshop so as to be most effective in gaining added district participation and commitment from this vital source. Program materials to support this highly critical phase of the total project are derived from the various component tasks of Activity #6.

ACTIVITY 3—CONDUCT PARTICIPANT SELECTION/ORIENTATION
(Percent of Total Project Effort = 4)
Experience has shown that the success of inservice training programs of this type
requires that a great deal more emphasis be placed on the critical aspect of ensuring
that the appropriate participants be identified and reliably assembled for purposes of
training. The term "appropriate" implies a participant who
- is highly motivated in seeking professional development via inservice training.
- has professional development "needs" which are aligned closely with the
objectives and purposes of the program.
- is supportive of the introduction of new ideas which can lead to change in
established procedures or approaches.
Initially, suitable descriptive program materials are developed in a brochure format
for the purpose of informing the vocational educator staff, in districts served by the
county office consortium member, of the availability, nature, scope, format, and
content of the inservice training program. Concurrent with the release of this
program information, an orientation session will be scheduled at each consortium
member site for the purpose of briefing key district decision makers (including board
members and superintendents). It has been generally agreed among host directors
that this session would prove exceedingly helpful in building needed, local "top level"
support and encouragement to district staff who would ultimately be participating. A
tentatively assigned number of participant "slots" would be provided to each
participating district. Participant nomination papers are to be distributed to each
district for completion and returned to the host county office of education.

Participant Selection
Participant selection criteria have been preliminarily established, and include:

        Criteria for Nominating and Selecting Participants
        1. Candidate requests to participate in the program
        2. Candidate shall have been employed by the district for at least one year
        3. Candidate expects to remain an employee of the district for at least two
more years
        4. In addition to his or her regular teaching, counseling, and/or adminis-
trative duties, candidate shall be serving at the present time or be appointed to serve
within the next academic year, in a capacity related to curriculum planning,
planning for special projects, operation of special projects, or professional staff
development.
A team involving the host director, key district staff and project staff will review
district nominations and develop the participant list at each site. A slate of alternates
will be developed in the event that a selected participant is unable to attend.
Notification of participants and alternates will then take place. Included in this
notification will be appropriate baseline testing instruments for completion and
return. As described in Activities 5 and 6, baseline participant data play an important
part in program materials development and subsequent program evaluation and
quality control procedures.
An initial workshop orientation session is planned (with participants) at each
consortium member location. This orientation session will have the specific objective
of establishing a firm participant expectation for program objectives, participation
format and details, university course credit arrangements (where applicable), and
final registration of participants desiring to participate in this inservice training
program. Program materials will be distributed and formal course orientation will
take place.

ACTIVITY 4—PLAN AND IMPLEMENT EVALUATION DESIGN
(Percent of Total Project Effort = 5)
It is proposed to utilize an independent, outside, third-party evaluation source to
conduct the program impact evaluation component. It is anticipated that much of the
participant data and information collected in the course of instituting program

quality control procedures will be of value and use to the evaluation activity. However, it should be emphasized that this data collection is not done (primarily) for evaluation. For this reason it is necessary to cause the involvement of the evaluation team at an early stage, and not retrospectively (after the fact), as is often done. Documents and specifications detailing the anticipated outcomes of the evaluation activity will be developed in collaboration with the Consortium Advisory Committee. These documents will be made the basis of solicitations of interest and capability by qualified individuals or agencies to accomplish the evaluation objectives.

An additional diagnostic component of this evaluation effort will seek to determine the validity of key assumptions made during project formulation and development. Specifically, for example, trends or occasions of missed assignments, poor attendance, etc. will be analyzed and interpreted thereby providing valuable insight into the planning for future programs of this type.

The combined implementation of Activities 4 and 5 make up the total project evaluation as described in Section 2.0.

ACTIVITY 5—IMPLEMENT QUALITY CONTROL (ON-GOING ASSESSMENT)
(Percent of Total Project Effort = 6)

This activity involves a number of tasks specifically designed to insure the effective use of the coordinated instructional systems approach utilized in the project design. The purpose of project quality control is to assess the extent to which the project is meeting its objectives during the conduct phase and to make necessary any required adjustments to training materials, methods and the procedures employed in the use of those training materials. Experience has demonstrated that close scrutiny of the degree of participant learning, the way in which that learning takes place and the factors which serve to strengthen and weaken the participants' motivation are essential in guiding the corrective action which insures the achievement of training objectives.

The tasks which comprise this activity include, but are not limited to the following:

a. Participant testing to determine extent of learning. A series of tests are administered at the start of training and again at the end of training to measure increases in participants' skills and knowledge. These surveys will identify the need for training reinforcement, if any, and the need to alter materials or conduct methods for participants in subsequent workshops.

b. Participant attitudinal survey data. At the conclusion of each training session participants are surveyed to determine both positive and negative factors which may affect their motivation to learn. Negative factors are, wherever possible, corrected for subsequent conduct of training at the same and other locations.

c. Staff Briefings and Debriefings. Prior to the conduct of each training activity, training development staff conduct a technical briefing which serves to identify the means and procedures specified for meeting the training objectives. This briefing considers information obtained from the other tasks in this activity and results in a carefully prescribed instructional strategy. At the conclusion of training activities conduct staff participate in a structured debrief designed to assess strengths and limitations experienced by groups of participants and by individual participants during the session(s). Consideration is also given to unsolicited comments made by participants, the host coordinators, guests and others as well as to the adequacy of facilities and other matters related to the conduct of the session(s).

d. Preparation of the Session Report. The briefings, debriefs, summary of test and survey results, and the individual impressions of the session leader (the senior member of the training conduct team who is held responsible for meeting the training objectives) are documented for use in subsequent training activities at all locations. The applicable session reports from previous training activities, news clippings of local educational interest and related resources are reviewed in depth by training conduct staff prior to delivery of a training activity.

e. Meetings with Host Directors and the Project Director. Meetings between the conduct and development staff and the project director and host directors serve to further modify training materials and conduct to optimally insure participant learning. The combined implementation of Activities 4 and 5 make up the total project evaluation as described in Section 2.0.

ACTIVITY 6—FORMAT TRAINING MATERIALS
(Percent of Total Project Effort = 12)
As previously mentioned, this program has been developed and formulated with the expectation of a high degree of utilization of materials, techniques, and procedures from a successful predecessor program (Project No. _____). In addition to the technology represented by the predecessor program, additional improvements to the training delivery approach have been made and tested and are incorporated into this project design.

Overall Primary Training Program
The overall primary training program (as presented at any one of the consortium member sites) is comprised of six (6) of seven (7) possible modules. The six modules to be conducted at a given site are selected on the basis of the six priority needs identified to exist n a given region. A description of the seven modules is provided in the boxed sections on the right.

Program Format
The key to the overall training program format is individualization. A training delivery model has been developed and tested which has proven highly effective in achieving attitudinal and behavioral change among this participant group. This result is made possible on an extremely cost-effective basis by carefully arranging the training delivery sequence as described below. A corollary benefit of adopting this approach is that a much more effective and efficient use is made of workshop time. In addition the individualized approach resolves a significant number of barriers to delivering the required training arising from such sources as:

- cost of substitute teachers
- availability of substitute teachers
- local impact of releasing large numbers of district staff simultaneously
- inflexibility in session make-up provisions for nominal absence.

Training Session Components
The inservice training requirement for each module is not treated by means of a single training format. Careful analysis has shown that a more effective approach would give recognition to the fact that three distinct components of a training requirement exist within each module. Each, in turn, requires a distinct training format as follows:

    6.1 Information Passing Component
    6.2 Task Familiarization/ Orientation Component
    6.3 Interactive Workshop Component

MODULE 1: JOB PERFORMANCE REQUIREMENTS

DESCRIPTIVE OBJECTIVE: To upgrade teacher and counselor skills in identifying the specific job performance requirements of employers, in the LEA's job market, so as to insure that vocational education programs adequately prepare students to satisfy employer entry skill demands.

WORKSHOP DESCRIPTION: Utilizes task analysis techniques to determine the cognitive and psychomotor skills required for successful on-the-job performance. How to treat employer tendency to upgrade entry level requirements. Primarily intended for vocational instructors having lesson plan responsibility and Work Experience Coordinators having vocational job development responsibility. Vocational counselors will find useful methods of adapting a variety of published information to the purpose of student guidance.

MODULE 2: DETERMINATION OF STUDENT NEEDS
DESCRIPTIVE OBJECTIVE: To upgrade teacher and counselor skills in indentifying student needs and insuring that vocational education programs are influenced in a positive way so as better to meet these needs.

WORKSHOP DESCRIPTION: Treats communications styles of today's stu-

6.1 Information Passing Component

The information passing component serves to provide the information necessary for use during the subsequent development and exercise of skills required to achieve the competencies stipulated in the project objectives. It is planned that each participant will spend one to two hours (for each module) interacting with highly motivational information passing presentations designed to provide him with this required information. The print format of the information passing component is designed to appeal to both inductive and deductive participant learning processes. Useful long-term resource materials and references are automatically provided. The success of information passing segments is not dependent upon maintaining a group environment.

6.2 Task Familiarization/ Orientation Component

Once the participant has interacted with the information and resources provided in the Information Passing Component he or she is adequately prepared to respond for two to three hours in the task formulation/orientation component of the module. This component causes the participant to assess specific problem situations and to make an initial, independent attempt to synthesize the previously derived information. This is accomplished in the context of the exercises, tasks and problems encountered in the Task Familiarization/Orientation Component which are appropriately individualized to allow each participant to apply the topical information to problems from his or her own realm of experience. Thus, the participant, while engaged in this component does not require, and indeed may be impeded by, group interaction. This component also serves to prepare the participant for the (third) Interactive Workshop Component.

6.3 Interactive Workshop Component

The interactive workshop component is designed to provide in-depth subject matter penetration for participants who have been previously oriented and resourced as a result of Component 1 and 2. In addition to an in-depth critique of participant identification and analysis of problems and problem solutions, the opportunity is provided to effectively and

dent population. Methods of quantifying and interpreting expressions of need and the implications for vocational education program development, including individualization of instruction. Appropriate techniques are introduced for insuring that student needs are made to positively impact curriculum development including such factors as: performance objectives, lesson plans, demonstrations and testing.

MODULE 3: CAREER EDUCATION OPPORTUNITIES FOR THE HANDICAPPED

DESCRIPTIVE OBJECTIVE: To upgrade teacher and counselor skills to modify vocational education programs so as to increase career education opportunities available to handicapped students who elect such programs.

WORKSHOP DESCRIPTION: Reviews the current state of knowledge concerning the capability of the handicapped student in the context of factors which influence vocational placement suitability and factors which impact the design of effective learning experiences. Techniques are developed to foster expanded career objectives for the handicapped student.

MODULE 4: IMPROVING SCHOOL/ INDUSTRY ARTICULATION

DESCRIPTIVE OBJECTIVE: To upgrade teacher, counselor and administrator skills which serve to improve articulation between the vocational education delivery system and employers, to insure that employers have high confidence in the "products" of career and vocational education.

WORKSHOP DESCRIPTION: Primarily designed to improve participant skill in adequately representing and projecting vocational education to the hiring community. Review of industrial practices relative to hiring, determining entry level skills, and establishing mobility criteria (including promotion). The extent and purpose of formal in-plant training and OJT. Techniques of involving the hiring sector in gaining favorable education training objectives.

efficiently interact with other participants to develop mutual understanding
and practice of highly appropriate solution approaches. The workshop component of each training module is scheduled for completion in 4 hours and
involves small group interactive learning processes including simulation, case
study, task completion, problem identification and small group discussion.

This component of the training module
also provides a close tutorial diagnostic
activity to closely monitor participant
learning. This monitoring activity begins at the start of the workshop with a
debrief and review of participant pre-
session work in component 2, Task
Formulation/Orientation, and continues
until workshop conclusion.

Participant Orientation

Prior to the delivery of the selected training modules, a three-hour participant
orientation session is conducted as described in Activity 3. Supporting materials are developed to meet the objectives
of this pre-program session, as described.

Key Administrators Workshops

In addition to the seven modules and
orientation session of the primary workshop activity, two additional workshops
for key administrators are planned. One
of these workshops occurs prior to th
primary training program and serves to
foster district "top level" support for participant involvement. In addition, information resources will be developed together with small-group exercises to
foster the understanding of the vital role
played by the existing vocational education delivery system and the critical importance of continuing professional staff
development to the effective operation of
this system.

The second administrators workshop, at
the conclusion of the primary training
activity, is designed to provide key district decision makers with specific
knowledge and skills to allow them to
make effective and significant use of the
increased capability represented among
the participant group. Topical areas will
include program results, organizational
management for new and/or special
projects, fostering an encouraging environment for program and curricular

MODULE 5: CAREER OPPORTUNITIES
FOR THE DISADVANTAGED
DESCRIPTIVE OBJECTIVES: To improve teacher, counselor and administrator skills in appropriate modification of vocational education
delivery so as to serve the needs of the
disadvantaged student.
WORKSHOP DESCRIPTION: Review of
techniques of student capability profile
analysis. Techniques of instructional
program individualization are developed as a proven effective means of
circumventing barriers to successful
learning. Techniques for expanding the
use of work-experience approaches to
provide occupational preparation for
the disadvantaged student.

MODULE 6: MAXIMIZING PROGRAM
ARTICULATION
DESCRIPTIVE OBJECTIVES: To provide incentives among teachers, counselors and administrators for improving information dissemination and
articulation leading to the improved
regional delivery of vocational education, thereby insuring more effective
and uniform achievement of career
and vocational education program
goals and objectives.
WORKSHOP DESCRIPTION: Techniques of goal-setting and delivery
system analysis for the development
of uniform vocational program goals
and objectives. Program response to
follow-up studies indicating IN/OUT
student migration patterns. Techniques of fostering realistic expectations and enthusiastic support for vocational education from students,
parents, and community.

MODULE 7: FORMULATING
PROGRAM OBJECTIVES
DESCRIPTIVE OBJECTIVES: To upgrade teacher skills in specifying appropriate learner performance objectives, and further, to cause the setting
of such objectives to positively impact
the curriculum design so as to insure
that students receive relevant instruction.
WORKSHOP DESCRIPTION: The establishment of learner performance objec-

change, and fostering a positive environment for increased accountability. In addition, availability of the learning packages at cost from the project director, is communicated to administrators in order that they may be made aware of the long-term resource capability that has been provided for their staffs.

tives with emphasis on what to do with them once they are set. Application to: competency based testing, lesson planning, graded difficulty laboratory exercises, etc. The use of a coordinated instructional approach and validation testing to determine acceptable criterion levels of performance.

ACTIVITY 7—CONDUCT TRAINING PROGRAM
(Percent of Total Project Effort = 70)

Upon completion of training materials development, participant recruitment/ selection and orientation, baseline testing, and finalization of logistics, facilities, and arrangements, primary training begins. Training activities will be conducted at 10 locations during the period of XXXXXXXXXX 1973 through XXXXXXXX 1973 and at the remaining 9 locations during the period of XXXXXX 1973 until XXXXXXX 1974. Training activities consist of one program for teachers, counselors, work-experience and cooperative education personnel, administrators and related personnel and a second, related program for key district decision makers. The former program begins with a three-hour training program orientation session followed by six four-hour workshop sessions. Each of the six workshop sessions is preceded by participant exposure to an individualized learning package of training materials. This demonstratedly effective training delivery approach is highly cost-effective. The learning package serves to provide information necessary for meeting training requirements through innovative, motivational presentation formats. Additionally, these learning packages are designed to properly orient participants to the workshop activity by providing practice exercises which reinforce understanding of the information passed and enable practice in associated skill development.

The learning package is designed to motivate, prepare and orient the participant for making effective use of his or her time in the workshop. Workshop activities take place in the context of small work groups led by expert trainers who facilitate learning through the use of participant expertise and experience to identify problems and reach solutions. Reliable process techniques demonstrated to be effective in the solution of problems impacting vocational education delivery are explained and practiced. These techniques, as opposed to formal lecturing, have been demonstrated to foster positive behavioral change because they permit experience in application rather than the mere provision of information.

The workshops are provided through one of basically three delivery models at the option of each consortium member.

    a. At __11__ of the 19 locations participants will receive the first workshop in the morning and the second workshop that afternoon. The third and fourth workshops will be conducted at the same time approximately one month later. The final two workshops will follow on a day about one month later.

    b. At __4__ of the 19 locations participants have elected to receive the first workshop in the afternoon and the second workshop that evening. The third and fourth as well as the fifth and sixth workshops will follow the same schedule respectively, approximately one and two months later.

    c. At the remaining __4__ locations participants have elected to receive the first workshop in the late afternoon or evening followed the next day at the same time by the second workshop. An one-and two-month intervals the third and fourth and fifth and sixth workshops, respectively, will be conducted.

These alternative delivery models have been devised to meet differing local district needs related to the availability of substitutes and participant commitments and motivations.

Two workshops for key district decision-makers are also planned. The first workshop of three hours duration, provided in each of the 19 locations prior to training of teachers and counselors, serves to identify specific local issues, examine the area delivery system for vocational education, and inform such decision-makers of the changes to vocational education delivery in their area that teachers and counselors are skilled and prepared to provide.

Monthly newsletters provided to all participants during the course of training activities serve to maintain motivation and interest while simultaneously providing important reinforcement and follow-up information useful for successfully meeting training objectives.

ACTIVITY 8—SUBMIT FINAL REPORT
(Percent of Total Project Effort =   1   )
Upon the conclusion of all project activities a final report is prepared. This final report provides for the documentation of all project activities and the dissemination of results of the independent, third-party evaluation. This report serves to identify the extent to which the project objectives have been met and also provides diagnostic information useful for the conduct of future inservice training activities.

ATTACHMENT 5

INFORMATION ON THE CONSULTING ORGANIZATION

OVERVIEW

_____ designs, develops and conducts professional development and applied research programs. Representative clients include local, state and national agencies and organizations--in both the private and the public sectors. In assisting a client to identify and secure appropriate program funding, to document the need for a program, and to develop a workable program solution approach, _____ will work extensively on a no-cost, shared risk basis.

_____ has already provided more than 12,000 participant days of inservice training in more than fifty separate programs. The professional staffs participating in these programs have included local, state and federal agency and government personnel, educators at all levels, as well as private industry management personnel. Most participants in these programs have earned advanced academic credit at leading colleges and universities by their participation.

Applied research programs, including those emphasizing evaluation, are a significant part of _____'s activity. Some programs place needed and vital information into the hands of key decision makers. Other research programs create workable solutions to critical problems arising in education delivery, manpower utilization, information dissemination and decision making.

To guide the development of new programs, _____ conducts intensive ongoing need analyses. Currently, _____ is engaged in studies of manpower utilization, public education delivery, municipal and state government, health services and criminal justice. These studies are serving to identify changing priorities of local, state, and federal communities. They are now guiding the formulation of new programs which will effectively meet these high priority needs, through either a professional development approach or a basic restructuring of existing procedures and delivery systems.

SERVICES

Problems which arise in trying to meet society's increasing need and demand for such services as education, municipal government, etc., are ongoing and dynamic. Organizations committed to the "delivery" of such services find that effective organizational response must involve timely change. _____ assists organizations to effect such needed change by formulating and implementing effective training or research programs.

_____ programs currently serve the needs of federal, state, county and local agencies, colleges and public school district and private business organizations. Often _____ is engaged directly by an organization in order to extend its own staff capabilities. More often, however, a client organization will engage services on behalf of another or several other organizations within the client's jurisdiction. This latter pattern is particularly effective in providing uniform support across several agencies. In any case, needed program responses either will or will not be adequately supported by some existing technology. In the former case, a professional development program is often indicated. In the latter case, research is usually required before needed changes can occur. Major _____ efforts can be described in terms of these two kinds of program:

PROFESSIONAL DEVELOPMENT PROGRAMS....
improve the client's or the sub-agency's capability by upgrading professional staff skills. Such programs seek to modify participant behavior, knowledge level or attitudes.

APPLIED RESEARCH PROGRAMS....
prepare the client organization to design and plan responsive improvements. Research programs collect and interpret data (evaluative studies), test feasibility of proposed approaches (feasibility studies), and design optimum systems and procedures to meet stated objectives (planning studies).

_____ has a recognized capability for planning and implementing effective

• Program Planning Studies
• Feasibility Studies
• Technical Studies
• Technical Resource Identification/Selection
• Inservice Training (Including Train-the-Trainer)
• Program Evaluation
• Training Material Development
• Media Methods—Design and Selection
• Instructional Television Programming

CONTRACTUAL APPROACH
To identify and secure appropriate funding, _____ works extensively on a no-cost, shared risk basis with a prospective client.

_____ then enters into prime or subcontract agreements with the client organization. Under such agreements, a fixed fee is earned in return for satisfactory accomplishment of the prescribed scope of work.

_____ is experiencing increased demand for its program services. This demand arises from two areas:

• former client organizations, funding agencies, and individual program participants who have additional need for program assistance, and
• organizations and agencies identified by ongoing studies as having priority need for specific program assistance.

Individual organizations, agencies, and jurisdictions often lack adequate local funds to meet their real needs for program support. In addition, they may have difficulty in justifying and obtaining the necessary categorical funds even when eligible. By creative application of our system analysis approach, program development methods, and innovative contractual techniques, _____ can assist in forming a "consortium" of several client organizations with similar needs. This is often done for the sole purpose of conducting a single program. Such an increased program commitment and impact permits an extremely high level of support which can be maintained more economically than would otherwise be possible.

ORGANIZATIONAL CAPABILITIES
The effectiveness with which _____ programs assist a client organization is best measured in terms of:

• the management system which applies the resources and quality controls necessary to fully carry out program commitments
• the people who conceive and execute programs

The management system employed by _____ integrates the technical skills of its staff with available resources within the client organization. _____ engages both full-time and consulting staff with expertise in analysis techniques, program development, conduct methods, and specific subject matter areas. _____'s staff brings required expertise, otherwise unavailable on a program basis, into collaboration with the client organization's own resources. This ensures that resulting programs are both practical and workable. Modern methods of quality control and manpower planning are an essential part of_____'s program planning approach. Carefully developed quality control procedures provide for the technical monitoring of programs. A series of checks and balances provides program directors, managers, coordinators, and program staff with optimal latitude in exercising individual technical judgment.

OFFICERS OF THE CORPORATION

_____ — President

_____ founder of _____ provides extensive expertise in system analysis, program conceptualization, and program development. He has been successful in guiding a corporate development program which continues to attract top professional talent to the organization. _____ continues to actively assist prospective client organizations in formulating and articulating their requirements and to qualify needed programs for support under the auspices of entitlement or categorical funds. Prior to founding _____ _____ was Assistant Professor at the _____, during which time he was also honored by appointment to a Fulbright-Hays Lectureship in _____. In addition, _____ has managed the _____ of a public corporation working primarily in the areas of behavior science research, national defense, and manpower utilization.

_____ — Executive Vice President

As General Manager of the Corporation _____ directly influences the planning and implementation of all _____'s programs. His background in research management and education administration provides vital resource expertise to a majority of the programs. _____'s extensive experience in the fields of career guidance and personnel services is proving of fundamental value in several new programs being developed for institutions of higher education. He has been instrumental in the development of program management and product quality control systems which have encouraged the sustained and viable growth of _____. _____ has previously been an Assistant Professor of _____ at the _____.

_____ — Vice President

Formerly Chairman of the Department of Management at _____ _____, _____ is Technical Director of _____. 's extensive background in program evaluation and management, business administration, and finance has significantly shaped and influenced the procedures which successfully implement programs on behalf of client organizations. He has been successful in the application of process analysis techniques to new and highly effective programs dealing with public administration in the municipal government sector. _____ continues to be active in graduate level training and higher education.

_____ — Vice President

_____ serves as Director of Public Relations for _____. As such he brings to bear an extensive background in personnel administration, industrial relations, and public service. His responsibilities include the full spectrum of communications between _____ and its client organizations. _____ has established innovative and highly effective programs for professional staff development which have fostered integration of resource skills in facilitation, program development, coordination, and evaluation. He has pioneered programs which foster the application of diverse process technologies in such areas as special education and cooperative education. Previously, _____ served in management and administration for several national firms. Recently he concluded a variety of consulting services in the personnel and industrial relations fields.

THE TECHNICAL STAFF

As a group and on an individual basis, the qualifications of _____'s technical staff are impressive. Of the many thousands of technical employee staff days logged per year, over 80 percent are by individuals who have earned the Doctorate or Masters degrees. A like percentage of technical staff employees have successful backgrounds in both private industry and teaching at higher education levels. The academic fields of specialization among the technical staff are divided evenly between system sciences, social sciences, and education.

During program development and conduct, _____ is able to draw effectively upon this staff diversity and talent. Additionally, _____ draws upon a pool of professional consultants during the course of specific programs. This group is carefully selected from among those possessing outstanding qualifications for effective program work. _____ takes a great deal of pride in the caliber of its consultants and in the rigorous management procedure followed in effectively employing this resource potential.

_____ employee staff brings a wealth of process expertise to bear on its programs. Specifically, a staff experiences include the design or conduct of programs involving:

- community action
- career guidance systems
- improvement of employment opportunities for the handicapped
- improvement of interpersonal relations and communication
- improvement of opportunities for minority students in cooperative work-experience programs; fostering of higher job placement success among minority groups
- improvement of acquisition and interpretation of data used by decision makers
- organizational effectiveness evaluations; studies leading to the restructure of organizational units
- A statewide model of vocational education delivery adopted as the required district planning disclosure format for all secondary and community college districts
- staffing patterns and procedures
- improvement of the administrative management skills of higher education personnel; project management training for key educational decision makers
- research on the effectiveness and responsiveness of educational programs for the handicapped
- training of participants to prepare commercially programmed instructions
- evaluative analysis of individual components of an educational delivery system
- increase of articulation between secondary and community college delivery agencies
- fostering of more responsive urban governments

PROGRAM DEVELOPMENT

A basic organizational problem is typically realized through the problem's impact, not its components. Therefore, the first step in_____'s program development approach is to conduct an analysis, to give needed visibility to the components of the problem. A succeeding series of program development steps leads to the specification of procedures to resolve the problem.

The program development approach typically begins long before the establishment of a formal contractual arrangement; substantial program development is the bulwark of an effective project application or proposal.

The program development approach provides for:

- specification of the unmet need
- determination, in measurable terms, of intermediate and overall program objectives
- analysis of the organizational setting within which the planned program will have impact

- analysis to find applicable technology, to avoid rediscovery
- specification of those procedures which provide maximum assurance that the program objectives will be met
- completion of a program plan which includes performance and cost schedules, manpower allocation and logistical arrangements

If state-of-the-art technology will fully support solving the problem, it usually proves most effective to share that technology with the individuals within the organization who are in a position to implement change. In such a case, the program development approach would lead to a PROFESSIONAL DEVELOPMENT PROGRAM.

Alternatively, if the state-of-the-art technology is insufficient to totally resolve the problem, there is a need for additional knowledge or information as a preliminary step in effecting the needed change. Thus, the program development approach would lead to an APPLIED RESEARCH PROGRAM.

PROFESSIONAL DEVELOPMENT PROGRAMS

Professional development programs improve the client organization's responsiveness and effectiveness by upgrading the professional skills of central or subagent staff. Programs use a coordinated instructional systems approach, with measurable performance objectives, to modify behavior, knowledge level, or attitudes. The entering expertise of the participant is identified and utilized in a structured program of individual and group accomplishment.

In the program development phase, training needs are identified. These needs, together with program constraints and participant characteristics, serve to dictate the development and/or selection of appropriate materials and presentation means. To successfully accomplish this requires continuous attention to detail. On every program of _____, this attention begins with a preliminary search of contemporary works to avoid rediscovery of an already existing technology. A reference and periodical library is maintained in the corporate office in , California. Additionally, staff are kept up to date and aware of new developments in professional program development through in- house seminars which often involved invited faculty to apply highly unique skills as dictated by specific program needs.

_____supports its clients' professional development programs with extensive program materials. These are always of reference quality and are typically designed to serve as a continuing resource for participants.

Using state-of-the-art techniques and the diverse resources of the development staff, training sessions are designed which insure the participant's positive interaction with the chosen technical material. This is typically done through small group workshop sessions. However, each program has different training requirements and a variety of innovative techniques are used as required. These techniques include formal presentation, small and large group discussion or critique, multimedia instruction, structured problem solving, role playing exercises, and simulation methods. In addition to workshops, professional programs may take the form of pre-service or train-the-trainer activity, self- instructional material or prepared audio-tutorial presentation packages.

_____ does not maintain instructional facilities or extensive commitment to instructional hardware. Conduct of professional development programs typically takes place at or near the client organization's facilities.

Adhering to the philosophy that to create dependency is not training, _____ finds it desirable to create a mechanism through which the client organization can continue to conduct a professional development program once _____ has provided the needed professional assistance. Individuals selected by the client organization may be trained by _____ staff to replicate all or part of the program as required.

Follow-up training allows participants to focus attention on the reinforcement of methods and techniques which are proving most effective. This training is often provided subsequent to the workshop, to further assure the achievement of specified behavioral change.

Final reports and evaluation results, which synthesize and document valuable contributions to the state of the art, are carefully detailed by_____. retains excellent resources for conducting evaluations of professional development programs. Additionally, _____ maintains a full-time editorial staff which works with the program development and conduct staff to provide consistent and effective report disclosures.

EXEMPLARY PROGRAMS

The following synopses of current _____ professional development programs are by no means exhaustive. They are, however, descriptive of the breadth and diversity of the programs which provide assistance to client organizations.

STATE DIRECTORS OF VOCATIONAL EDUCATION AND THE DESIGN OF A MANAGEMENT INFORMATION SYSTEM

The Problem. State Departments of Education seek improved systems of data and information to assist in the optimum management of fiscal and educational manpower resources, and to meet the public's need for effective educational programs.

The Program. An intensive workshop series for State Directors of Vocational Education, State Board Chairmen, and key administrative staff from more than 45 states. Held to identify requirements for and to conduct, design, and plan implementation of a management information system to meet the unique needs of each participating state.

FOSTERING EFFECTIVE MUNICIPAL GOVERNMENT

The Problem. City managers and staffs of small to medium-sized city governments find that difficult crisis management situations are becoming the rule rather than the exception.

The Program. A series of interactive workshops, involving a large consortium of urban cities, responding to the need for more effective management practices. Brings top municipal decision makers and their key staffs together in a structured situation to evaluate specific decision-making and personnel administration techniques. Creative use is made of instructional television.

ADVANCING COMMUNITY COLLEGE ADMINISTRATIVE RESOURCES

The Problem. Community colleges face the dilemma of becoming more eligible for state and federal assistance to meet special student needs, but increasingly finding these funds unavailable in a practical sense because they lack specific programs and qualified resource personnel.

The Program. A series of several intensive training programs, serving the western states under various sponsorship. Individual programs include qualified campus resource persons involved in financial aid administration, students, and individualized instructional programs for low income and minority students.

STRENGTHENING ARTICULATION BETWEEN COMMUNITY JUNIOR COLLEGES AND FEEDER HIGH SCHOOLS

The Problem. Community colleges experience increasing difficulty in developing curricula and guidance processes which respond uniformly to the needs of a widely divergent student input mix from feeder high schools.

The Program. A statewide program providing more than 4,000 participant days for training to secondary school and community college vocational education teaches, counselors, and administrators. Program topics include vocational education delivery system analysis, task analysis and job performance analysis, student capability assessment, deriving training requirements and objectives, instructional program design, determining entry level requirements, creating placement opportunities, expanding student career horizons, and effective follow-up techniques.

LOCAL EDUCATION AGENCY PROGRAM PLANNING

The Problem. Local education agencies (LEAs) require increasing administrative and managerial assistance in meeting requirements of entitlement support, accountability, categorical funds solicitation, and intermediate and long-range planning.

The Program. A series of statewide programs for state department of education and regional education personnel, consultants, and resource specialists, under various sponsorship. Topics include analysis of the delivery system, effective resource and manpower utilization, project and district planning techniques, evaluation, and program management.

THE PREPARATION OF PROCEDURALIZED INSTRUCTIONS

The Problem. Personnel who operate and maintain equipment have difficulty in using manufacturer-supplied technical information. The result is often needless repair, equipment damage, or prolonged downtime.

The Program. An intensive training program for both writers of technical publications and training personnel from commercial airlines, aerospace equipment suppliers, and training organizations, on use of job and task analysis and the development of proceduralized instructions. Specific applications include training materials, complex equipment operations and maintenance.

THE EMERGING ROLE OF COMMUNITY COLLEGE, JUNIOR COLLEGE, AND SECONDARY DISTRICT VOCATIONAL EDUCATORS AS PROJECT MANAGERS

The Problem. Top educational administrators are increasingly called upon to act as project managers, a position for which there is typically inadequate skill preparation.

The Program. A statewide program for education deans and directors from community college and secondary districts. Employs a multimedia case study method to treat such topics as crash program management, assessing data adequacy, forecasting, etc. Participants learn how to use workshop materials, including additional multimedia packages, to conduct programs for local staffs.

APPLIED RESEARCH PROGRAMS

Applied research programs make creative use of existing research findings through ongoing investigation of contemporary knowledge and results, and through application of these findings to needs for new information, interpretation, and procedures. This approach often involves adapting and using findings from several disciplines or fields. A reference and periodical library is maintained in the corporate office in California. Additionally, staff members are kept up to date and aware of new developments in applied research and evaluation through in-house seminars which often involve invited resource persons. _____ uses its diversified consulting faculty to apply highly unique skills as indicated by specific needs.

On the basis of the program development phase, a research program's testing hypotheses are developed. A research design is then constructed to indicate the nature and quality of data, as well as the type of research techniques applicable (historical, descriptive, analytical, experimental, or predictive). From this experimental design, researchers develop the data collection procedures which lend themselves best to the study. During actual data collection, initial hypotheses are constantly tested against findings. Analysis methods may involve manual or computer-based processing. The conclusions of a research program may take the form of actual data, advisable courses of action, or recommendations which indicate the need for new systems and procedures.

_____ evaluation programs serve to identify and document the effectiveness with which systems, procedures, or programs respond to the stated needs. Evaluation program designs, like all other applied research designs, are based upon the program development phase. The documentation of _____ applied research programs includes description and citation of factual data, discussion of implications drawn from the data, and possible recommendations indicating the need for new systems, procedures and their anticipated impact. _____ maintains a full-time editorial staff which works with the staff in order to provide an effective final report format.

A CASE STUDY:

A SIGNIFICANT RESEARCH PROGRAM UNDERTAKEN BY_____
Public and private vocational education and manpower training programs make it possible for any person to prepare for entry into the world of work. To provide trainees with this preparation, career educators use several approaches. One of the most promising and popular of these approaches is work experience education, which combines a trainee's regular classroom and laboratory activities with actual on-the-job learning experiences.

To gain the full benefit of the work-experience approach, the trainee must perform actual job duties and tasks. However, this poses a problem since the trainee is, admittedly, unskilled at this stage of occupational training. Job supervisors are often reluctant to allow the trainee to fully engage in the tasks and duties of the assigned job, particularly in jobs requiring complex skills.

Recognizing this problem, a major agency engaged _____ to conduct a research program to strengthen such career programs.

Previous research evidence has shown that when using simplified step-by-step, written and illustrated instructions on-the-job, an inexperienced person can in certain cases perform better than someone highly skilled in the job procedure. This evidence suggested that introducing a "job guide" approach to work experience education programs could be highly effective in increasing the training opportunity. The research program, testing this job guidance approach, involved the separate consideration of:

- selection of jobs for trainees
- specific job guides for specific sites
- selection of trainees for assignment to each job, one using a job guide, one not using it
- collection and analysis of data to evaluate the impact of the job guide approach

RESEARCH PROGRAM OBJECTIVES

This research program has the objectives of assessing the impact of job guides on:
- the variety of jobs for assignment to trainees
- the variety of trainees who may benefit from a work experience approach
- the range of job demands with which a work experience education trainee may deal
- the level of community support and commitment for career education

POTENTIAL IMPACT OF THIS RESEARCH PROGRAM

It was possible to foresee several areas of local, state, and national concern which may be impacted by the results obtained here. Specific application of these results are possible in connection with programs to:

- increase the effectiveness of manpower systems
- increase worker mobility in times of widespread job displacement
- decrease the demand for a highly skilled work force
- decrease the number of unemployed and unemployable persons
- increase the available manpower pool from which an employer may draw in meeting employer commitments
- increase the educational opportunities for all trainees

WHERE TO START: JOBS

The allied health occupations provide a virtually unlimited variety of jobs having relatively "higher skill" requirements. For this reason, sponsorship of jobs in these occupations was sought for test consideration.

_____ researchers immediately began analysis to select specific jobs for the testing program. To ensure that resulting trainee job experiences would be sufficiently challenging, jobs were selected from among those which trainees might late seek when looking for actual employment; jobs which provide an opportunity to advancement into higher positions.

More than 95 different departments and 900 job operations were studied. The selected jobs were then subjected to further analyses to identify specific job performance requirements, job procedure, environment, etc. The jobs selected for testing involved the following departments:

- Central supply
- Medical laboratory
- Medical records
- Orthodontic laboratory
- Physical therapy
- Radiology

It was determined that none of these jobs had ever been performed in connection with any work experience education program in the test area.

DEVELOPING JOB GUIDES FOR TESTING

_____ has extensive knowledge and experience in the development of proceduralized and programmed instructional materials, including the development of job guides. An extensive amount of theory derived from the fields of psychology and behavioral science underlies the design and development of the job guide format. Based upon this expertise, _____ created a specific job guide format for this project which combined text and illustrations to convey the information needed to perform a job. The entire set of job guides were written at _____. Prior to their use, trained employees verified accuracy during actual use.

Actual job guides are illustrated here. In operation, the trainee follows the job guide to do a specific task. The job guide is designed so that the user is not asked to make independent decisions on what should be done next. This allows, for example, a trainee who has no understanding of photographic principles to develop X-ray film. In developing the job guides for this project, it was necessary to first develop a standard vocabulary. All words and phrases used on the job were identified. Different words were never used to convey the same meaning. For each job it was necessary to use precise wordings to convey information to the trainee.

A PRESENTATION KIT

_____ has developed an audio-visual presentation kit in response to growing demand for information about the 12 Function Vocational Education Delivery System Model. The multimedia material in this kit offers an understandable and clear explanation of the 12 function delivery system concept and is designed for use in presentations to state department staffs, district staffs, local boards, advisory committees, industrial and business groups, service organizations, and community agencies.

In addition, the kit is designed to properly orient new and existing staff in vocational education and to encourage their active participation in vocational education program planning. The kit was produced in close coordination with leading authorities in vocational education.

The 12 function vocational education delivery system is a precise description of how vocational education happens today at the local level. It provides education planners with a framework to develop future plans and has proven extremely useful to local boards, administrators, counselors, and instructional staffs. The 12 function model is fully compatible with existing planning techniques such as Program Planning and Budgeting Systems (PPBS), goals and objectives, evaluation and accountability.

The 12 function vocational education delivery system approach has been used as a basic element of district and state plans which respond to Vocational Education Act (VEA) entitlement requirements.

APPENDIX D

Sample Letters of Agreement and Engagement

This section contains four sample letters of agreement, a statement of consulting terms and conditions that can be appended to a letter of agreement, and a letter of engagement. The first letter of agreement is very general and can be applied to many different consultations. Next there is a letter of agreement for providing engineering services.

The last two letters of agreement are for marketing services. The first relates to marketing products and services and the second to marketing intellectual products. These are followed by an example of a statement of terms and conditions that can be added to a letter of agreement. This is a more formal document that to some extent resembles a contract.

Finally there is an example of a letter of engagement for a presentation. This gives an opportunity to compare the situations that call for letters of agreement as opposed to letters of engagement and shows that a letter of engagement is less formal.

LETTER OF AGREEMENT ON THE CLIENT'S LETTERHEAD

[Client's Letterhead]

_____, 19xx

[Name of Consultant]
[Street Address]
[City, State, Zip]

Dear _____:

We are pleased to inform you that we have selected you as a [type] consultant to work for us on [specify project or nature of work] on the following terms:

1. Term. This agreement will be for a initial period of [specify, e.g., two years], commencing on _____, 19xx, and may be extended for an additional period by mutual agreement in writing. This agreement may be terminated at any time by either of us by [specify, e.g., giving thirty (30) days' written notice to the other party].

2. Duties. Your duties will include [specify, e.g., the rendering of consultation and management services in connection with [name of project]. You will consult with our board of Directors, officers, and department heads concerning the organization and fiscal policy of our company. You will further have complete authority and power over the management of [project], including the direction and supervision of the administrative staff. You may at your discretion arrange to assist in management duties and may delegate to management such duties as you may deem proper.

3. Hours. You will devote a minimum of _____ hours per month to your duties under this agreement, and you may, if you desire, devote any additional time. You are free to represent or perform services for any other clients, provided that it does not interfere with your duties under this agreement.

4. Compensation. For your services rendered you will receive a reasonable monthly sum which shall be at least _____ dollars ($_____) per month but which shall not exceed _____ dollars ($_____) per month. We will pay you on the fifteenth (15th) of each month an amount mutually agreed on for services rendered during the preceding month. If we fail to agree on the amount to be paid for any given month, we shall pay you the minimum compensation provided and submit the dispute to a panel of three (3) arbitrators, one chosen by each of us and the third chosen by the other two, and their determination shall be final and binding.

5. Assignment. Because of the personal nature of the services to be rendered, this agreement may not be assigned by you without our prior written consent, but, subject to the foregoing limitation, it will insure to the benefit of and be binding on our respective successors and assigns.

If this agreement meets with your approval, please sign and return the original and one copy of this agreement. You may retain the additional copy for your own records.

Very truly yours,

[Signature]
[Typed name and title]

Accepted this_____
day of _____, 19xx
[typed name of consultant]

LETTER OF AGREEMENT ON THE
CONSULTANT'S LETTERHEAD

[Consultant's Letterhead]

_____ , 19xx

[Name of Client]
[Street Address]
[City, State, Zip]

Gentlemen:

Engineering Services

Report on [name of project] System

Submitted herewith is our proposal for services in connection with an engineering study and report on [name of project] system.

The engineering study and report will include the following items:

1. General field examination of the system.
2. Preparation of base map showing the location and size of [major items in system].
3. Analysis of system based on current volume and estimated future growth.
4. Recommendations for general development of system including observations regarding alternate possibilities for future system development including:
   a. System [volume].
   b. Number and general location of [outlets].
5. Establishment of priorities for necessary work to bring system up to ultimate design condition.
6. Estimates of probable investment required for initial improvements, together with maps showing initial improvements to system.
7. Estimates of probable investment required for future improvements, together with maps showing ultimate system layout.
8. Comments on condition and practices of present system and recommendations as to improving conditions of present system.
9. Comments on generally accepted practices of [components], construction, and maintenance.
10. Comments on [type of equipment] and recommendations, with cost estimates, on necessary rehabilitation or replacement of existing gear. Recommendations to include ratings and general arrangement of major components of plan offered.

A written report will be prepared and presented in person to you. This report will summarize our findings and recommendations which will serve as the basis for determining appropriations necessary for required facilities.

The report will be presented to and discussed with you within approximately [number] days after acceptance of this proposal.

It is understood that you will make available to us all plans, records, and other pertinent information from your files which will be of assistance to us in our work and will also provide the services of a [type of employee] to assist us during the time required to make the field examination of the system.

Our fee for the services outlined above will be $ _____ which will be due and payable on presentation of the report.

This letter may be made a contract on your approval by affixing the date of acceptance and the appropriate signature in the space below.

This letter may be made a contract on your approval by affixing the date of acceptance and the appropriate signature in the space below.

Respectfully submitted,
[typed name of engineers]
By [signature]
[typed name and designation of
person signing]

Accepted this_____
day of _____, 19xx

[typed name of client]
By [signature]
[typed name and designation of person signing]

AGREEMENTS FOR MARKETING CONSULTATIONS

The two following letters deal with agreements to consult on marketing of physical products and of intellectual products. With the proliferation of communication media, contracts must cover a broader spectrum of media than previously. This is in line with the responsibility of the consultant to offer state-of-the-art approaches to client's needs.

Agreement to Market Products and Services

[Date]
[Name of Consultant]
[Street Address]
[City, State, Zip]

Dear _____ :

1. This letter shall serve as an agreement between [Client's name], hereinafter the "Client," and [Consultant's name], hereinafter the "Consultant," governing services to be provided by the Consultant in connection with the development and marketing of products and services and general business and management advisory services related to existing products and services and future products and services during the term of this agreement.

2. The Consultant shall provide services as determined necessary and appropriate for the general benefit of the Client as generally described in the proposal provided to the Client and attached hereto and thereby incorporated into this agreement. All services will be provided with the highest and best state of the art known to the Consultant. The parties to this agreement understand and acknowledge that the marketing, sale, licensing, distributing, syndicating and such other means of capitalizing on the Client's business ventures is a speculative venture with uncertain outcomes and that no promises or assurances, warranties or representations regarding the success of such activities, the services to be provided, or the amount of income to be derived can be projected or are relied upon in the execution of this agreement.

3. The parties to this agreement shall use their best efforts to obtain the maximum income from such properties to the benefit of the Client and agree to communicate all relevant information about leads, opportunities, contracts and associated plans and offers which may be relevant to the performance of this agreement. It is understood that either party as well as third parties not associated with this agreement may receive invitations, overtures and offers pertinent to the objectives of this agreement

5. In consideration of the services provided by the Consultant, the Client agrees to compensate the Consultant as follows:

A fee equal to a share of all pretax income derived by the Client or any entities (such as corporations, joint ventures and partnerships) established by the client to receive income from all properties, sales, fees, royalties, commissions and services on all business ventures and activities equal to [specify percentage] percent due and payable on or before the fifteenth (15th) day of each month for the prior month.

6. In addition, the Client agrees to reimburse the Consultant for any and all direct expenses which may be incurred in the performance of this agreement within fifteen (15) days of the receipt of an invoice for such expenses. The Consultant agrees to obtain prior approval from the Client for any expense item greater than [specify amount].

7. This agreement may be terminated by the Client upon ten (10) days written notice and by compensating the Consultant at the rate of [specify amount] dollars per hour for time expended until termination, less any funds received by Consultant under the terms of Paragraph 5.

8. The Consultant shall have reasonable right, at its own expense, to inspect the books of account of the Client in connection with the terms of paragraph 5. In the event that such inspection determines that fees due the Consultant under the terms of paragraph 5. have been underpaid by an amount equal to Three thousand dollars ($3,000.00) or more, the Client agrees to reimburse the Consultant for the costs associated with such inspection up to a maximum of Two thousand Five hundred dollars ($2,500.00).

9. This agreement is binding upon and enures to the benefit of the parties hereto and their respective heirs, assigns, successors, executors, administrators and personal representatives and shall be governed by the laws of the state of [name state].

10. In the event of a dispute relative to this agreement, either party may request and require that such dispute be resolved by arbitration under the procedures established by the American Arbitration Association, with the site of such arbitration being [specify place] or such other location as the parties may mutually agree.

11. This agreement is the entire and complete agreement between the parties. No reliance is made by either party regarding any warranties or representations not included within this agreement and this agreement may be extended in duration and/or scope by mutual written agreement.

12. No waiver of any provision herein shall be deemed or shall constitute a waiver of any other provision of this agreement. In the event that any provision of this agreement shall be determined to be unenforceable or voidable, all other provisions of this agreement shall remain in full force.

13. If any legal action or other proceeding is brought for the enforcement of this agreement, or because of an alleged dispute, breach, default or misrepresentation in connection with any of the provisions of this agreement, the successful or prevailing party or parties shall be entitled to recover reasonable attorneys' fees and other costs incurred in that action or proceeding, in addition to any other relief to which it or they may be entitled.

14. If a signed copy of this agreement is not returned to the Consultant by [specify date] it shall be voidable at the option of the Consultant.

If the terms and conditions of this agreement meet with your approval please sign and return a copy of this agreement for my files.

I look forward to a long and mutually beneficial working arrangement between us.

Sincerely,
[Consultant's name]

Accepted for [Client's name]

_____

Date_____

AGREEMENT TO MARKET INTELLECTUAL PRODUCTS

[Date]
[Name of Consultant]
[Street Address]
[City, State, Zip]

Dear _____:

1. This letter shall serve as an agreement between [Client's name], hereinafter the "CLIENT," and [Consultant's name], hereinafter the "CONSULTANT," governing services to be provided by the Consultant in connection with the development and marketing of intellectual properties to be developed and made available to the market by the Client on the subject of [specify subject].

2. This agreement relates to the development and marketing of intellectual properties to include audio tapes, video tapes, training programs, books, seminars, newsletters, consulting methodologies/packages, lectures, computer software, databases, articles, columns, syndications, manuals, and such other intellectual properties which may be determined to be appropriate for communicating and marketing the information on [specify subject] and related topics developed by the Client.

3. The Consultant shall provide services as defined in the proposal submitted in connection with this project and attached hereto and thereby incorporated within and made a part of this agreement. All services will be provided with the highest and best state of the art known to the Consultant. The parties to this agreement understand and acknowledge that the marketing, sale, licensing, distributing, syndicating and such other means of capitalizing on the Client's intellectual properties determined appropriate is a speculative venture with uncertain outcomes and that no promises or assurances of the success of such activities or the amount of income to be derived can be projected or are relied upon in the execution of this agreement.

4. The parties to this agreement shall use their best efforts to obtain the maximum income from such properties to the benefit of the Client and agree to communicate all relevant information about leads, opportunities, contracts and associated plans and offers which may be relevant to the performance of this agreement. It is understood that either party as well as third parties not associated with this agreement may receive invitations, overtures and offers pertinent to the objectives of this agreement and that efforts by the Consultant, the Client or third parties may result in the creation of income for such intellectual properties.

5. In consideration of the services provided by the Consultant, the Client agrees to compensate the Consultant in the following fashion:

    a. A monthly retainer in the amount of [specify amount] for a period of [specify time period] months due and payable on or before the first day of the month, commencing on [specify date] and

    b. A share of all pretax income derived by the Client or any entities (such as corporations, joint ventures and partnerships) established to receive income from all intellectual properties and subsidiary rights thereto defined in paragraph 2, above, equal to [specify percentage] percent until such time as the Consultant has received a total of [specify amount] income, including the fees received as a monthly retainer for services provided and excluding any other fees which the Consultant may receive as a result of additional services requested by and provided to the Client. A statement of income received, payments due and a check for payments due shall be provided to the Consultant by the Client quarterly on or before the fifteenth (15th) day of January, April, July, and October for the previous three months.

6. The Client agrees to reimburse the Consultant for any and all direct expenses which may be incurred in the performance of this agreement within fifteen (15) days of the receipt of an invoice for such expenses and may establish a requirement that any expenses in excess of Three hundred dollars ($300.00) per month be approved in advance.

7. This agreement shall end on [specify date] but the Client shall be responsible to the Consultant for the fees due under the terms of paragraph 5.b., above, until such time as the maximum payments due have been received. This agreement may be terminated by the Client upon thirty (30) days written notice to the Consultant. In the event of termination, the payments due the Consultant under the terms of paragraph 5.b., above, shall be as follows:

　　a. If termination occurs within the first ninety (90) days, the Consultant shall continue to receive income under the terms of paragraph 5.b. up to a maximum of Fifteen thousand dollars ($15,000.00) including monthly retainer income received until thirty (30) days following receipt of notice of termination.

　　b. If termination should occur after ninety (90) days, the Consultant shall continue to receive income in full accordance with the provisions of paragraph 5.b..

8. The Consultant shall have reasonable right, at its own expense, to inspect the books of account of the Client in connection with paragraph 5.b. In the event that such inspection determines that fees due the Consultant under the terms of paragraph 5.b. have been underpaid by an amount equal to Three thousand dollars ($3,000.00) or more, the Client agrees to reimburse the Consultant for the costs associated with such inspection up to a maximum of Two thousand Five hundred dollars ($2,500.00).

9. This agreement is binding upon and enures to the benefit of the parties hereto and their respective heirs, assigns, successors, executors, administrators and personal representatives and shall be governed by the laws of the state of [name state].

10. In the event of a dispute relative to this agreement, either party may request and require that such dispute be resolved by arbitration under the procedures established by the American Arbitration Association.

11. This agreement is the entire and complete agreement between the parties and may be extended in duration and/or scope by mutual written agreement.

12. No waiver of any provision herein shall be deemed or shall constitute a waiver of any other provision of this agreement.

If the terms and conditions of this agreement meet with your approval please sign and return a copy of this agreement along with the first monthly retainer payment due.

I look forward to a long and mutually beneficial working arrangement between us.

Sincerely,
[Consultant's name]

　　　　　　　　Accepted for [Client's name]
　　　　　　　　_____
　　　　　　　　　　Date_____

STATEMENT OF CONSULTING TERMS AND CONDITIONS

Some consultants prefer to prepare a general statement of their professional terms and conditions and incorporate it by attachment to a letter of agreement. A sample of such a statement is presented below:

[Name]
[Address]
[City, State, Zip Code]
[Telephone]

GENERAL TERMS AND CONDITIONS

All time, including travel hours, spent on the project by professional, technical, and clerical personnel will be billed. The following approximate ranges of hourly rates for various categories are currently in effect:

CATEGORY	HOURLY RATE
Senior Consultant	$95.00—$105.00
Staff Consultant	$85.00—$ 95.00
Junior Consultant	$75.00—$ 80.00
Staff Analyst	$55.00—$ 60.00
Staff Technician	$45.00—$ 50.00
Technical Typist	$25.00—$ 30.00

Hourly rates will be adjusted semiannually to reflect changes in the cost of living index as published by the United States Department of Labor. If overtime for nonprofessional personnel is required, the premium differential is charged at direct cost to the project. Unless otherwise stated, any cost estimate presented in our proposal is for budgetary purposes only and is not a fixed lump-sum bid. The client will be notified when 75 percent of any budget figure is reached, and the budget figure will not be exceeded without prior authorization from the client.

Reimbursable Expenses

The following expenses will be billed at direct cost plus 10 percent:

a. Travel expenses necessary for the execution of the project including air fares, rental vehicles, and highway mileage in company or personal vehicles at 20 cents per mile. Air travel will be by economy class except between the hours of 11:00 P.M. and 6:00 A.M. and when economy class service is not regularly available.
b. Telephone and telegraph charges.
c. Postage.
d. Printing and reproduction.
e. Computer services.
f. Other expenses directly attributable to the project.
Subcontracts will be billable at cost plus 20 percent.

Invoices and Payments

Invoices will be submitted monthly and payment is due within 30 days of date of invoice. A one and one-half percent per month service charge will be added to all delinquent accounts. In the event [name of consultant] shall be successful in any suit for damage for breach of this agreement including for nonpayment of invoices, or to enforce this agreement, or to enjoin the other party from violating this agreement, [name of consultant] shall be entitled to receive as part of its damages its reasonable legal costs and expenses for bringing and maintaining any such action.

Rates for foreign contracts are negotiable and the above rates do not apply.

Warranty
Our professional services will be performed, our findings obtained, and our recommendations prepared in accordance with generally and currently accepted engineering consulting principles and practices. This warranty is in lieu of all other warranties either expressed or implied.

Limitation of Professional Liability
The client agrees to limit any and all liability or claim for damages, cost of defense, or expenses to be levied against [name of consultant] to a sum not to exceed $10,000, or the amount of our fee, whichever is less, on account of any error, omission, or professional negligence.

Respectfully submitted,
[typed name of engineers]
By [signature]
[typed name and designation of
person signing]

Accepted this_____
day of _____, 19xx

[typed name of client]
By [signature]
[typed name and designation of person signing]

LETTER OF ENGAGEMENT FOR A PRESENTATION

The last letter is a letter of engagement that covers the arrangements for a presentation. It is a simple, straightforward document that covers the details of a short-term consultation. This highlights the kind of situation in which a letter of engagement is preferable to a letter of agreement. The letter of agreement covers a moderate-sized project that lasts for a period of weeks or months. The letter of engagement is more appropriate for a smaller project that lasts for a period of a week or less.

[Date]
[Name of Client]
[Street Address]
[City, State, Zip]

Dear _____:

This letter shall serve as an agreement between [Client's name], hereinafter the "Sponsor," and [Consultant's name], hereinafter the "Consultant," governing the development and conduct of [project name] for [specify organization] on [specify date].

The Consultant shall supply camera ready masters of materials to be provided to participants for duplication by the Sponsor and distribution to participants on or before [specify date].

The Sponsor shall supply a head table, speaker's podium, hand-held microphone and overhead projector for transparencies.

The Sponsor agrees to provide the Consultant with the names, addresses and telephone numbers (when available) of all participants.

The Sponsor shall compensate the Consultant in an amount equal to [specify amount]. This compensation shall be for professional services and travel expenses and shall be paid as follows:

a. Upon acceptance of this agreement _____ [specify amount]
b. On or before [specify date] _____ [specify amount]

If this agreement is not signed and returned along with the initial payment due at the time of execution on or before [specify date] it shall be voidable at the option of the Consultant.

If the terms of this agreement meet with your acceptance, please return a signed copy of the agreement along with your check.

Sincerely,
[Consultant's name]

Accepted for [Client's name]
By_____

Date_____

APPENDIX E

Samples of the Formal Written Contract

As with the letter of agreement, the formal written contract may be prepared by either the client or the consultant. Both parties should have competent legal authority review the general form of a specific contract. The same is true for letters of agreement.

THE BUSINESS CONSULTANT AND MANAGEMENT CONTRACT

This contract is an example of an agreement for a consulting firm to give advice and supervision on the management of a business, in this case a hospital. This form constitutes an agreement between consultants and their clients governing a complex business transaction to be undertaken by the client but with detailed advice and supervision to be provided by the consultants. The consultants not only advise the client on the proper method of carrying out the project involved, but are also given specific management authority over most aspects of the project. This type of situation may be necessitated by the requirements of a third party, such as a lender or lessor, who believes the services of the consultant are necessary to the successful operation of the project involved.

Provision is made for compensation of the consultants based on the amount of work they perform for the client with a minimum and maximum dollar amount of compensation provided for each month. The consultants also agree to provide a minimum number of hours of service to the client and to spend additional time at the sole discretion of the consultants.

If disputes arise under the agreement, provision is made for arbitration in accordance with the rules of the American Arbitration Association. In order to protect the reputation and good name of the consultants, the contract contains a provision declaring the uniqueness of the services to be provided by the consultants and the irreparable harm to them which would result if such services were not fully performed. It provides that equitable remedies, including injunction and specific performance, may be obtained by the consultants if the contract is breached by the client. In this situation, the main force of this provision is to insure that the consultants will continue to manage the client's project so that the third party investor may be fully protected. This agreement can be altered to cover a wide variety of management consultation situations.

AGREEMENT

AGREEMENT made this _____ day of _____, 19xx, between [name of client], (e.g., a Delaware corporation), hereinafter referred to as the "Corporation", and [name of consultant(s)], (both jointly and severally,) hereinafter referred to as the "Consultants":

Recitals

The Corporation is presently in the process of negotiating [description of project, e.g., to build or lease and to conduct and operate a general hospital at the following location]:

It is the desire of the Corporation to engage the services of the Consultants to perform for the Corporation certain functions in the management and operation of [e.g., the hospital] and to consult with the Board of Directors and the officers of the Corporation and with the administrative staff concerning problems arising in the fields of [e.g., hospital management fiscal policies personnel policies purchases of equipment, supplies, and services] and other problems which may arise from time to time, in the operation of [e.g., a general hospital].

Agreement

Term

1. The respective duties and obligations of the parties hereto shall commence on the date [e.g., that the Corporation enters into said lease].

Consultations

2. The Consultants shall make themselves available to consult with the Board of Directors, the offices of the Corporation, and the department heads of the administrative staff, at reasonable times, concerning matters pertaining to the organization of the administrative staff, the fiscal policy of the Corporation, the relationship of the Corporation with its employees, and in general, concerning any problem of importance concerning the business affairs of the Corporation.

Management Authority of Consultants

3. In addition to the consultation provided for in Paragraph 2 above, the Consultants shall be in complete and sole charge of the administrative staff of [e.g., the hospital]. The administrative staff of the hospital shall include all the employees of the Corporation directly, or indirectly engaged in the affairs of the hospital other than the Board of Directors of the Corporation, the president, vice president, secretary, and treasurer of the Corporation, and the medical staff of the hospital. The medical staff of the hospital is defined as those persons who are licensed by the State of Delaware to perform, and are performing, services as physicians, surgeons, nurses, physiotherapists, social workers, psychologists, psychiatrists, pharmacists, and other services of a professional standing in the healing arts and sciences.

Management Power of Consultants

4. The business affairs of the Corporation which affect directly or indirectly, the operation of [e.g. the hospital], and which arise in the ordinary course of business, shall be conducted by the administrative staff. All the members of the administrative staff shall be employees of the Corporation however, the Consult-

ants shall have the sole and complete charge of the administrative staff, and shall have the absolute and complete authority to employ (on such terms and for such compensation as they deem proper) discharge, direct, supervise, and control each and every member of the administrative staff. It is the intention of the Corporation to confer on the Consultants all the powers of direction, management, supervision, and control of the administrative staff that the Consultants would have if the members of the administrative staff were direct employees of the Consultants.

Business Manager

5. The Consultants, in their sole discretion, may employ, in the name of the Corporation, a business manager. If such a business manager is employed, he shall act as administrative assistant to the Consultants and as the chief administrative officer of the administrative staff. The business manager shall be under the direct control and supervision of the Consultants. The Consultants may, from time to time, delegate to the business manager as much of the Consultants' authority as they deem proper with respect to the employment, discharge, direction, control and supervision of the administrative staff, and the Consultants may withdraw from said business manager, at any time the Consultants deem it expedient or proper to do so, any portion or all of the said authority theretofore conferred on the business manager.

Fiscal Policy

6. The Corporation recognizes the necessity for a sound fiscal policy in order to maintain and promote the solvency of the Corporation. To this end, it is hereby agreed by the parties hereto that the Corporation will establish reserve accounts for the following purposes:
    a. A reserve account for the payment of any and all taxes that may be charged against the Corporation by any governmental jurisdiction.
    b. A reserve account for the payment of all sums withheld from the salary or wages of the employees of the Corporation and for which the Corporation is chargeable under the laws of any and all governmental jurisdictions.
    c. A reserve account for the payment of all obligations due [name of lessor] pursuant to the terms and conditions of the above referred-to lease.
    d. A reserve account for the purchase of equipment necessitated by the wearing out or obsolescence of the equipment in use, or by the development of new equipment.
    e. A reserve account for building maintenance and for the expansion of the physical facilities. The Consultants shall, from time to time, advise the Board of Directors of the amounts of corporate funds that shall be deposited in each of said reserve accounts. This determination on the part of the Consultants shall be based on the principles of sound business management and the availability to the Corporation of said funds. The Corporation agrees to deposit corporate funds in said reserve accounts pursuant to the recommendations of the Consultants, and the amounts recommended by the Consultants. The reserve accounts shall be deposited in one or more national banks, or branches thereof, located within [county and state]. All checks, drafts, or other instruments by which funds are withdrawn from said reserve accounts, in addition to any other signature that may be required, shall bear the signature of one of the Consultants.

Consultants to Act as Agents

7. From time to time, the Corporation may deem it advisable to enter into agreements with [e.g., insurance companies, prepaid medical plans, and other firms and associations which pay all or part of the expenses incurred or to be incurred by the hospital patients for the care and treatment afforded them while patients in the Corporation's hospital]. With regard to said agreements, the Consultants shall be the exclusive agent of the Corporation for the purpose of

negotiating the terms and conditions of the said agreements. However, the Consultants shall not bind the Corporation to said agreements without first obtaining the approval of the terms of said agreements from the Board of Directors of the Corporation.

Authority to Contract

8. From time to time, the Corporation may wish to expand the physical facilities of [type of facility] or remodel or modify the same. If the costs to be incurred by the Corporation for such expansion, modification, or remodeling are less that $, then the Consultants may contract for the performance of the same in the name of the Corporation under the authority given them in Paragraph 4 above however, if such expansion, modification or remodeling is to be of such extent that the cost to be incurred by the Corporation for the performance thereof is $_____ or more, then the terms and conditions of said contracts for said expansion, modification, or remodeling shall be negotiated by the Consultants, and the Consultants shall be the exclusive agents of the Corporation for said purpose, but the Consultants shall not bind the Corporation to said contracts without first obtaining the approval of the terms and conditions of said contracts from the Board of Directors of the Corporation. The provisions of this paragraph shall apply with equal effect to the purchase of equipment and supplies.

Employment of Certified Accountants

9. It is understood and agreed by the parties hereto that the services to be performed by the Consultants do not include the auditing of the books of the Corporation or of [name of project], the preparing of any financial statements, the preparing of any tax returns or other documents required to be prepared by any governmental body having jurisdiction to tax, or any other acts or services normally performed by public accountants. The Consultants may engage, hire, retain, and employ, in the name and for the account of the Corporation, one or more, or a firm of, certified public accountants to perform for the Corporation the services denoted above in this paragraph. Said accountant or accountants may be employed, hired, engaged, and retained on such terms and conditions and for such compensation as the Consultants deem reasonable [e.g., It is understood by the Corporation that the Consultants are partners of a firm of certified public accountants known as [name of firm]. It is specifically agreed that the Consultants may be, and the Consultants are, hereby authorized to employ said partnership, or its successors in interest, to perform for the Corporation the services denoted above in this paragraph, and the Consultants may obligate the Corporation to pay to said partnership, or its successors in interest, a reasonable amount for the performance of said services.]

Employment of Assistants

10. If it is reasonably necessary for the Consultants to have the aid of assistants or the services of other persons, companies or firms in order to properly perform the duties and obligations required of the Consultants under this agreement, the Consultants may, from time to time, employ, engage, or retain the same. The cost to the Consultants for said services shall be chargeable to the Corporation and the Corporation shall reimburse and pay over to the Consultants said costs on demand.

Limited Liability

11. With regard to the services to be performed by the Consultants pursuant to the terms of this agreement, the Consultants shall not be liable to the Corporation, or to anyone who may claim any right due to his relationship with the Corporation, for any acts or omissions in the performance of said services on the part of the Consultants or on the part of the agents or employees of the Consultants except when said acts or omissions of the Consultants are due to their willful misconduct. The Corporation shall hold the Consultants free and harmless from any obligations, costs, claims, judgements, attorneys' fees, and attachments arising

from or growing out of the services rendered to the Corporation pursuant to the terms of this agreement or in any way connected with the rendering of said services, except when the same shall arise due to the willful misconduct of the Consultants, and the Consultants are adjudged to be guilty of willful misconduct by a court of competent jurisdiction.

Compensation

12. The Consultants shall receive from the Corporation a reasonable monthly sum for the performance of the services to be rendered to the Corporation pursuant to the terms of this agreement; however, in no event shall the compensation paid to the Consultants by the Corporation be less than $_____ per month nor more than $_____ per month. The Corporation and the Consultants, by mutual agreement, shall determine the compensation to be paid the Consultants for any particular month by the fifteenth (15th) day of the next succeeding month. The final determination of the monthly compensation shall be based on the reasonable value of the services rendered by the Consultants, and within the range prescribed above in this paragraph. If the Corporation and the Consultants fail to agree on said compensation within the said fifteen (15) days, the amount of monthly compensation due the Consultants shall be determined by arbitration pursuant to the provisions of Paragraph 14 below. Anything contained in this agreement to the contrary notwithstanding, the minimum monthly remuneration of $_____ shall be paid to the Consultants on the first day of the month of each and every month during the term of this agreement and the acceptance of said minimum amount by the Consultants shall not in any way diminish, affect, or compromise their rights to additional compensation as provided for herein.

Minimum Amount of Service

13. The Consultants shall devote a minimum of _____ hours per month to the affairs of the Corporation. Anything to the contrary notwithstanding, the Consultants shall devote only so much time, in excess of said _____ hours, to the affairs of the Corporation as they, in their sole judgment, deem necessary and the Consultants may represent, perform services for, and be employed by such additional clients, persons, or companies as the Consultants, in their sole discretion, see fit.

Arbitration

14. Any controversy or claim arising out of or relating to the compensation to be paid by the Corporation for the Consultants for the services rendered by them pursuant to the terms of this agreement shall be settled by arbitration in accordance with the rules of the American Arbitration Association, and judgment on the award rendered by the arbitrator or arbitrators may be entered in any court having jurisdiction thereof. Any party to this agreement may submit to arbitration any said controversy or claim.
[The following paragraph may be used where more than one consultant is a party to the agreement.]

Failure to Act by One Consultant

15. It is understood and agreed that any direction or consultation given or service performed by either one of the Consultants, pursuant to the provisions of this agreement, shall constitute the direction or consultation or the performance of service of both of the Consultants. If, for any reason, one or the other of the Consultants is unable or unwilling to act or perform pursuant to the terms of this agreement, such event shall not void this agreement or diminish its effect, and the performance on the part of the other consultant shall constitute full and complete performance of this agreement on the part of the Consultants.

Legal and Equitable Remedies

16. Due to the uniqueness of the services to be performed by the Consultants for the Corporation, and due to the fact that the Consultants' reputation in the commu-

nity as business managers may be affected by the financial success or failure of the Corporation in the operation of the [project], in addition to the other rights and remedies that the Consultants may have for a breach of this agreement, the Consultants shall have the right to enforce this contract, in all of its provisions by injunction, specific performance, or other relief in a court of equity. If any action at law or in equity is necessary to enforce or interpret the terms of this agreement, the prevailing party shall be entitled to reasonable attorneys' fees, costs, and necessary disbursements in addition to any other relief to which he may be entitled.

Right to Manage

17. Except as specifically provided to the contrary herein and to the greatest degree allowable under the Corporation Code and other laws of the State of Delaware, it is the intent of the Corporation to confer on the Consultants the exclusive and absolute right to manage and direct all the business affairs of the Corporation which in any way concern the operation of [project] and which arise in ordinary course of business of [project]. Should any one or more of the provisions of this agreement be adjudged unlawful by any court of competent jurisdiction, the remaining provisions of this agreement shall remain in full force and effect. Further should one or more of the provisions of this agreement be adjudged invalid by a court of competent jurisdiction, such determination shall have no affect whatsoever on the amount or amounts of compensation to be paid to the Consultants pursuant to the terms of this agreement.

Governing Law

18. This agreement shall be binding on and shall be for the benefit of the parties hereto and their respective heirs, executors, administrators, successors, and assigns, and shall be governed by the laws of the State of _____.

Executed at [name of State] on the day and year first mentioned above.

CLIENT
[typed name of client]
By [signature]
[typed name and designation of person signing]
CONSULTANT
[typed name of consultant]
[signature]
[typed name and designation of person signing]

FORM OF AGREEMENT FOR TECHNICAL SERVICES

The following illustrates a typical contract for the delivery of technical consulting services. This basic format is typical of contract forms used by engineers, architects, educational consultants, design consultants, marketing consultants, etc.

This form constitutes a formal contract for complete engineering services in connection with a major project. It tends to minimize subsequent disagreements and constitutes compelling evidence as to the agreement of the parties if legal controversy should arise. The agreement contains recitals indicating the background of the document.

In the illustrated form, a preliminary engineering report has been made on the project to be undertaken. It is therefore possible throughout the form to refer to this preliminary report in connection with the services to be provided. The engineers agree to represent the client in all engineering matters involved in the project. It should be noted that the consulting engineers, although independent contractors, act not only as advisors on engineering matters, but also are required to take affirmative action in implementing the client's project.

Except for a few specialized types of advisors, who might better be called analysts, it is usual for consultants/advisors to come up with a concrete work product helpful to clients in addition to merely telling the client what action to take. For example, an attorney advises on the possible provisions to be inserted in a will and on their legal effect, but does not leave the drafting and execution of the will to the client. Instead, the attorney produces a formal document called a will and arranges for its proper execution.

The main promise made by the client is to pay the consultant. Many bases of compensation are possible. In this form an example is given for compensation based on a percentage of cost excluding engineering and legal fees, land and rights-of-way, and the client's overhead. Such an arrangement is sometimes used in contracts with certain government agencies, although such a basis of compensation is sometimes made illegal because of the temptation to the contractor to increase costs in order to increase the fee.

In this agreement, the problem of runaway costs is partially overcome by providing that the percentage of compensation is reduced as the amount of cost increases. The form also provides compensation on the basis of employees' salary plus a fixed percentage of such salary. Such an arrangement is subject to the same objection mentioned before. Provision is made for payment to the consultants of specified percentages of their compensation as various stages of the work are completed. The agreement provides for additional compensation to the consultants if changes in plans and specifications are made after they are approved by the client. The standard per diem charge of the consultant is used to determine the additional compensation.

ENGINEERING SERVICE AGREEMENT

AGREEMENT made this _____ day of _____, 19xx between [name of client], hereinafter referred to as the "Client", and [name of consultant], hereinafter referred to as the "Engineers."

Recitals

The Client now owns [and operates] [type of structure].

The Engineers have heretofore prepared and submitted to the Client a report entitled "[e.g., "Preliminary Report, (name of project)"].
The Client desires to retain the Engineers to provide complete engineering services on the project.

Agreement
It is hereby agreed that the Client does retain and employ the said Engineers to act for and represent it in all engineering matters involved in the project. Such contract of employment to be subject to the following terms, conditions, and stipulations.

Conditions of Agreement
1. The scope of the project shall include the improvements recommended in the [e.g., "Preliminary Report, (name of project] as prepared by the Engineers.

Plans and Specifications
2. The Engineers shall prepare such detailed plans and specifications as are reasonably necessary and desirable for the construction of the project. The specifications shall describe in detail the work to be done, materials to be used, and the construction methods to be followed.
   The Engineers shall obtain approval of the plans and specifications from [e.g., State Department of Health].
   Duplicate copies of plans and specifications shall be submitted to the Client.

Advertisment for Bids
3. After the Client has approved the plans and specifications, the Engineers shall assist in the preparation of notice to contractors and shall provide plans and specifications for prospective bidders.

Awards of Contract
4. The Engineers shall have a representative present when bids and proposals are opened, shall prepare a tabulation of the bids and shall advise the Client in making the award. After the award is made, the Engineers shall assist in the preparation of the necessary contract documents.

Resident Inspection
6. The Engineers shall furnish competent resident engineers or inspectors to supervise the construction of the work. Said resident engineers or inspectors shall be assigned to the project during such periods as are mutually agreeable to the parties hereto. Such personnel and their salaries and expense allowances shall be subject to the approval of the Client.

Tests and Final Inspection
7. After the construction is completed, the Engineers shall perform such tests as are necessary to make certain that all equipment and construction fully complies with the plans and specifications. The Engineers shall make a final inspection of the work and shall certify its completion to the Client.

Plant Operations
8. The Engineers shall supervise initial operation of the [structure] and shall [e.g., instruct the Client's operating superintendent in the proper operation of the plant.]

Records and Reports
9. The Engineers shall not be required, under the terms of this contract, to make property surveys necessary for acquisition of right-of-way or property. The Engineers shall, however, make all topographic and construction surveys.

Property Surveys
10. The Engineers shall not be required, under the terms of this contract, to make property surveys necessary for acquisition of right-of-way or property. The Engineers shall, however, make all topographic and construction surveys.

Time of Completion
11. The Engineers shall complete the plans and specifications within _____ days after date of execution of this contract.

Compensation
12. The Client shall compensate the Engineers for their services by the payment of the following fees:

A. For surveys, preliminary plans and estimates, final plans and specifications, and general supervision of construction a percentage of construction costs in accordance with the following schedule:

The first $15,000 of construction cost	10%
Next $385,000 of construction cost	6%
Next $400,000 of construction cost	5½%
All over $800,000 of construction cost	5%

B. For resident supervision and inspection, a fee equal to [e.g., the salary paid the resident engineer and inspectors plus seventy-five (75%) percent of such salary paid, and plus any expenses incurred by the resident engineer and inspectors in connection with the job and paid by the Engineers].

Construction cost is defined as the total cost of the project exclusive of the cost engineering, legal service, land and right-of-way, and Client's overhead.

The fee shall be due and payable in the following manner:

The amount of _____ dollars ($_____) previously paid for the preliminary report will be considered as part payment of the fee stated above.

On completion of plans and specifications, their approval by the [e.g., State Department of Health] and presentation of plans and specifications, their approval by the [e.g., State Department of Health] and presentation of plans and specifications to the Client an amount equal to seventy (70) percent of the computed fee in accordance with Schedule A above based on estimated construction cost and less amounts previously paid.

During the period of construction and proportionally with the progress of construction an amount equal to twenty (20) percent of the fee in accordance with Schedule A above based on contract construction cost.

On completion of the project and final inspection, an amount equal to the total fee outlined above based on final construction cost, less amounts previously paid.

The fee for resident supervision and inspection as provided under Schedule B above will be billed and payable monthly.

Services Not Included
13. If, after the plans and specifications are completed and approved by the Client and [e.g., State Department of Health], the Engineers are required to change plans and specifications because of changes made by the Client, then the Engineers shall receive an additional fee for such changes which shall be based on their standard per diem fees.

Assistants
14. It is understood and agreed that the employment of the Engineers by the Client for the purpose aforesaid shall be exclusive, but the Engineers have the right to employ such assistants as they may deem proper in the performance of the work said assistants to be employed subject to the approval of the Client, and the services of said assistants are to be paid for by the Engineers.

Assignment
15. This Agreement, and each and every portion thereof, shall be binding on the successors and assigns of the parties hereto, but the same shall not be assigned by the Engineers without written consent of the Client.

Executed, in duplicate, at [state], on the day and year first written above.

CLIENT
[typed name of client]
BY [signature]
[typed name and designation of
person signing]

ENGINEERS
[typed name of engineers]
BY [signature]
[typed name and designation of
person signing]

SAMPLE OF AGENT AGREEMENT

The following contract form is typical of the type of contract used where the consultant will act as an external agent for the client, usually with respect to selling or representing. This form of agreement is also typical of the forms of agreement which are used between a consultant and those individuals retained by the consultant to serve as subconsultants.

CONSULTANT AGREEMENT

THIS AGREEMENT made and entered into this _____ day of _____, 19xx, by and between _____ (hereinafter referred to as "Company") and

IN CONSIDERATION of the mutual agreement herein contained, it is mutually understood and agreed by and between the parties as follows:

I. NATURE OF SERVICE
  A. Consultant is hereby authorized to procure clients for the Company. All funds received by the Consultant shall be received in trust for the Company and be delivered immediately to the Company. All checks or other negotiable instruments received by Consultant from client shall be made payable to the firm or firms designated from time to time by the Company.
  B. Consultant shall have the exclusive right to establish his own working hours and determine his own days of work.
  C. Consultant shall not be required to perform his services upon the Company's premises.
  D. Any business expenses incurred by Consultant, including but not limited to automobile, and the like shall not be reimbursed by the Company.
  E. Consultant agrees to use his best efforts in conducting all of the activities referred to in this Agreement.
  F. Consultant agrees to refrain from taking any action to injure the Company or its reputation.
  G. Nothing contained herein shall be construed to create the relationship of Employer and Employee or Agent and Principal between the Company and Consultant. Consultant shall conduct his business as an Independent Contractor and shall have no authority to create, alter or amend any agreements or representations on behalf of the Company or to incur any liabilities for the Company. Consultant acknowledges that he is not an employee of the Company, and said Company is not obligated nor charged with the responsibility of withholding income taxes from any commissions due the Consultant nor is the Company obligated to pay Social Security taxes nor F.I.C.A. taxes upon or for the Consultant.

H. Consultant agrees to adhere to fair business principles and comply with all
Federal, State and local laws and regulations either existing or pending.
Consultant further agrees to file applications for licensing, bonding or other
permits, and pay all fees pertaining thereto as may be required by any
regulatory body.

II. SOLICITATION AND TERMINATION

A. Consultant shall not make any misrepresentations or offer warranties or
guarantees of any kind to its clients, the effect of which would be to induce the
prospective clients to enter into an agreement with the Company. If a lawsuit
should arise from misrepresentations made by the Consultant, the Consultant
shall indemnify the Company for any and all damages incurred thereby,
including court costs, legal fees and any judgments rendered or settlement
costs incurred therefrom.

B. Consultant agrees that he will not issue, distribute or circulate any advertising
or promotional material, circulars or pamphlets relating to the Company
unless and until it has been authorized and approved in writing by the
Company. The Consultant shall withdraw any said material and discontinue
its use immediately upon the Company's written request to do so.

C. This Agreement may be terminated by either party upon giving written notice.
Upon the giving of said notice, the Company shall cause to be paid to
Consultant any monies due Consultant, as herein provided, and Consultant in
turn shall reimburse the Company for any monies it advanced not earned, and
return to the Company any material, products, stationary, samples, etc., which
Consultant may have which belong to the Company. Upon termination of this
Agreement for any reason, the Company shall have a secured lien over any
accrued or accruing commissions due Consultant under the provisions of this
Agreement or any amendment or addendum attached hereto, for monies owing
from Consultant to Company, and for any damages sustained by the Company
from conduct of the Consultant.

III. COMPENSATION

In consideration of the functions performed hereunder by the Consultant,
Company will pay Consultant $200.00 of the fees, and/or deposits collected from bona
fide clients acquired by the Consultant for the Company.

The above stated commission shall constitute the only source of compensation to the Consultant by the Company.

IV. CONTRACT ENFORCEMENT

A. This Agreement constitutes the entire agreement about understanding between the parties and supersedes any and all other agreements between the
parties.

B. No remedy granted to the Company by virtue of the Agreement shall be
exclusive of any other legal or equitable remedy available to the Company
existing by laws of statute.

V. MISCELLANEOUS

A. The parties agree and intend that all questions concerning this Agreement,
including the validity, capacity of parties, effect interpretation and performance shall be governed by the laws of the State of _____.

B. The rights, privileges, duties and obligations of both the Company and the
Consultant to each other shall be limited to those specifically set forth herein.

C. This Agreement and the terms, conditions and obligations herein contained
shall be binding upon the parties hereto, their assigns, transferees, heirs and
legal representatives.

D. This Agreement shall not vest in Consultant, his heirs, estate, or legal
representatives, any right, title, or interest in any assets in the Company itself,
its name, good will or other market business activities other than as set forth

in this Agreement and only for so long as the Agreement has not been terminated, and not longer.

E. This Agreement constitutes the complete Agreement between the Consultant and the Company. No representation or promise, either oral or written, has been made except as specifically set forth herein. Should any part of this Agreement by declared invalid, such invalidity shall not affect the remainder of this Agreement. It is the intention of the parties that they would have executed the remaining portion of this Agreement without herein including any portion which may hereafter be declared invalid.

F. The forebearance or neglect by either party to insist upon the performance of this Agreement, or any part thereof, shall not constitute a waiver of any rights or privileges.

IN WITNESS WHEREOF, the parties have executed this agreement on the day and year first above written.

THE FOREGOING IS HEREBY AGREED TO:

> Consultant
> [Company Name]
>
> by_____

SAMPLE FORM OF A SUBCONSULTING CONTRACT

The following form is included as an example of a contract which a consultant might use in retaining the services of a second or subconsultant. The primary or master consultant is referred to as the "Company" and the assistant or subconsultant as "Consultant."

It will be obvious that this agreement form could be used by a client in retaining the services of a consultant, as well.

CONSULTING AGREEMENT

The _____ was formed to serve the continuing and specialized education of technical and other professional groups and individuals. Through its unique programs of publishing seminars and workshop offerings, the _____ provides quality education tailored to the specialized needs of professionals in a real-world, performance-oriented environment. In the furtherance of this work, the president of the _____ (hereinafter called the President) desires to utilize the expert assistance of

_____

(hereinafter called the Consultant) in the field or fields in which the Consultant has professional qualifications.

A. Character and Extent of Services

1. It is the mutual intent of the parties that the Consultant shall act strictly in a professional consulting capacity as an independent contractor for all purposes and in all situations and shall not be considered an employee of the _____(hereinafter called the Company).

2. The Consultant reserves full control of his activities as to the manner and selection of methods with respect to rendering his professional consulting services to the Company.

3. The Consultant agrees to perform his activities in accordance with the highest and best state of the art of his profession.

4. The Consultant is an independent contractor and shall provide worker's compensation insurance or self-insure his services. He shall also hold and keep blameless the Company, its offices, agents and employees thereof from all damages, costs or expenses in law or equity that may at any time arise due to injury to, death of persons, or damage to property, including Company property, arising by reason of, or in the course of performance of this agreement nor shall the Company be liable or responsible for any accident, loss or damage, and the Consultant, at his own expense, cost and risk, shall defend any and all actions, suits, or other legal proceedings that may be brought or instituted against the Company or offices or agents thereof on any claim or demand, and pay or satisfy any judgment that may be rendered against the Company or officers or agents thereof in any such action, suit or legal proceeding.

B. Period of Service and Termination

1. The period of service by the Consultant under this agreement shall be from through _____ and may be renewed upon the mutual agreement of the parties hereto.

2. Either the Company or the Consultant may terminate this agreement by giving the other party 30 days written notice of intention of such action.

3. The President reserves the right to halt or terminate the conduct of a seminar/workshop by the Consultant without prior notice or claim for additional compensation should, in the opinion of the President, such conduct not be in the interests of the Company.

C. Compensation

1. Upon the Consultant's acceptance hereof, the Company agrees to pay the Consultant according to the following schedule:
   [insert compensation rate or fixed fee and any allowance for or schedule of allowable expenses, if any].

2. In the event that the Company desires, and it is mutually agreed to by the Consultant, the Consultant's services may be used in the conduct of seminars/workshops not specifically identified in paragraph C.1. In such cases, the Company agrees to pay the Consultant on the basis of the following schedule:
   [insert appropriate schedule]

3. In the event of special circumstances, variations to the fee schedule of paragraphs C.1 and C.2 will be allowed as mutually agreed to in writing by the parties hereto.

4. Notification. The Consultant will be notified by the President in writing to engage his participation in specific seminar(s) and/or workshop(s) to which the fee schedule of paragraphs C.1 and C.2 apply. Such notification will include a statement of the time(s) and place(s) of intended seminar/workshop conduct together with other information contributing to the successful conduct of the seminar/workshop sessions.

5. The Consultant, as an independent contractor, shall be responsible for any expenses incurred in the performance of this contract except as otherwise agreed to in writing prior to such expenses being incurred. The Company will reimburse the Consultant for reasonable travel expenses incurred with respect thereto.
   [a specification of "reasonable" may be inserted here]

D. Method of Payment

1. Having proper notification the Consultant shall be paid as provided for in paragraphs C.1 and C.2 hereof, on the basis of a properly executed "Claim for Consulting Service" form.

2. The "Claim for Consulting Service" form is to be submitted at the end of the calendar month during which consulting services are performed. Exception to this arrangement are allowed with the written approval of the President.

3. Payment to the Consultant will be made by check, delivered by certified mail postmarked no later than _____ days subsequent to receipt of the "Claim for Consulting Service" form as provided for in paragraphs D.1 and D.2.

E. Copyrights

1. The Consultant agrees that the Company shall determine the disposition of the title to and the rights under any copyright secured by the Consultant or his employee on copyrightable material first produced or composed by the Consultant in the performance of this agreement but which is incorporated into the material furnished under this agreement, provided that such license shall be only to the extent the Consultant now has or, prior to the completion or final settlement of this agreement, may acquire the right to grant such license without becoming liable to pay compensation to others solely because of such grant.

2. The Consultant agrees that he will not knowingly include any copyrighted material in any written or copyrightable material furnished or delivered under this contract without a license as provided in paragraph E.1 hereof or without the consent of the copyrighted material is secured.

3. The Consultant agrees to report in writing to the Company promptly and in reasonable detail any notice or claim of copyright infringement received by the Consultant with respect to any material delivered under this agreement.

F. Drawings, Designs, Specifications

1. All drawings, sketches, designs, design data, specifications, notebooks, technical and scientific data, and all photographs, negatives, reports, findings, recommendations, data and memoranda of every description relating thereto, as well as all copies of the foregoing, relating to the work performed under this agreement or any part thereof, shall be subject to the inspection of the Company at all reasonable times and the Consultant and his employees shall afford the Company proper facilities for such inspection and further shall be the property of the Company and may be used by the Company for any purpose whatsoever without any claim on the part of the Consultant and his employees for additional compensation, and subject to the right of the Consultant to retain a copy of said material shall be delivered to the Company or otherwise disposed of by the Consultant, either as the Company may from time to time direct during the progress of the work, or in any event, as the Company shall direct upon the completion or termination of this agreement.

G. Assignment

The Company reserves the right to assign all or any part of its interest in and to this assignment. The Consultant may not assign or transfer this agreement, any interest therein or claim thereunder without the written approval of the Company.

IN WITNESS WHEREOF, the parties have executed this agreement.

CONSULTANT

COMPANY

Date_____   Date_____

SAMPLE OF A FIXED PRICE SERVICE CONTRACT

The following agreement serves as an example of a consultant providing a specific set of services within a definite time period for a fixed dollar sum. In this example, the consultant is referred to as the "CONTRACTOR" and the client, an institution of higher education, as the "UNIVERSITY."

AGREEMENT

THIS AGREEMENT is made, this _____ day of _____, 19xx by and between _____, hereinafter referred to as the "University" and _____, hereinafter referred to as the "Contractor."

WITNESSETH:

WHEREAS, the University desires to develop and conduct a training program for its personnel and the personnel of such other eligible education agencies as may become participants in this program, and

WHEREAS, the purposes of said training program are to:

Upgrade the managerial and technical skills of career counseling and placement personnel and increase the professional stature of career counseling and placement personnel and provide a cadre of trained professionals and appropriate materials to continue further training as required with minimum funding support needed, and provide a vehicle for the ongoing assessment of in-service training needs of career counseling and placement personnel.

WHEREAS, the Contractor is particularly skilled and competent to conduct such a management training program, and

WHEREAS, funds for this contract are budgeted for and included in a federal project plan approved under _____, and as described in the program prospectus identified as Grant _____, which is hereinafter referred to as the "Project", and

WHEREAS, said Project was approved [date] and project expenditures approved on [date]

NOW, THEREFORE, it is mutually agreed as follows:

1. The term of this Agreement shall be for the period commencing [date], continuing to and until [date].
2. The Contractor agrees to develop and conduct a training program consisting in part of a series of three workshop session presentations. Each of said workshop presentations shall be of eight hours' duration and shall be conducted at [place]. The aforesaid training program shall be developed and conducted by the Contractor in accordance with the project prospectus submitted by the University for funding under _____ and in particular with the "attachment" to said program prospectus, which is marked Exhibit "A," attached hereto and by reference incorporated herein.
3. The aforesaid workshop presentations shall include three days of intensive training using an approach which has demonstrated considerable success working with career counseling and placement personnel of this type. Specific workshop topic coverage shall include the following:
   a.
   b.
   c.
4. The aforesaid training workshop will be conducted during the contract term in accordance with a schedule mutually agreed upon by the University and the Contractor.
5. In connection with the conduct and development of the aforesaid training program, the Contractor agrees as follows:
   a. The Contractor will plan for and prepare such necessary materials as are needed to conduct the various program sessions as described. Such material preparation and development will include the preparation of participant resource material, development of worksheets, orientation materials, participant guides and handbooks. All materials developed will reflect the highest standards of quality applicable to educational material development state of the art.
   b. The Contractor will provide expert session facilitation staff as follows:
      A minimum of one (1) expert staff for the first twelve (12) participants in attendance at each session. Further the Contractor will provide one (1) additional expert staff for each additional twelve (12) participants in attendance at each session to a maximum of 48 total participants per session.

    c. The Contractor will regularly consult with designated personnel of the University for the purpose of monitoring program progress and planned activities so as to improve and strengthen the overall program.

6. The Contractor further agrees to:
   a. Furnish the University on or before [date] with a final report. This report will describe all relevant aspects of program activity and will be in such style and format as to comply with the requirements of the enabling grant.
   b. Prepare appropriate pre-session and post-session participant testing materials to enable the ongoing assessment of the overall program activities. The Contractor shall collect, analyze, and interpret these findings as an integral part of the program development and conduct activity.
   c. Conduct, within 4 to 6 months after the conclusion of the workshop presentations, a post-test follow-up survey which will seek to discover what difficulties, if any, the participants in the program have encountered in applying the principles developed in the workshop training activity to career counseling and placement problems. A component of the follow-up survey will probe for participant attitude and individual assessment of the relevancy of the workshop training activity and the topic material in the context of program administration experience during the intervening period.
   d. Furnish the University with copies of all written and visual materials produced for distribution to the workshop participants. The Contractor will retain no proprietary rights to such materials, said rights being vested to the University.

7. The University agrees as follows:
   a. To designate one of its staff members as Project Director to represent the University in all technical matters pertaining to this program.
   b. To arrange the necessary pre-program advertisement and participant notification so as to encourage participation.
   c. To provide or otherwise arrange for facilities which are adequate to conduct the workshop sessions.
   d. To limit session attendance, exclusive of Contractor staff, to the maximum eligible number of participants _____ plus up to three (3) additional non-participating persons.
   e. To make the necessary arrangements with the participating educational agencies to make personnel available as participants in all specified training activities.
   f. To arrange for the use on an as-available basis of University instructional equipment including 16mm sound projectors, overhead transparency projectors, 35mm slide projectors, tape recorders, and/or related audiovisual equipment, as requested by the Contractor in response to program requirements. The University agrees to provide competent personnel to operate all such equipment. The University will provide adequate maintenance and care of such equipment and will provide operational assistance to the Contractor as requested.
   g. To distribute to the program participants at the request of the Contractor, various project materials which are relevant to the program. Such materials may include training session handout material, descriptive information, questionnaires and announcements.
   h. To provide or arrange for assistance to the Contractor at training session locations as mutually agreed in connection with facility arrangements, scheduling, and other matters pertaining to the successful conduct of the program.

8. It is expressly understood and agreed by both parties hereto that the Contractor while engaging in carrying out and complying with any of the terms and conditions of this contract is an independent Contractor and is not an office, agent or employee of the University.

9. The Contractor shall provide worker's compensation insurance or self-insure his services. He shall also hold and keep harmless the University and all offices agents, and employees thereof from all damages, costs of expenses in law or equity that may at any time arise or be set up because of injury to or death of persons or damage to property, including University property, arising by reason of, or in the course of the performance of this contract, nor shall the University be liable or responsible for any accident, loss or damage, and the Contractor, at his own expense, cost and risk, shall defend any and all actions, suits or other legal proceedings that may be brought or instituted against the University or officers or agents thereof on any claim or demand, and pay or satisfy any judgment that may be rendered against the University or offices or agents thereof in any such action, suit or legal proceeding.

10. In consideration of the satisfactory performance of the Contractor, the University agrees to reimburse the Contractor in the amount of Fifteen Thousand Dollars ($15,000) in accordance with the following schedule:

30 May 19xx	$ 5,000.00
30 June 19xx	$ 5,000.00
30 July 19xx	$ 5,000.00
	$15,000.00

IN WITNESS WHEREOF, each party has caused this agreement to be executed by its duly authorized representative on the date first mentioned above.

CONTRACTOR   UNIVERSITY

_____   _____

NAME   NAME
TITLE   TITLE

PROFESSIONAL SERVICES AGREEMENT

Often a consultant will offer services to an organization which may involve government regulations. In this case some projects may be covered by the regulations covering classified information. You will notice this in Clause 7. Otherwise the contract is typical of a contract for professional services.

This Agreement is made this _____ day of _____, 19xx by and between _____, hereinafter referred to as the COMPANY and _____, hereinafter referred to as CONSULTANT.

1. STATEMENT OF WORK: During the terms of this Agreement, CONSULTANT will perform service as requested from time to time by the COMPANY, at such place or places and at such times as shall be mutually agreeable to the parties hereto. The services shall relate to preparing contract or subcontract draft documents for review by COMPANY attorney.

2. PAYMENT: The COMPANY shall pay CONSULTANT according to the following schedule:
   a. Hourly fee of $_____ or flat fee as agreed to in writing by the parties.
   b. Travel Expense: The COMPANY shall reimburse CONSULTANT for the actual cost of transportation (except for normal commuting), lodging and subsistence as authorized by _____. Travel expenses will be paid only in

accordance with the effective policy of the COMPANY covering such expenses.

  c. Other Expenses: The COMPANY shall reimburse CONSULTANT for all other reasonable actual expenses incidental to the services performed hereunder which have been approved in advance by _____.

  d. Invoices: Payment for compensation and reimbursement for expenses incurred will be made 30 days after submission by the CONSULTANT of invoice. The invoices should be submitted at least monthly and should specify the period for which compensation is claimed, and travel costs and other expenses claimed must be itemized. The invoices must be substantiated by receipts for transportation and lodging and all other items of expenses amounting to more than $10 where receipts are normally issued. The invoices should be submitted to _____.

  e. Total costs under this Agreement may not exceed $_____ unless approved in advance by the COMPANY in writing.

3. OTHER OBLIGATIONS: The CONSULTANT represents and warrants to the COMPANY that he is now under no contract or agreement, nor has he previously executed any documents whatsoever with any other person, firm, association or corporation that will, in any manner, prevent his giving, and the COMPANY from receiving, the benefit of his services and related inventions or contrivances that may be devised by him, or developed under his direction, in accordance with the terms of the Agreement. The COMPANY agrees that, during the term of this Agreement or any extension or renewal thereof, the CONSULTANT may be employed by other persons, firms or corporations engaged in the same or similar business as that of the COMPANY, provided, however, that the provisions of Section 5f hereof shall be strictly observed by the CONSULTANT with respect to such other persons, firms or corporations.

4. TERMINATION: This Agreement commences on the date written above and shall terminate on [date]. By mutual agreement, the Agreement may be extended for an additional period or periods of _____ . Either party may terminate this Agreement at any time by giving written notice to the other party.

5. PATENTS AND DATA:

  a. Title: CONSULTANT agrees that the COMPANY shall have sole ownership and title to all rights and legal interest in:

    (1) All data, drawings, designs, analyses, graphs, reports, products, tooling, physical property and all other items or concepts, computer programs, and

    (2) All inventions, discoveries and improvements, whether patentable or not, which are conceived or reduced to practice during the terms of this Agreement, relating to subject matter prepared, procured, produced or worked on by CONSULTANT, his associates or employees, arising out of or relating to the service or work performed hereunder.

  b. Disclosures and Assignments: CONSULTANT agrees to make full disclosure to the COMPANY of all items included in Section 5a above and, to the extent that CONSULTANT may be so requested by the COMPANY, CONSULTANT agrees to execute and deliver to the COMPANY assignments, in forms satisfactory to the COMPANY of such items. CONSULTANT also agrees to do or perform, or cause to be done or performed, with the COMPANY bearing all legal and all out-of-pocket expenses, therefore, all lawful acts deemed by the COMPANY to be necessary for the preparation and prosecution of applications for and the procurement, issuance, maintenance, enforcement and defense of patents and/or copyrights, throughout the world, based on inventions and/or subject matter included in Section 5a above. The COMPANY will bear all expenses incurred in the enforcement and defense of all such patents and/or copyrights.

  c. Information made available to CONSULTANT or which CONSULTANT becomes privy to, or produced by or for him pursuant to this Agreement, during the term of this Agreement, shall be considered proprietary information supplied in confidence, and shall not be disclosed to others, or used for manufacture or any other purposes except as required under this Agreement, without prior written permission by the COMPANY.

d. Nothing herein shall be construed as an implied patent license under any patents of the COMPANY.

e. CONSULTANT agrees to obtain an agreement similar to this Section 5 from any agent, employee or associate of this Agreement.

6. SECURITY: CONSULTANT will comply with all applicable security regulations of the United States Government and of the COMPANY.

7. GOVERNMENT CONTRACT REQUIREMENTS: This Agreement is/is not issued pursuant to Government contract _____. If this Agreement is for an amount in excess of $2,500 and a Government contract number or the word CLASSIFIED is stated, the following is applicable:

a. Audit and Records: CONSULTANT agrees that his books, records and such of his facilities as may be engaged in the performance of this order shall at all reasonable times be subject to inspection and audit by the Government Department having jurisdiction of the prime contract noted. The Controller General of the United States or any of his duly authorized representative shall, until the expiration of three years after final payment under this Agreement, have access to and the right to examine any directly pertinent books, documents, papers and records of CONSULTANT involving transactions related to this Agreement.

b. Security: In the event this order requires access to any classified information or material which information is classified as "Confidential" or higher, the provision of DAR clause 7-104.12 shall be applicable. The COMPANY reserves the right, and CONSULTANT agrees to such reservation, to terminate this Agreement at any time if the CONSULTANT is not at all times authorized to handle such classified matter by the appropriate Government agency.

8. SUBCONTRACTING: CONSULTANT will not subcontract or assign any of the work or rights hereunder without prior written approval of the COMPANY.

9. RELATIONSHIP OF CONSULTANT: CONSULTANT will serve as independent contractor, and this Agreement will not be deemed to create a partnership, joint enterprise, or employment between the parties. CONSULTANT is required to make appropriate filings with the taxing authorities as a self-employed person to account for and make all payments required by the local, State and Federal taxing authorities to include income tax, social security and SDI payments, and CONSULTANT further agrees to indemnify and hold the COMPANY harmless for any claims made by the above-mentioned taxing authorities resulting from performance made by CONSULTANT in performance of this Agreement. If the COMPANY determines that taxes should be withheld, the COMPANY reserves the right to unilaterally withhold as appropriate and notify the CONSULTANT accordingly.

10. INTERPRETATION OF CONTRACT: This Agreement may not be changed except in writing, signed by CONSULTANT and authorized procurement official of the COMPANY. This writing contains the entire agreement between the parties. The validity, performance, construction and effect of this Agreement shall be governed by the laws of the State or Commonwealth in which the COMPANY has an address and place of business as set forth in the first paragraph of this Agreement.

IN WITNESS WHEREOF, the Parties hereto have executed this Agreement as of the day and year first above written.

The COMPANY
By:_____

Title:_____

The CONSULTANT
By:_____

Index